Heathen Pilgrim

Heathen Pilgrim

Walk Across Turkey

by Matt Krause

Edited by Ruth Anne Krause

Cover design by Alper Rozanes

Delridge Press
Seattle MMXVII

BISAC: TRAVEL / Special Interest / Hikes & Walks

For Pryor

Choose your suck.

No matter what you do, part of it is going to suck.
So don't look for something that doesn't suck.
Choose the suck you want.

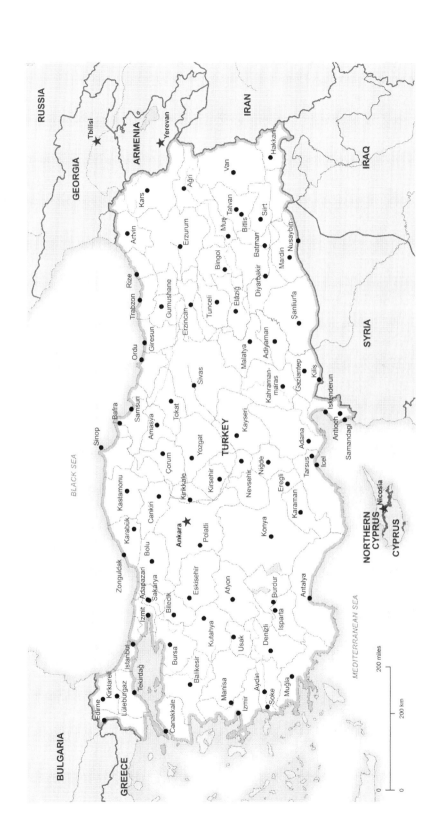

Contents

WHERE AM I?

I wake with a start. *Where am I?* Through the parting fog of sleep I remember that I am in İstanbul. A hot sun is shining through the window. I am sweating in the humidity. My walk starts in a week.

I want to go back to sleep. I want the walk to be over. I wish my plan had been a dream. I wish that this morning I could shake it off, shower, drive to work at a familiar office, sit at a familiar desk, and click away on a familiar computer emailing familiar people.

Instead, in one week I will lace up my boots, pull on my backpack, and walk out onto a hot, dusty highway — my home for the next 7 ½ months until I reach the barbed wire fence that separates Turkey from Iran.

God, this bed is soft. Can't I just stay here?

I've mapped out the route in great detail. I've even made a spreadsheet breaking the entire thing down into 11-kilometer (7-mile) segments. For every one of those segments, I know the beginning elevation, the ending elevation, and the average temperature of that area for that time of year. For every one of those segments I know if there is a gas station or a village, and whether the road bends to the left or to the right.

I have gone out of my way to eliminate as much of the unknown as possible, but there are two things I can't answer beforehand:

1. Where am I going to sleep at night?
2. Am I going to die from a scorpion sting on the Central Anatolia plateau?

I laugh nervously when I tell people that last one, about the scorpion. What I don't tell them is that I actually have two bigger fears:

Will someone kill me in my sleep? Will my death prove all those others right who said, "But it's dangerous."

The second is that the next decade of my life will look like the previous one. I had been planning to build a small business empire — not huge, just large enough to sustain my family and me. I was going to find "The One," settle down, get married, and have children. I would come home at the end of the day to a house filled with people who loved me. I would eat dinner with children who called me "Daddy." At night I would fall asleep next to the woman I loved and wake up next to her in the morning.

I started a couple businesses, but they struggled, and I closed them down. I found the woman I thought was The One. We got married, but by the end of the decade we divorced.

I want to hit the reset button on my life. Is this walk the right way to do it? Or am I about to engage in a colossal waste of time?

HALF-COOKED CHICKEN

Thursday, 30 August

At 10:30 a.m., at the walk's starting point in Kuşadası, I stepped off an overnight bus from İstanbul. The other bus passengers scurried to taxis or cars driven by loved ones. Car doors banged shut. Cars sped away. Even the bus driver pulled away in his bus. I stood alone in the parking lot not knowing what to do next.

A voice in my head said, "Welcome to your new reality. It's going to be like this for a while."

Another voice chimed in, "You are not of this world now, get used to it."

I wandered around the parking lot aimlessly for a minute or two, and then sat down on a bench in the shade. I pulled out my phone and texted Elif, a friend of mine back in İstanbul, "Arrived in Kuşadası, see you in Denizli in three weeks."

I stuffed the phone back into my pocket and focused on walk operations, logistical things I'd need to do: "I'll need to put my feet in the sea before the walk starts, maybe I should head down to the sea now."

The shoreline was about 3 kilometers away. I stood up and began walking. It was hot. I remembered why I was starting on 1 September, and not earlier: In July of last year a friend who lived in the area had posted on Facebook that her car was covered with tar from the road melted by the summer sun. I didn't want to walk in that kind of heat.

Kuşadası is a tourist town, with a permanent population of about 70,000, swelling to as much as half a million during the summer months, depending on how many cruise ships are docked at the port. Walking through it is a little like walking through the cantina in the movie *Star Wars*, a place filled with thousands of people just passing through from distant galaxies. People who will be gone in a few days. People like me.

I reached the sea and noticed that because of the cruise ship docks I was still about 30 feet above the waterline. So I turned left and began walking south along the coast, looking for a place closer to the water.

One or two kilometers later I spied a narrow gravel road about half a kilometer long heading toward the water. I walked down the road to a dirt embankment rising about 3 meters above the water.

I pulled off my boots, dropped my pack, and eased myself down the rocky embankment into the ankle-deep water. The water was cool and clear. I took a picture of my feet in the water.

A family walking by on the gravel road above watched me as they passed. I smiled up at them sheepishly. It's probably perfectly normal to take a photo of your feet in the water, but for some reason I was ashamed to be walking across the country. Friends back home had told me it's a great undertaking, but I thought, *Normal people don't do stuff like this.*

After I took the photo I climbed back up the embankment to the gravel road. I dried my feet with my socks, put my boots back on, and eased into my pack.

Finding a place to sleep on the first night had been a major fear. *Maybe,* I thought, *I should tackle that next. Get it out of the way.*

I walked a few steps and scanned the area. A couple hundred meters away I saw a man and a woman sunbathing on a dry grassy area with a building nearby. I thought I saw a few places to camp on the grassy area. I walked toward the couple. I couldn't tell what the building was, maybe an old house.

The man, about 55 years old with matted salt-and-pepper hair, looked like he had lived a life in the sun without sunblock. The years had not been kind to him.

The woman looked to be in her mid-20s. She was reasonably attractive, or perhaps I was just lonely.

She had seen me coming, but the man had not, so as I drew near I called out in Turkish, "*Merhaba!*" (Hello!)

The man looked up. "Merhaba!" he called back and waved me over.

I wondered if I had stumbled into a situation where I would be the third wheel. Were this man and woman together? I felt like a lost little boy stumbling onto the adults at a late-night party. I was wearing baggy knee-length shorts, a sweaty black t-shirt, and was wearing my oversized backpack.

As I approached them I blurted out in my very bad Turkish that I was looking for a place to camp that night, was it okay for me to set up my tent on the grass nearby? The man answered immediately in English that of course I could stay, no problem, and he waved his arm across the realm to signal that I could camp wherever I liked.

He motioned to me to take a seat in one of the empty lounge chairs next to the two of them, and he asked me if I wanted something to drink. I was hot and thirsty. I told him that an iced tea would be great if he had some. "Sure!" he said, jumping up from his lounge chair. "Peach or lemon?"

"Peach," I said, and he disappeared into the building to get my iced tea.

I turned to the young woman. I had since gathered that she and the man were not together.

My eyes settled briefly on the strings of her bikini pressing against the flesh of her hips. I quickly looked away.

Keep it in your pants, Matt! You have a job to do!

I focused my eyes on her face and asked her, "What brings you to Kuşadası?"

She replied that she worked for a cruise line and had come from Moldova with her Moldovan clients. She told me the boat was docked in the nearby city of İzmır and she had a couple days of shore leave. She had decided to spend those days sunbathing by the sea.

The man brought back a can of Lipton peach iced tea.

I thanked him and took it. The can was warm, but I kept my mouth shut.

I could see through the open doors and windows of the building that this was not a house but an empty restaurant building. I didn't see a stick of furniture — no tables, no chairs, no cash register. Just a large, cavernous, empty shell of a building surrounded by large windows that looked like they hadn't been washed in 30 years.

I asked the man his name. "Murat," he said.

Murat made me a little nervous. He had offered me a place to stay, a chair, and some tea, but I sensed that his offers weren't coming from a place of hospitality or kindness. He had a hungry look in his eyes that said, *I have a need. Business is slow.*

The three of us sat on our lounge chairs making small talk. Strangely, the chairs faced away from the sea.

After about an hour the young woman got up and left. She had to go back into town to meet some friends, she said. So she left me alone with Murat, the two of us sitting in our lounge chairs facing away from the sea, I, "sipping" from my now-empty can.

Later that afternoon I needed to leave to go meet Orhan, a friend of a friend of mine. I stood up and told Murat I would be back later that day.

Orhan was a local TV celebrity, and as I walked the few kilometers back into town to meet him I recognized his picture on posters at bus stops. He picked me up in his car at the city center and took me for a short tour of Kuşadası, then we stopped at a grocery store to pick up a few things for lunch.

From the grocery store, we went to Orhan's home, where his wife prepared a delicious lunch of *köfte* (meatballs), *sigara boreği* (deep-fried cigarette-shaped pastries filled with cheese), a cold soup of squash and yogurt, and *çoban salata* (tomatoes, cucumbers, and peppers). We ate lunch and a dessert of cold watermelon while sitting on their balcony overlooking the sea, enjoying as much of a conversation as my rusty Turkish would allow.

After lunch, Orhan dropped me off back at Murat's place where I went for a swim in the bay.

After swimming and lounging in the shade with Murat, I pitched my tent. A new camper had arrived, a university student named Göksel who was setting up his camp nearby. Göksel was hitchhiking south along the Aegean coast in order to walk the Lycian Way before school started again.

After our tents were set up, Göksel and I walked into town and drank a couple beers. Then I headed back to camp while Göksel continued touring around Kuşadası. For him, 9 p.m. was way too early to turn in.

That night the palm trees above me blew gently in the sea breeze, the Aegean waves lapped at the shoreline, and the salt air blew gently through the mesh roof of my tent. I began to relax with the exciting thought of living a nomadic life for a while, and I slept one of the most peaceful sleeps I'd slept in years.

Friday, 31 August

The next day, the day before the walk began, Murat and I sat in the lounge chairs most of the day while Göksel did some sightseeing in town. Neither of them seemed as impressed with me as I was. Murat was just happy to have a customer of any sort, and Göksel had his own adventures to think about. The day before, the Moldovan woman had not seemed very impressed either.

Around mid-afternoon Murat suddenly sat up on his lounge chair, turned to me, and eagerly asked, "Would you like some dinner? Could I fix you some chicken?"

Chicken sounded good, sure, but never had I seen anyone get so excited about a poultry dinner. Since I seemed to be the only customer Murat had seen in awhile I said, "Yes, that sounds great."

Murat sprang up and ran inside to call some domestic help for the evening.

Later, a woman arrived to help Murat grill the chicken on an inside grill.

Murat asked me if I wanted salad. I told him yes. There was no refrigerator, of course, as the whole building was empty. He went into the pantry, brought out some wilted greens, and began chopping them up for the salad. To drink, he offered me the choice of either a beer or juice. I chose the juice, and he brought me a can of warm fruit juice to go with my wilted salad and half-cooked chicken.

I stared down at the plate of food Murat had just placed before me. Should I complain or should I trust that all would be well and dive in? I dove in.

After dinner I retired to my tent and fell asleep.

Saturday, 1 September

On the big day, Saturday, 1 September, I woke up with my alarm at 6 a.m.

I wanted a shower. It would be my first shower in a couple days and might be my last one for some time.

I broke camp and crammed everything into my backpack. I asked Murat where the shower facilities were. He pointed in their direction. When I got to the facilities I found no running water. I brought that to Murat's attention.

"Oh, you want running water!" he said.

"Yes, that would be nice," I replied.

"I'm sorry. There isn't any. You can use the buckets in the restaurant vestibule," he said.

The vestibule floor was made of stone with a drain pipe in the middle. A small plastic pitcher sat next to the water bucket, presumably to use as a ladle.

I tasted the water first, to see if it was salt water from the sea or freshwater. It was freshwater, so I picked up the pitcher and gave myself a sponge bath.

After I bathed and dried off, I pulled on my best black T-shirt (gotta look nice for the start of my walk!). I asked Murat what I owed him. He waved his hands and said I could pay him whatever I thought it was worth. I rummaged through my wallet, found 50 lira, and gave it to him. He looked disappointed.

"Just 50 lira?" he asked.

"Sorry, that's all I have."

It was 6:40 a.m. The sun was peeking over the hills to the east. I left Murat behind and headed for the cruise ship docks, the official start of the walk. The sea and the sky were a clear blue. No one was out yet. I had the road to myself. I had been preparing for this for almost a year.

WALKING WITH JOY

When I arrived at the docks Joy Anna was already there, playing fetch with a mangy stray dog while she waited to join me for the first day.

Joy Anna was a 30-year-old American woman from Florida who had moved to Ankara and worked for Turkayfe, a group that promoted Turkey on the internet. They had called me when I was in İstanbul to let me know they would like to help sponsor me for the walk. They also wanted one of their people to join me for the first day. Joy Anna was that person.

We greeted each other. Then, while Joy Anna continued playing with the dog, I reached into my pocket and pulled out a small scrap of yellow paper on which I had scrawled my pre-walk checklist of things I had to do before the walk. I had made this checklist months before, knowing that I would be too nervous at the start of the walk to remember what I needed to do.

The checklist said:

1. Take whiteboard and marker out of pack and write "This day's walk is dedicated to the employees at the Starbucks in Reedley." Put on Fowler Nursery's mesh cowboy hat with the leather hatband, and take a selfie.
2. Erase the Starbucks message.
3. Write on the whiteboard "This walk is dedicated to Pryor Gibson" and take selfie.

When those tasks were finished, I stuffed the whiteboard and marker back into my pack, and crumpled up the note and stuffed it into my pocket. I relaxed a bit and made some more small talk with Joy Anna. Two nearby taxi drivers stood around watching us idly, probably bored by their early morning wait for fares. I smirked to myself, noting that I was about to embark on the biggest journey of my life, and my send-off party consisted of a stray dog, two bored taxi drivers, a bunch of cruise ship passengers sleeping on the ships a few meters away, and Joy Anna.

Joy Anna asked one of the taxi drivers to take our photo. "I'm sure these drivers have no idea who they are taking a picture of right now," Joy Anna commented under her breath.

I thought, *Well yes, that's probably true.*

In order to get to this point, I'd already convinced myself that no one else really cared or needed to care who I was or what I was doing, because nobody else was going to do the walking for me. I had to be motivated to do the walk by myself. Being known could not be one of the motivations for it.

I handed the camera to one of the taxi drivers. Joy Anna and I stood next to the dog, cruise ships behind us, and tried not to squint into the sun while the driver took a few photos.

A local newspaper had asked if they could be there to start the walk with me. But they hadn't arrived yet.

"It's 8 o'clock," Joy Anna said. "Should we get started without them?"

"Yeah," I said, "Let's do it."

So Joy Anna and I started walking through Kuşadası, negotiating the traffic, the potholes, and the hills. The dog and the two taxi drivers stayed behind at the docks.

Once outside Kuşadası, we began climbing some especially steep hills. This was my first experience climbing hills with my huge backpack, and I immediately began to realize that I wouldn't be able to move quickly to dodge traffic, so I would probably need to stay off the road, on the left shoulder where I could see oncoming traffic approach.

As we were climbing one of the grades, two young men rode up on a motorcycle and stopped. They were the journalists who were going to cover us for the local Kuşadası newspaper. They found us walking past a private rest stop with a restaurant that had shade and a place to sit and drink tea. I asked them if they'd like to interview me sitting in the shade at the rest stop, but they said they preferred to do it by the side of the road for authenticity.

They spoke only Turkish and asked us if we were boyfriend and girlfriend. We told them *no*.

They asked me why I was doing the walk. I had thought about it plenty of times before, but I had never been able to explain it to myself, never mind others, so I hesitated for a moment while I searched for the words. One of the journalists filled the momentary silence with "You must be walking for peace," and I said "Yes, that's it" and let it go at that.

After the journalists rode off, Joy Anna and I were thirsty, so we sat in the garden at the restaurant for a while and shared a bottle of water. Then we started walking again. We walked through a number of small villages of about 1,000 to 2,000 people.

I was sweating like a pig by that time and had soaked through my black T-shirt, but Joy Anna decided that it was time to take a picture, so I posed next to one of the village entrance signs hunched underneath my heavy pack, while Joy Anna took a photo.

As we walked through the village we saw a bus full of high school students. The bus was parked at the side of the road and the driver had run into a nearby market. I left Joy Anna at the side of the road and walked up to the bus. As soon as the students inside saw me, they got excited and stuck their hands through the windows. I shook some and gave high fives to others. With the students worked up now, I turned towards the side of the road with a big grin and walked back to Joy Anna.

"Do you know them?" Joy Anna asked me, puzzled.

"No, of course not," I said.

"Then why did you do that?"

"I don't know, that's just what I do. I don't think about it."

Joy Anna and I walked together until at 1 p.m. we came to Havutçulu, a small village of about 700 or 800 people and my destination for the day. Now I would have to find a place to spend the night.

Earlier in the day Joy Anna had taken some of the fear out of that task by telling me that it was perfectly fine for strangers to use the mosques to wash up and to rest. In fact, it was expected and welcomed.

I'd once been told a story about Abraham that is popular in Turkey, and Joy Anna reminded me of the story.

A stranger comes and pokes his head in Abraham's tent door and says, "I'm a stranger out walking from point A to point B. Would it be alright if I come in and have some tea with you and your family?" Abraham invites him in and they are sitting around the stove eating their dinner and drinking their tea when this guy says something bad about God. Abraham is famous for being a big devotee of God and Abraham gets really angry and says, "No one can come into my house and badmouth God and be welcome here. You must go now." Abraham throws the guest out and the guest walks off into the darkness. Then God appears to Abraham and says, "You know, I've been working on that guy for all of his life and he badmouths me and still I'm patient with him, so who do you think you are to decide this for yourself and kick this guy out? It's your job to welcome him also.

Turks grow up on this story. They refer to any stranger or unknown person as a "guest of God." I was happy that Joy Anna had reminded me of this.

Before I set up my tent in the garden, I left my backpack at the side of the mosque and walked Joy Anna out to the main road where I waited with her for a *dolmuş* (mini-bus) to take her back to Kuşadası. After a few minutes one stopped and I said goodbye to her as she boarded.

Then I walked back alone to the mosque to set up my tent.

FIRST BLOOD

Back at the mosque, I pulled my sleeping bag and tent out of my pack, feeling like an imposter, marveling as I set up camp that no one walked up to me to tell me "No, you're not allowed to do this! You can't walk across Turkey and you can't sleep at our mosque!" It wasn't supposed to be this easy.

There was even an outlet nearby for me to charge my iPhone. I sat on a bench, staring at the outlet, wondering if anyone would be angry at me for stealing electricity. I decided to take that risk.

As my phone charged I moved to one of the benches facing the water fountain. The fountains at the mosques tend to be about ten feet high, octagonal, with a faucet on each of the faces. Each faucet on the octagon has a bench facing it like the one I was sitting on. When people came to the mosque to pray they could sit to wash their feet and their hands and their faces before entering.

I felt pretty sacrilegious using the fountains to simply rest and wash, and as I turned the faucet handle and cupped my hands under the flowing water I wondered if God was about to strike me down for using His water to wash my dusty face.

I looked around to see if anyone was watching. I saw no one; the mosque seemed deserted; the village seemed deserted. Havutçulu is a small agricultural village, and I figured the farmers were probably out working their fields. Also, it was between calls to prayer.

As I sat on the wood slat bench waiting for the sun to set, a man about 55 years old drove up in a fancy car with plates from one of the big cities in another province of Turkey. He got out of the car, and as he started walking toward the mosque he looked over at me and blinked, surprised. Then he greeted me in English.

"Hello! Where are you from?" he asked.

"California," I said.

"Is everything ok?"

"You mean with California?"

"No, with you."

"Yeah," I said, "everything is great."

"Can I help you with anything?"

"No, thank you. I'm just sitting here resting. Is it okay if I sit here?"

"Yes, of course it's okay." He added, "You're also welcome to use the faucets to clean up or to do your laundry."

"Excellent, thank you."

I asked him a little more about himself. He told me that he was passing through and had stopped at the mosque to pray. He had been living in Los Angeles for a few years now, and he was visiting family in a nearby village.

I had so far been impressed with myself being a foreigner alone on an exotic adventure, existing in a land where I didn't speak the language. Now here I was speaking English to a man from Los Angeles.

The man walked into the mosque to pray, and I continued sitting in the shade charging my phone. I had expected his permission to make me feel at home, but I still felt like an imposter.

Except for the praying man from Los Angeles and a few passersby, it was pretty quiet. I sat on the bench as still as I could, trying not to disturb the silence around me while my phone charged.

I watched and nodded hello as one man walked by on the street and looked over at me apologetically, as if waiting for me to give approval for his intrusion. Several others who passed by had no reaction to me at all other than a glance. There were a few, though, who stared wide-eyed, then hurried off. I wondered if I scared them. Maybe they thought of me as a ticking time bomb, and if they just treated me quietly and peacefully I would go away and not turn this into an international incident. Or, maybe, I thought, there was an angry mob hiding somewhere waiting for me, ready to appear at any second with their flaming torches, and these passersby were just trying to sneak a peek before the mob appeared.

But there were two or three who stopped and greeted me. They seemed perfectly okay with a stranger sitting in their mosque garden. They told me I was welcome to camp there, wash up in the running water, and use the restrooms. This reception surprised me. I still felt like an imposter, and couldn't accept the idea that it was so okay for me to be there.

Sitting by myself on the bench in the shade was starting to make me feel uncomfortable, so after my phone had charged I ventured out of the mosque gate to explore the streets near the mosque. I came upon a group of young men in a nearby cafe playing Okey (Turkish dominoes) and stopped to watch. I expected them to ask me what I was doing and to send me to some village official to get approval for being there. But they just smiled at me and seemed happy to show me their game.

I watched for a few minutes and then walked back to the mosque. At one point several farm workers all riding together on one tractor drove by the mosque. They slowed down to stare at me and kept staring as their tractor crept past. A few minutes later they reappeared, apparently having circled the block so they could come back and stare some more. I didn't know how to read the blank expressions on their faces. I thought maybe they were going to return again to run me out of town. I stood waiting, but they didn't come back.

As the sun began to set I walked back into the village and had my first dinner of the walk. There was no restaurant. The village was too small to support a restaurant but it was large enough for a *bakkal* (corner market). I walked into the bakkal and bought a container of yogurt, a loaf of white bread, and some cheese. For dessert I bought the local version of a Kit Kat.

Three or four small tables with dirty tablecloths were set up under a grape arbor outside the bakkal. Even though the late summer sun was setting, it was still rather hot, and I was grateful for the shade under the arbor. I sat down at one of the tables, brushed some of the dirt away, and ate my first dinner of the walk as I watched the men and women of the village come home on their tractors.

I thought to myself, *Wow, I am going to survive this.* I had survived the first day. I had walked; I knew where I was going to sleep that night; I had talked to someone; nobody had killed me; I was sitting at a table having my dinner, and the farmers were going back to their homes to have their dinners. I was okay!

After eating, I lingered at the table a few minutes to watch the sun set behind a semi truck parked across the street. Beyond the truck the green of the fig trees and farms on the rolling hills began to darken and cast long shadows.

When I'd finished lingering, I stood up, said goodbye to the people in the market, and thanked them. I walked back to the mosque, but before I crawled into my tent, a guy driving a tractor towing a wagon full of farmers stopped at the mosque, waved, and said hello. After he had explained me to the people in the wagon, he drove away.

Then, though it was early, I crawled into my tent and fell into a peaceful sleep within an arm's reach of the mosque wall, happy and relieved to have "first blood" out of the way.

THE TWO POLISH GUYS

At 5:15 a.m. the wail of the *muezzin*'s call to prayer from the loudspeakers of the minaret rising over me stirred me out of my sleep. Not only was sleeping next to a mosque safe and convenient, the mosque came with an alarm I couldn't ignore. I pulled on my boots and stumbled about 20 meters (22 yards) to the little outhouse in the mosque's garden. Then I knocked down my tent, brushed off the dirt, and stuffed it into my pack. All was quiet. There was no one to say good morning to. I figured most of the adults in the village were probably already on their farms tending to their fig trees since no one came to prayers that morning.

I felt a momentary stab of self-pity. Here I was on the second morning of my big cross country event that was going to take months of my life and there was no one around to share it with. I hungered to hear a simple "Hey, Matt, safe journeys on your second day!" or "Bravo! You made it through the first night!"

I let the feeling pass, pulled on my pack, and walked out to the main road a few hundred meters away, and began walking east towards the sunrise. A few hundred meters later, once I started to feel the call of the day's adventure was stronger than the pull of my warm sleeping bag, I stopped, pulled off my pack, and, for the second time of the walk, I pulled out my small whiteboard, a black marker, and my camera. I scrawled "Today is for Mason Waters," photographed it, stuffed everything back into my pack, and resumed walking.

About 200 meters later, I realized I was hungry. I looked at my watch. It was 6:30, time for breakfast.

I spotted an outdoor tea garden up ahead on the left side of the road. Outside was a dusty handwritten sign advertising *gözleme*. Gözleme, a popular food in Turkey and a favorite of mine, is a layered flatbread stuffed with a choice of crumbled white cheese, mashed potatoes, or spinach. The place seated only about twenty people, and I was their only customer. I asked the owner if he was open. He was. The morning air, though still crisp and fresh, was starting to warm up, so I took a seat under one of the shade trees and ordered gözleme and *çay* (tea).

I was hungrier than I thought, so I greedily tore into my breakfast, scraping the plate to make sure I got every last crumb of gözleme.

When I finished I pushed back from the table, feeling smug and proud of myself for being probably the only person in the world who dared take on an adventure of this magnitude.

At that moment two other men breezily stepped into the tea garden wearing backpacks. I could see by their freshly-pressed t-shirts, cargo shorts, and white Nikes that they were not locals.

I greeted them and invited them to sit down with me for breakfast. They ordered çay and gözleme too. I asked what they were doing and where they were from. One of them spoke a little English; the other spoke none, and neither of them spoke Turkish, but we did the best we could to find words we all knew. I asked them what they were doing and where they were from.

One was named Darek and the other was Piotr. One was a Catholic priest and the other was a diamond-tipped industrial saw blade salesman. They were from Poland and were best friends on an extended walking pilgrimage from Poland through southeast Europe, east through Turkey, south through Syria and Jordan, and finishing in Israel. Their operational model was that they would work at their regular day jobs during the year, and then during their two- to four-week vacation they would leave Poland and walk a portion of the journey. They had already been engaged in this project for some years and had been through Poland, the Czech Republic, Romania, Bulgaria, and northwestern Turkey. The year before, they'd walked from İstanbul to İzmir. This year they were walking from İzmir to Denizli.

The previous night, they told me as we sipped our çay, they had slept in a large, steel ocean shipping container.

I looked at their backpacks and was amazed that they were so small. I wanted to compare weights, so I stood up and walked over to their packs, asking if I could pick them up and look at them. My own pack weighed about 18 or 20 kilos (40 or 44 pounds). Their two packs together weighed half of what my single pack weighed. I asked them what was inside the packs, and they rattled off a brief list of the main contents. I realized I was carrying a lot of equipment that they didn't have. For example, they carried sleeping bags, but no tent. I thought, *man I have a lot to learn.*

At that time, September 2012, Syria's civil war was heating up, and I asked them if they were going to have trouble walking through that country. They didn't seem too worried. They said that because they were walking only two weeks at a time, they would be walking into Syria in five years, and by that time Syria would probably have its problems sorted out.

I sat back down and ordered another tea. Darek and Piotr gave me tips for life on the road, and I told them a little about the country. They finished their breakfast and asked the owner of the restaurant to take a photo of us. Then the three of us shouldered our packs and walked back to the road together. Though we would be walking in the same direction, I let them go ahead first, pretending I had business to tend to before setting out. They took off down the road, and I followed a few minutes later so I could see them off in the distance. I felt a mild sense of comfort being able to see them ahead of me. After about an hour of walking I couldn't see them anymore.

NAUGHTY BOYS AND CIRCUMCISION

It was fig harvest season in the valley, and there was rack after rack of figs drying by the side of the road. Early in the afternoon while I walked, a local farmer waved me over to his side of the road. I went over and shook his hand. He introduced himself as Nasuh and motioned to me to sit down in the shade of his garden's awning. He offered me some chilled watermelon. We sat in the shade eating the chilled watermelon and dried figs, but I was mainly interested in the pitcher of cold water sitting on the table. I greedily drank what water he offered, and was disappointed that he didn't seem to realize just how much I wanted the rest of it.

He spoke only a little English and I spoke only a little Turkish, so we limited ourselves to friendly small talk.

As Nasuh and I were in the middle of chatting I spotted the two Polish guys walking down the road towards us. Somehow during the day I had passed them and not realized it. I called them over, introduced them to Nasuh and invited them to sit with us in the shade.

Since Darek and Piotr didn't speak Turkish, I ended up translating into Turkish what they said and translating into English what Nasuh said. Because of my poor Turkish and their poor English, communication was difficult, and sometimes Nasuh would look at us as though we had said something kind of rude or had turned down his hospitality.

After our snack Darek, Piotr, and I resumed our walk, chatting together for about 3 kilometers (2 miles). Darek and Piotr liked to walk faster than I did, and it was probably easier for them with their lighter packs, but I was finding that the weight of my pack didn't matter as much as long as I walked in a straight line and on flat ground.

When we crossed through a grassy area with some shade trees I told them I was going to take a break under one of the trees. So we said our goodbyes and they continued on.

I took off my pack and rested under one of the trees for about 10 minutes. When I stood up to begin walking again, I felt relaxed. The small villages I had been walking through had thinned out, revealing an idyllic little valley surrounded by hills and full of trees and farms.

After walking for another hour, I came to the edge of Germencik, a small town of about 10,000 people. Two boys, 10 or 12 years old, stood at the side of the road underneath the city limit sign watching me as I approached. The younger one was leaning on a bicycle.

The older one swaggered across the road and asked me for money, eyeing my backpack and the few possessions I had dangling from it such as my evening sandals, my jacket, and a couple of other items. None of it was valuable to anyone else, but if I lost my evening sandals I would have to wear my hiking boots in the evening and I definitely did not want to do that. Everything I was carrying was valuable to me.

When I told him I had nothing for him, he began to grab at the objects dangling off my backpack. I started walking faster, telling him again that I had nothing for him. He started to fall back, and I thought I was rid of the boys. But then they both seemed to realize they could use the bicycle to harass me more efficiently.

The older boy called back to the younger boy to bring the bicycle forward and ride alongside me so he could take over while the older boy rested. The younger boy started pedaling towards me. However, the bicycle was too big for him and he had to stand up in order to pedal. When he did finally wobble up to me begging for money, he tried batting at the backpack with one hand while hanging onto the handlebars with the other. Since he had only one hand free, he had to resort to words rather than actions, and his begging became more and more desperate. I figured I could outlast him as long as he was on the bicycle, and after a few more minutes they both gave up on me. I entered Germencik alone and relieved, but in a bad mood.

There is a commuter train that runs between Denizli and İzmir, two of the larger cities in western Turkey. The tracks that run between the two cities generally run parallel to the highway I was walking on that week. On the other side of the railroad tracks, a couple hundred meters to my left, I saw a large mosque. I thought, *Okay, I'll go check out the mosque, even though it's kind of early to settle down for the night.*

I walked onto the mosque grounds. Soft, cool, green grass grew underneath huge shade trees. The grass was long enough to reach my mid-calf. I could use the fountains and the bathrooms. There was food nearby, everything I needed for the night was there.

I plopped down next to the fountains and gulped water from my bottle. I wiped my chin dry and turned on one of the faucets to clean up a bit. I figured I would wait until the sun went down and then find a place on the mosque grounds to camp.

Just then a man walked up, apparently to pray in the mosque. "Merhaba," he said. He introduced himself and asked what I was doing.

I said, "I'm walking across Turkey, and I started just a couple of days ago."

I expected him to smile and laugh and not take me seriously. Instead, he matter-of-factly said that he had come to the mosque to do his prayers. He invited me to a feast his family was giving—a *sünnet* (circumcision ceremony) for his son. He was headed there after prayers, he said. I eagerly accepted his invitation. As a stranger, I felt quite honored to be invited to such a personal family event.

"Wait a few minutes while I pray," he said, and went inside the mosque.

When he came out from his prayers, I pulled my pack back on and walked with him the couple hundred meters to his house. There were dozens of people milling around in his packed-dirt courtyard, waiting for the chicken to come off the grill. A few dozen people were also seated at long folding tables with white paper tablecloths tacked to the tables.

The man proudly showed me to a seat and walked over to the grill so he could get me the first plate of chicken. I began to make small talk with the people seated around me while I waited. The man brought the first plate of chicken to me and handed it to me with a flourish. It was still pink inside. I smiled and took the plate anyway, because I wanted to be a gracious guest.

I quickly became the center of attention as the other guests turned to me and questioned me about my walk and who I was.

I took part in the festivities for about an hour and a half until my belly was full of chicken, rice, and çoban salata. There was also plenty of *rakı* (aniseed liquor) going around and I drank my fill of that, which was a mistake as I am not much of a drinker.

At about 5:30 p.m., just before the ceremony itself, I began to feel a little embarrassed that I might become the guest of honor at someone else's party, so I told them I needed to go as I needed to finish my walking for the day. I put on my backpack and walked unsteadily out of the yard, shaking a lot of hands as I went. I walked to the main road, which was only about 100 feet away, and leaned against a wall because my head was spinning from the rakı.

I had wanted to go back to the mosque for the night, because it was so comfortable there. However, I had just told everyone I was leaving town.

I continued leaning against the wall for 15 or 20 more minutes, trying to clear the cobwebs from my head before walking on to the next town, Erbeyli, a small village of about 2,000 people.

MY FIRST IMAM

It took me about an hour of walking to reach Erbeyli.

In most of the towns I had passed, the mosque was within 200-500 meters of the highway. In Erbeyli it was a little further off the road, but I could spot the minaret rising into the sky about a kilometer away, on a road perpendicular to the main road. I had picked this as the spot to stay for the night even before I arrived in the village. I heard the call to prayer begin as I entered town, so I stepped up the pace a bit.

I turned left off the highway and crossed the tracks of the Denizli to İzmir train. On the other side of the tracks was a bakkal. These markets are often the social hub of the village, so I popped my head into the market to say hello and tell them I was walking through and would like to go rest a bit at the mosque. I asked if that would be okay, and the owner of the bakkal said that yes, of course, it was fine for me to rest there.

I left the bakkal quickly. I was in a hurry. I wanted to be waiting in the mosque garden when the men came out after prayers.

As I walked deeper into the village towards the mosque, I encountered many families out for a relaxed late-afternoon stroll. Happy, well-dressed boys and girls circled around on shiny new bicycles, welcoming me to their village. I returned their smiles and greetings.

When I arrived at the mosque, I was relieved to see the men were still inside for prayers. I found the fountain, set down my pack, turned on one of the spigots, and washed up as best I could. Then, as I took a look around, I noticed that the garden was completely tiled over. The previous night's well-kept mosque garden had plenty of dirt and grass to sleep on. This one might be more challenging, but with my sleeping pad it wouldn't be too much of a problem.

The men finished their prayers and emerged from the mosque. When they saw me standing there they looked at me questioningly. Who is this unidentified stranger with a backpack standing by the fountains? They didn't seem suspicious, just curious. I smiled at them and nodded and said hello. The larger group dissipated, leaving a smaller group of six behind. They walked over to me, we shook hands and started chatting in Turkish. They asked me who I was and what I was doing there. When I told them I was walking across Turkey they began laughing. "Well, you're just beginning!" they said.

As we made small talk, I commented on the farms in the area and asked what they were growing. The men replied that in this area they grew peaches and figs mostly.

One of the older men, who seemed to be a leader in the group, questioned me further about what I was doing. I told him more about my walk and that this looked like a very comfortable place to stay for the night. "Would you mind if I set up camp here?" I asked. "I have everything I need in my backpack."

"It's probably not suitable," said the older man. "Look, it is all tiled over."

The sun was getting low, and I didn't want to have to move on to the next village, so I pressed a bit more and asked, "Is there another place I could sleep instead?"

The men eyed each other uncertainly. I started to feel uncertain myself. Was it not cool for me to stay at a mosque after all? Was it not cool for me to stay in this village? Then they began explaining that the problem was that the tiled-over mosque grounds weren't really a suitable place for me to sleep. They wanted me to have a roof over my head and a couch to sleep on, they said.

I insisted that I had a sleeping pad and that the tiles were no problem. The older man said, "No, we will find you another place to stay."

Most of the men in the group were elderly, 65-75 years old. One of the six, though, was a younger man in his early twenties. He stood out in the group, not only because of his age, but because he was wearing jeans and a light blue polo shirt with horizontal stripes. He spoke in a clearer Turkish that was easier for me to understand than the slurred Turkish of the older men. The older man I'd been talking to motioned to the younger man in the blue polo shirt and told him to call the *muhtar* (village administrative head). The young man tapped a number into his cell phone and called the muhtar. I overheard him telling the muhtar my story.

"Do we have a place for him?... Yes, he has all his camping gear — sleeping bag, tent, everything.... We don't want him to stay at the mosque. The yard is all tiled over. So what should we do?... No, that space is all used up.... Okay, I'll do that."

The young man hung up.

"We don't have any space here," he said to me, "but would you want to stay at my place?"

I don't know what he thought "space" was, but an offer to stay in someone's home was fine by my book. I nodded yes.

The young man motioned to me and said, "Come with me." So I said goodbye to the older men and started walking down the street with the younger, blue polo-shirted one.

As we walked to his house I asked him some questions about himself. His name was Enes. He was 23 years old, and he was the village's imam.

I had never met an imam before, but my image of imams was that they had long gray beards and mustaches. They wore skull caps and long flowing gowns.

Enes was twenty-three years old and wore polo shirts.

I asked, "Am I going to stay at your place tonight?"

He said, "Yes, of course!"

When we walked into his apartment I saw that he lived like a typical twenty-three-year-old young man who had just gotten his first job and apartment. It was basically a bachelor pad with no furniture to speak of except for a spindly little table in the kitchen, one chair, and a futon mattress on the floor of the living room. Enes dragged the mattress into my room so I could spread my sleeping bag on it. Later, when I opened his refrigerator, I saw only a bottle of ketchup and a jar of mayonnaise.

After a few minutes, Enes needed to leave to take care of some unspecified imam business. I stayed behind, alone in his empty apartment.

I decided to wash up in the bathroom. It was a good thing I wasn't very dirty that day, as the only items in the bathroom were a worn toothbrush, a half-used tube of toothpaste lying by the sink, and a few sheets of toilet paper on the back of the toilet, no spare roll in sight. There were also no towels anywhere. I washed as well as I could and dried off with my t-shirt. Then I laid out my sleeping bag on the futon and checked my emails on my iPhone.

Enes came back to the apartment after dark, about 9:30 p.m. He was talking to a friend on his cell phone. I was sitting in the dark because I hadn't been able to find a light switch. I thought maybe there wasn't even a lightbulb in the apartment, it was so barren.

When he finished the call, he said to me that he was going into the next town to hang out with some of his friends. Would I like to come?

I said, "Sure, of course."

We went to his car, a rundown red subcompact. He cleared some debris from the passenger seat and I plopped down as he went over to the driver's side. While we drove the 10 kilometers (6 miles) to İncirliova, I asked him about the process of becoming an imam in Turkey.

Enes had graduated from an imam school, which is similar to a seminary in the US, but it is run by the government. He was originally from a town about forty miles from Erbeyli. When we graduate from imam school, he told me, the government ministry in charge of placement assigns us to a village, and Erbeyli was the one he had been assigned to after he graduated.

I asked him, "What is the salary of an imam?"

He said that the salary wasn't great. It was about two thousand lira per month, which comes to about one thousand US dollars per month. It's not a lot, Enes told me, but the village provides a house for the imam.

In İncirliova we found his friends sitting outside a restaurant. They were also in their early twenties and were also government employees, but from other departments such as sanitation and postal. I found it strange that an imam and a garbage man got their paychecks from the same personnel office.

We sat on wooden chairs around a little wooden table on the sidewalk and drank tea and talked about girls, fast cars, and vacations, probably what all young men in their early twenties would talk about.

Later, while driving me back to the house, Enes mentioned that he was going out that night to attend a friend's wedding, and he invited me to go along. I told him thank you, but it had been a long day and I would like to turn in. He said he would probably be out late, and suggested that before I leave in the morning we should meet up for breakfast. I told him that sounded good.

Before he left for the wedding he turned on the living room light and showed me where the other light switches were. Alone once again in the imam's unfurnished apartment, I went back to checking my emails and uploading photos onto my website. Around midnight, I turned in and slept soundly.

Monday, 3 September

I woke up the next morning in the early light, about 5:30, expecting to have breakfast with Enes, but he was nowhere to be found. I brushed my teeth, packed my things in my backpack, and walked out to the main road for my day's walk to Aydın, a larger town east of İncirliova, where we had met his friends the night before.

A couple kilometers down the road a red car honked at me and pulled over. It was Enes. He rolled down the window and said, "Hop in, we are going to breakfast!" He wanted to catch me before I got too far away. He apologized, saying he had wanted to have breakfast with me but had to leave early to do some imam business and was glad he had found me by the side of the road.

So we drove to İncirliova and Enes called his friends from the night before to meet us for breakfast. One of them was busy and couldn't make it. The three of us who could make it breakfasted on çay and *poğaça* (a plain, buttery white roll).

"How did things go at the wedding last night?" I asked the two of them.

They told me the wedding had been for a friend of theirs, so they had been out late drinking and had just woken up a few minutes before Enes had pulled up, honking, beside me on the side of the road.

I laughed at the image. Instead of a long-bearded holy man, here was this twenty-three-year-old kid in a light blue polo shirt and jeans getting drunk with his buddies, dancing until late at night at a wedding, and then passing out at a friend's house. I was a little puzzled though. Earlier that morning I had heard the call to prayer in the village.

I said to him, "When I heard the call to prayer I assumed you were at the mosque."

He said, "No, that wasn't me; it was a friend doing back-up for me."

After breakfast Enes asked me if I wanted him to drive me into Aydın. I told him, "No, I need to go back to the spot where you picked me up. I need to walk every meter."

He took what I said at face value. He took me back to the exact spot he had found me an hour earlier. We said our goodbyes, took a photo together, and on I went, walking east.

EAST OF AYDIN

Just a few minutes after saying goodbye to Enes, I met some truckers eating breakfast by the side of the road. They invited me to join them. I declined, saying I had just eaten.

"I read about you in the paper," one of them said.

"Could be. Thanks for the breakfast offer, *afiyet olsun* (bon appetit)," I told him as I resumed walking.

As the day wore on I entered Aydın, a larger city of 191,000 people where I'd planned to stay the night. I felt like a hick. This was my third day on the road and already the noise and grime of a larger city overwhelmed me. I stopped at a restaurant for some *ızgara köfte* (grilled meatballs), and, although I was overwhelmed by the big city, I relished the opportunity to eat my meal incognito, not having to let worries about politeness restrain me from greedily grabbing the last piece of cheese or cleaning out the rice dish. *Oh*, I thought, *the joy of eating unconcerned about abusing one's host's hospitality, eating him out of house and home.*

After my lunch I was so full I could have cried.

Later in the day I took a break from the sun at a mosque east of Aydın. I sat down in the shade on one of the wood slat benches in the garden to rest. It was hot and I was tired. I'd been considering staying at this mosque. The garden was partly tiled over but not completely like the garden back in Erbeyli. There were patches of dirt and grass, so I'd have a place to sleep.

I sat waiting for someone to come by. No one did. It was too early to camp, though, and I figured it would be best to move on.

Sitting in the shade though, I was too comfortable to move on so easily. So I sat for a while longer. I killed some time reflecting on a theory I had begun to develop, about the size of a village and how it affects the fortunes of a foot traveler. In general, I had been finding that I seemed to do better in villages of less than 5,000 people. Even better were villages of less than 3,000 people. There, the pace of living is significantly slower and the residents seem even more likely to engage a stranger in conversation. In a small village it is easier to find the people you need in order to get an invitation to stay.

Eventually, at about 5 p.m., I stood up, pulled on my pack and resumed my walk east. I would be able to walk another hour or two.

After about an hour I came to a village of about 2,000 people called İmamköy and decided I would try to stay there for the night.

As I crossed the railroad tracks to exit the highway and enter the village, I came alongside a group of women coming home from work in the fields. When they saw me they scattered, averting their eyes. In fact, as soon as I walked into the village all the women seemed to disappear. There was not a single woman in sight in the whole town. I realized then that this village would probably be more conservative than Erbeyli.

Shortly after entering the village I saw a bakkal where I could stop and say hello. Outside the bakkal was a little tea garden where a few elderly men sat at tables drinking tea and talking. I poked my head into the bakkal and asked if it was okay if I sat down and got a drink of water. The bakkal owner answered, "Sure, sit down. Have some water."

I bought a bottle of water, set my pack on the ground, and pulled up a chair beside some of the men. After we had made small talk for about twenty minutes, the bakkal owner joined us at the table. He seemed a bit standoffish toward me, and it felt like he was saying, *Just wait a few minutes and let us get to know you before you get too friendly here.*

I started to get nervous. I felt like I was having to audition for a role as a homeless person. And while I completely understood the need for getting to know a person who might be staying in one's village, daylight was burning and if the answer was going to be no I needed to get moving. I tried telling myself, *Okay trust in the universe and give it a little time with these people and things will turn out fine.*

But I couldn't help myself. I blurted out, "Is it okay if I stay in the village tonight?" and gave my usual spiel: "I've got everything I need. I've got my backpack. I've got my tent. I've got my sleeping bag. All I need is a space to set it up."

He looked at me closely and said, "Why don't you sit a little longer and then we will make a decision." The other men just looked at me silently.

I was surprised that the atmosphere in İmamköy could be so different from a village just 20 kilometers away, where I'd been welcomed so readily.

İmamköy suddenly felt empty, gray, and lifeless. Other than myself and these elderly men and the bakkal owner, there was no one in sight. I supposed the younger men were still out in the fields working — the women, too, aside from those who'd arrived in the village at the same time I had. And those women were nowhere to be seen.

There was still some daylight, though, so I sat around with these guys drinking tea. Since it was fig harvest time, trucks filled with flats of figs were coming in and out of the village. I watched the regular delivery trucks as they came by. I watched one truck go by with farm workers headed out to a field and another truck going by loaded with figs, heading for the wholesale market.

Then a truck came through and stopped in front of the bakkal to sell watermelons out of the back of the truck. A few of the villagers appeared on the street to buy some.

The driver of the truck noticed that I was sitting outside the bakkal watching. He picked up a long knife and slit one of the watermelons in half. He walked over to me. "Here, have some watermelon," he said and handed me one of the halves. I savored each bite and let the juice run down my throat and my arms.

When it began to get dark, farmers began returning to the village and the men I had been sitting with scattered to go back to their homes. Soon it was just the bakkal owner and I sitting in front of the bakkal. But his son, who was about ten, soon rode up on his bike with a few other village boys his age. It was getting on toward dinner time.

The bakkal owner called his son over to us and asked him to run upstairs and have his mother prepare some extra food. The family home was above the bakkal. The owner and I would be dining outside that night.

I asked the bakkal owner again if I could stay at the mosque, which was just across the street.

He said, "Well it's unkempt. We don't take very good care of it. So let's find you another space."

I assumed he meant I was unwelcome there in the village, and that I would need to move on to the next village. It was already well after dark, too late to move on, so I felt on edge, nervous that he might not let me stay there.

Then I heard the bakkal owner telling his son, who was still standing by us, that after he talked to his mother about dinner he was to take his friends and go clean out the very dirty storage room next to the unkempt mosque. "We'll put the foreigner in there for the night," he said in Turkish.

He turned to me, shrugged apologetically, and said that there was no electricity in the room and that there was a thick layer of dust over everything. However, there was also no clutter in the room.

I breathed a sigh of relief, knowing that I'd have a place to stay that night, regardless of how dusty it might be.

So the kids went into the storage room, swept out the dust and sprayed down the floor with a hose. Then the son said to me, "Okay, it's clean now. You can go in and get set up."

The room was very warm and wet and humid from being sprayed down. Bedding down in it felt like bedding down in a swamp. Since there was no electricity I set up my camp in complete darkness.

Soon the bakkal owner came out to get me for dinner, and we dined on green beans cooked in a tasty tomato sauce, a cucumber and tomato salad, and olives. We sat at a rickety table out in the open garden across from the bakkal and next to the mosque. His son appeared once in awhile to see if we needed anything from the house.

After dinner the bakkal owner went back inside to take care of his family, and the neighborhood boys came out to play a game of football (soccer) in the street. When they saw that a foreigner was sitting at the table, they came over to me and started asking questions about football. They wanted to know which was my favorite team and which players I liked. Since they were rabid football fans, they knew the names of many of the players and they wanted to know about my favorite team and players.

I told them my favorite team was Fenerbahçe, which is one of the two biggest teams in Turkey. As soon as I said Fenerbahçe their eyes lit up. They said, "Oh, we love Fenerbahçe, too," and they started listing names of players. Immediately the conversation was out of my league, since I don't really care about football, or any organized sport for that matter. But I know that the fastest way to kill a conversation in Turkey is to say you don't care about football, so I just smiled and let them fill my silence with their excitement.

After 15 minutes of discussing football, we played a card game which I didn't really understand. One of the boys was glad to sit next to me and actively play cards while I pretended to learn what was going on. When it was 10 p.m. I said, "Okay, it's about time for me to go to sleep. I've got to get up early and start walking tomorrow." The kids kept playing until midnight.

The bakkal owner had been right about the mosque grounds being unkempt. As in my room, the area around the mosque was completely dark, and I stumbled my way through the litter and debris to find the bathroom next to the mosque. Though I'd taken it personally at first, thinking the bakkal owner didn't want me in the village, I could see he'd had good reason to suggest I sleep somewhere else. This was downright dangerous.

After stumbling my way back out of the bathroom and fumbling my way into my sleeping bag in the storage room, I fell asleep to the sounds of the boys outside playing. I was still sweating. My sleeping bag was made for -20 degrees Fahrenheit, and even though it was completely open and I was laying on top of it, I was still hot.

Tuesday, 4 September

At 6:30 a.m. I was awakened by the sound of the steel door in front of the bakkal being rolled open by the bakkal owner. I wanted to get out of the village pretty quickly, because I wasn't feeling very welcome. So I hurriedly stuffed my things in my pack and walked out of the storage room.

I poked my head into the market to say goodbye and had a rare woman sighting. The man's first customer of the day was one of the village women who had come down for supplies for the morning. But I knew from the code of ethics in the village not to make eye contact or say hello. So I just said to the bakkal owner, "Thank you very much for your hospitality," and gave him my contact information. I walked the 200 meters out to the main road and took the morning picture of my whiteboard with that day's dedication.

As I walked away I thought about the strange lifelessness of İmamköy. I thought of the abandoned mosque. I thought of the women coming in from the fields the day before, turning their eyes away from me. I wondered how it would feel to be born a girl there and have to avert my eyes and to have it determined for me that my life was pretty much out of my control.

I contrasted that with Erbeyli, just 20 kilometers away. Enes was an imam but not like the bearded holy men I'd imagined imams to be. He wore jeans and polo shirts and got drunk. He had fun and talked about girls. I couldn't imagine women in his city averting their eyes in the presence of men. It was a village where people danced at weddings and had fun. It was a village where girls rode bicycles and greeted strangers. It was a village that had made me feel welcome.

I felt uncomfortable and disoriented as I realized that whatever I'd thought would be true of any given place was probably 95% wrong, whether it be about imams, or women in the villages, or people being friendly and hospitable in the west of Turkey and conservative terrorists in the east. Maybe this was how it would be for the months ahead of me. I was going to have to live with that disorientation, allowing the world to present itself to me as it was and not as I thought it was or should be. I'd have to be born a dumb-ass anew each day.

VEHICLE MAINTENANCE YARD

I reached the town of Kösk (population 9,900) early on Tuesday, 4 September. It was only 10:45 a.m. I had planned to spend the night in Kösk, but since it was so early I decided to keep walking right through it. Besides, I was learning that towns that large were too big for walkers like me.

Once I got through Kösk and had a broader view of my surroundings, I noticed the Menderes River valley beginning to narrow. In about four days I would begin the week-long climb onto the Central Anatolia plateau. Reaching that plateau would be a significant milestone for me. It would mark the end of the beginning. I would be well on my way and probably thinking that at some point I would finish this walk.

East of Kösk I found an evil eye charm on the shoulder of the road. The evil eye, known in Turkish as the *nazar boncuğu*, is a Mediterranean good luck charm that stares back at jealous spirits and wards their bad energy away from anyone who might be even remotely admired or known. I had meant to pick one up in İstanbul, but I got distracted and forgot. I leaned down, picked up the charm, and tied it to my pack, where I planned to keep it all the way to the other side of the country. My sunglasses were no longer the only piece of equipment I'd found lying on the side of the road.

The road that day had a very wide shoulder. But in Turkey a wide shoulder is not a safe place to walk, it's an extra lane to drive in when traffic is heavy or when tractors need a place to drive during harvest. Trucks also use them and one whizzed by me every couple of minutes. One of them even swerved toward me intentionally. Maybe the driver was bored and this was just his form of entertainment. He missed me by only a couple of feet. To have a semi trying to see how close it can get to you as it passes is a scary thing to have happen.

I'd learned from living in Turkey that when there is an open space you take it. But in the three years I'd been back in the US preparing for my trek by walking on the side of the country roads near Reedley, California, I'd forgotten that rule. There, people generally didn't drive on the shoulders. So, once back in Turkey, I had to remind myself, *Okay, you need to remember the local habit now or you're going to die before you reach the fence bordering Iran, evil eye or no.*

I stopped at a restaurant for a lunch of *kaşarlı köfte* (cheesy meatballs). The cook knew who I was and how long I'd been on the road. He'd seen me in the paper, he said.

Toward the end of the day I started looking for a place to sleep, but was having a hard time finding one. The first village I rolled into was more like a wide spot in the road, and there were barely enough people to support a bakkal. However, I was tired and I wanted to stop for the day, so I tried it anyway. I spotted a tea garden by the side of the road. I walked up and sat down for tea, took off my sunglasses, and tried to make eye contact with the people at the nearby tables. No one would meet my gaze though, and when I finally did catch someone's eye it was the waiter's.

He walked over to me, leaned toward me, and said before I could introduce myself, "Maybe you better just move on to the next village." I did take that personally, figuring that I was probably smelling pretty ripe.

How did he know I wasn't just there to order tea, I asked myself. I grudgingly stood up, shouldered my pack, and hit the road again.

As the late afternoon shadows grew long, I pulled off the road into Sultanhisar, a small town of 10,000 people in the eastern half of the Menderes River valley. There, I rested in the mosque garden for a bit before resuming my search for a place to stay.

A handful of people at the mosque told me that there was very memorable scenic camping at a set of ruins a couple of kilometers up one of the hills. I had heard about these ruins before — in fact, a number of people had recommended them to me in the past.

I climbed up the hill with my 45-pound pack, even though it was an extra 4 kilometers (2.5 miles) at the end of the day. I had hoped to be finished walking by then.

But I was looking forward to getting to the top. The site had been described to me as bucolic, ancient, and silent, and as having a great view. As I climbed, I thought about how I had made good progress in the last few days, and if I liked the campground I might stay at it an extra day. I had peaceful visions of hanging my laundry out to dry against a backdrop of ancient ruins, looking out over the valley below, sipping tea and feeling content.

There were guards at the gate, however, who told me camping was forbidden there. Tired and frustrated, I told the guards the people in Sultanhisar below had said there was plenty of camping up here. The guards just said, "They don't know what they're talking about."

Dejected, I hiked back down the hill and back into town. I returned to the mosque's garden and sat for a few moments wondering what to do. There was no hotel in Sultanhisar and daylight was burning.

Across the street I saw the city headquarters and a sign above the door: "Mayor's Office."

Sweaty, dirty, and wearing my backpack, I entered the mayor's office and told the staff in the front office that I would like a place to stay in Sultanhisar that night but couldn't find a place, and I told them about being refused entry at the "camping place" up on the hill. The person at the reception desk took one look at me and quickly ushered me into one of the back offices. Someone else came to the back office and said, "Follow me." I followed this person into the mayor's office. The mayor was on the phone — actually on two phones at the same time, looking very busy.

I took my backpack off and sat in the overstuffed leather couch in his office, leaning forward so my sweaty back wouldn't stick to the leather behind me. The attendant who had brought me into the room asked me if I wanted a glass of water. I said, "Yes, thank you very much," trying my best not to seem too eager.

When he finished his phone calls, the mayor pushed back from his huge oak desk, introduced himself to me, and shook my sweaty, dirty hand. I repeated my story to him and asked if he could help me find a place to stay. We chatted for a few minutes to get acquainted. Then he got on the phone again and made a call.

"I've got a foreigner here passing through. Can you find him a place to stay tonight?"

He spoke Turkish very quickly and I didn't quite get everything he said, but when he hung up he looked at me smiling. "I've found you a place to stay," he said. "Go with that guy over there." He pointed to an assistant standing in the doorway, and then picked up one of the phones, since they were both ringing again.

The assistant drove me across the village in a beat-up Toyota to the city's vehicle maintenance yard.

"Is this where I'm staying tonight?" I asked.

"Yes, it is," the assistant said.

I was happy to be assigned any place with a horizontal surface where I could stretch out and sleep, so it was fine with me that the mayor had arranged for me to stay at a maintenance yard that housed the village's stock of vehicles — a couple small buses, a snowplow that probably got used once every 20 years, and a couple garbage collection trucks.

The workers at the maintenance yard were very friendly and hospitable to me, a stranger who appeared suddenly. They invited me to use the yard's office, which had a soft couch I could sleep on, making it the first time in a week I wasn't on a hard surface (even at the imam's house I had been on the floor). There were no lights in the office, but there were electrical outlets where I could charge my iPhone and computer. It was quiet. There was running water. I washed three of my shirts and hung them out to dry.

After I'd settled in, the mechanics on the night shift invited me to join them for a dinner of pide and ayran. After dinner we sat around the table drinking tea and discussing the tensions building in Syria. At 8:30 p.m. I went inside to sleep on the soft couch.

The next morning my alarm went off at 6 a.m., waking me from a deep sleep. I had been dreaming. The last time I remembered dreaming was a week before in Kuşadası. It was hard to believe I had left İstanbul only a week before. I had been walking four days and four nights. It seemed a lot longer. I brushed my teeth, washed my face, and pulled on a freshly-washed shirt. This would be my fifth day walking, and I had not showered in those five days. I hoped to find a cheap hotel or a hostel in Nazilli, that day's destination, where I could celebrate the end of Week 1 by taking a steaming hot shower.

I left the vehicle maintenance yard and walked 3 kilometers to the main road.

Before beginning the day's walk, though, I ate a breakfast of *simit* (a round bagel-like roll covered with sesame seeds) and çay with Mehmet Bey, a dolmuş driver who would be driving the same route I would be walking.

A few hundred meters into the day's walk, I stopped to pull out my notebook and write the following note:

> *Things I learned this week:*
>
> •*Wash shirts at every stop, one at a time so they can dry while hanging from your backpack.*
>
> •*Mosques are great places to wash and rest up. They are like truck stops, but with religion.*
>
> •*Things I need to learn: How to shower more regularly.*

DAY FIVE AND SIX

It was lunchtime when I arrived in Nazilli, population about 120,000. I walked up to the first restaurant I saw and ordered a lunch of kaşarli köfte. Once again, the cook recognized me — he had seen me in the local papers or on the local TV, but he couldn't remember which one.

After lunch, I pushed back from the table, congratulating myself again on finishing five days of walking. I decided that instead of stressing out over finding a place to stay for the night, I would reward myself by staying at the hotel next door.

The lobby of the hotel was bright, the rooms clean. The water was hot, and breakfast was included. All this for $28 per night. Pure luxury by the standards of someone who was now used to sleeping in the dirt. I eagerly took a room.

My first act of celebration was to take a shower. After my shower, I lay down on the clean white sheets before falling asleep for a luxurious nap that started out as a 30-minute catnap but stretched into the rest of the day. I woke up at dusk, only to fall back asleep and sleep soundly through the night.

In the morning I lazily rolled out of bed at 10 a.m. and shuffled down the stairs to the veranda for breakfast. The waiter showed me to my table in the shade of a few large palm trees on the lawn just off the veranda.

I was not starving by any stretch of the imagination. I'd been eating plenty this week, but for breakfast I'd always wolfed down a quick gözleme and çay or simit and çay. This morning, however, I plugged my iPhone in to charge on a wall near the kitchen and then sat back in my chair to leisurely dine. While I waited for breakfast to arrive I nursed the steaming hot cup of çay the waiter had placed before me on the round glass tabletop. I heard water gushing from a fountain and, turning to look, watched it splash out onto the pavement, disappear into a drain, and then return to the fountain to gush again. I enjoyed the sound of the running water.

The waiter soon appeared carrying a platter filled with the traditional Turkish breakfast — bread, an array of jams and preserves, seasoned potatoes, sliced cucumbers and tomatoes, green olives, black olives, and three kinds of cheese. I greedily gobbled down every consumable morsel and then asked for more. When I finished my second plate, I sat for another hour drinking unlimited refills of tea and listening to the water splashing in the fountain.

After breakfast, I stepped off the patio and strolled out to the road to take in the scenery. The hills, palm trees, and farms nestled into the slopes reminded me of Santa Barbara and California's Central Coast. I pulled out my phone to check the Kickstarter campaign. It had reached 72% of its goal, with three weeks to go.

In the past few days, I had slept outside in a mosque garden, on the floor of an imam's apartment, on the floor of an empty storage room, and on the couch in the office of a municipal vehicle maintenance yard. I had learned some basic road skills, like:

•Be friendly.
•Get an early start.
•Drink a lot of water.
•Wear sunscreen.
•Wash a shirt at every stop. Keep a relatively clean set of clothes handy for after each day's walk.
•Mosques are like truck stops with religion — great places to rest up and wash.
•Pass up no opportunity to charge phone and camera batteries.
•Assume nothing; you know less than you think you do.
•Keep it in your pants.

I felt good, at ease with myself and with the world in general. I made a mental note that the next thing I needed to learn was how to shower more regularly.

By then it was shortly after noon, so I decided to head back to my room for a nap. On my way back to my room I realized that if I left the hotel that afternoon, I would need to find a place to stay for the night, so I decided to stay a second night too.

POLISH GUYS AND GAS STATIONS

On the morning of my seventh day on the road, I walked out of Nazilli and stopped at a tea garden near the village of Hamzalı to top off my water supply. The tea garden was tended by a hyperactive 15-year-old boy named Halil who couldn't stop talking about how fast his Peugeot scooter was and how rich he'd be after fixing it up and selling it.

His parting words to me as I left, yelled at the top of his lungs even though I was within an arm's length, were, "Don't forget me!"

"Okay Halil," I said, "I won't. I might even mention you in the book."

Later that day, I pulled into a Shell gasoline station for water and ended up resting in the shade drinking tea and chatting with the station manager.

He mentioned that two men from Poland had come walking through the day before and had camped under a nearby tree. He leaned forward and pointed at the tree.

"When were they here?" I asked.

"They left this morning."

I couldn't believe my ears. Did he just say the Polish guys were here the whole night and had slept just over there? *Man, they've got some mad hobo skills. I need skills like that,* I thought.

I leaned forward as he talked, frustrated that my Turkish was so rusty that even though I listened intently I might not be getting the whole story. I admired the two Polish guys so much I didn't want to miss anything that was said about them.

Darek and Piotr had taken on a kind of a star quality in my mind. I had been on the road a very short time, and was just beginning to learn what I called "hobo skills," things like how to find a place to stay at night and how to wash your t-shirt at a mosque.

I had seen a lot of gasoline stations along the way, but I hadn't been invited to sleep at one yet. *Boy,* I thought, *if I could only figure out how to break that code or learn the secret handshake, it would rock my world!*

When I realized the station manager was not going to teach me the secret handshake, I thanked him for the tea and shook hands with the station attendants. Then, as an afterthought, I asked the manager if I could lie on the grass and take a short rest before I continued on. "Of course you can," he said. So I lay down and took a nap on the grass where Darek and Piotr had slept the night before, hoping some of their hobo skills would rub off on me. And then I stood up, pulled my pack back on, and continued walking.

HORSUNLU

I stopped that day at Horsunlu, a small village at the eastern edge of the Menderes River valley. The river valley at that time of year is very beautiful. Figs and other crops are being harvested. The weather tends to be sunny still, but the heat of summer is breaking and people can comfortably sit out on their patios and their kids play in the streets. The hills leading to the plateau loomed in front of me, and I was looking forward to the change in scenery that would come in a few days as I began the climb up onto the plateau.

I spotted a park in Horsunlu that looked inviting, but first I wanted to get permission to sleep there. As I approached the tea garden a couple of guys waved me over and invited me to sit with them. We chatted for a few minutes, and then I launched into my standard spiel:

"Is it okay if I camp in the park tonight? I've got a tent, a sleeping bag, everything I need to sleep outside."

They said, "Sure. You are welcome to sleep in the park."

I asked them if there was anyone else I needed to speak to. One of the guys said that he was the administrator of the park and there was no higher authority.

I made a mental note to myself, *Excellent, that administrative task has been taken care of.* I could relax now, I had a place to sleep that night.

They recommended restaurants to me, but since there was still plenty of light outside and I wasn't hungry yet, I just continued drinking tea with them.

After about 30 minutes I carried my pack over to the park and set up camp. It was still light outside, so I leaned back into the soft grass, propped my feet up against a tree, and wrote in my journal for a while. Even though I was in a public park in plain sight of curious passersby, I felt comfortable and relaxed.

Shortly after sunset the farm workers began coming home from the fields. A young man and his mother emerged from one of the homes across the street and walked towards me carrying the largest plate of food I'd seen in a long time — figs, lentil soup, shepherd's salad, olives, yogurt, cheese, a plate of bread, and some çay. They introduced themselves (the young man was named Hüseyin) and offered the food to me.

I told them thank you very much, but I am not hungry. I had quickly learned that villagers were going to offer me whatever food they had, and I was too modest to accept, so I had started getting into the habit of eating before I arrived in a village. If I entered a village with a full stomach, I could politely refuse offers of food and still not go to bed hungry.

However, Hüseyin and his mother would not take no for an answer, and insisted on setting the plate of food on a bench for me to eat later. They scurried back to their house across the street and I sat on the concrete retaining wall at the edge of the park to eat from the huge platter of food.

When I'd finished all I could eat, I carried the tray back across the street and left it at their doorstep. Since there was still a little light, I continued writing in my journal.

Shortly after dark the park magically transformed. The place where I had been relaxing in solitude suddenly came alive. While I'd been writing, someone had set up chairs and tables and had created a tea garden. Villagers began congregating in the park for the evening social hour — groups chatting over çay, some playing games, kids playing ball on the grass. A couple of older men, whom I recognized from the mosque across the street, saw me and called me over to their table. I walked over and sat down with them.

"How long will you stay here?" one of them asked.

"One night. I'll leave tomorrow," I said.

I saw a look of disappointment briefly cross their faces. I wondered why they'd be disappointed I was only staying one night.

"Are you Christian?" the same man asked.

"I guess, sort of."

"Have you heard about Mohammed?"

I thought back to their look of disappointment a few moments before, and realized it was because they knew then that they had only one night to convert me to Islam.

"Yes, of course, I've heard of Mohammed," I said.

"Do you know that the Bible is broken?" one of the others asked.

"No, how it is broken?"

"The Koran is a better, cleaner version of God's word. It was dictated directly to Mohammed from God."

"That's nice," I said.

"Given this, how could you not be a Muslim?"

In my broken Turkish I tried to tell them that their logic was good only if you believed in the premise. I didn't believe the premise so I didn't reach the same conclusion.

They tried the same argument again. I didn't know if they didn't understand my clumsy Turkish or if they just didn't want to accept my answer.

I said again, "Your argument is logical if you accept the premise, but I don't believe the premise, so your argument doesn't resonate with me."

We went through this three times. They pushed. I resisted. It became clear a conversion wasn't going to happen that night, so we all got frustrated and agreed to disagree. We finished our tea. I smiled, said goodnight, and went back to my tent.

I slept soundly, falling asleep about 9:30 p.m., even though the park was still full of noisy villagers blowing off steam from the day's labors.

Saturday, 8 September

The next morning I woke up about the same time the villagers were leaving for the fields. I wrote a note to Hüseyin and his mother, thanking them for their hospitality and telling them my mom would be very happy to know her son was being taken care of. Since they had both already left for work, I left the note on their doorstep, pulled on my pack and walked out to the main road.

THE DAY BEFORE SOMETHING WENT WRONG

Saturday, 8 September

About 3 hours out of Horsunlu, I started the climb out of the Menderes River valley. The predictable pattern of farm after farm began to end, and the mile after mile of flat road began to give way to gently-rolling hills.

About 3 p.m. I was climbing up one of those rollers. There were no villages nearby. I thought I was alone, so I was surprised when a boy about 12 years old suddenly appeared alongside me.

"Where are you from?" he asked.

"California," I responded.

"Can I have your sunglasses?"

"No, I need them."

He spotted the sandals dangling from the back of my pack, and pointed at them.

"Can I have those?"

"No, sorry, I need those too."

He started grabbing at my sandals, trying to pull them off the pack. They were attached to the pack with a climber's carabiners, so I didn't worry too much about losing them.

I said, "Sorry man, I need those. They're mine, you can't have them."

I sped up, walking faster and then faster, hoping to leave the boy behind. However, he walked faster too.

I briefly considered trying to break into a run to leave him behind, but I knew that because I was walking uphill with a heavy pack, I would be at a disadvantage. Trying to run would only highlight how vulnerable I was.

Finally, after a few minutes of walking faster and faster, the boy seemed to give up, drifting off to the side and disappearing into the trees.

I was alone once again, but now feeling nervous, realizing how vulnerable the hills and solitude made me. I knew the population would become sparser and sparser the further east I went, and my vulnerability wasn't going to decrease. In fact, the further east I went, the more I would depend on other people. Would they bring me food, or would they try to take my sandals?

About 30 minutes later, shortly after my nervousness had subsided and I had settled back into the calming rhythms of walking up and down the rolling hills, I realized I was getting hungry and that it was about time to eat my evening meal.

I spied a small restaurant and decided I would eat there. Coming closer to the restaurant, I saw that it looked nearly deserted, with only one other customer, and nothing seemed to be happening in the kitchen.

I poked my head in the door, waited for an employee to appear, and called out, "Are you open?"

"Not really. I guess we could make some toast though, how about that?"

"Toast would be good, I'll take it," I said as I found a chair, pulled off my pack, and took a seat. The restaurant overlooked a valley below, in which there were two or three small villages of probably a couple thousand people each.

"Can I get some çay too?" I called out to the employee, who was now busy making my toast.

"Sure, of course."

While I waited for my toast, the one other patron in the restaurant walked over to me. His gait looked a little uneven and his eyes a little crazed.

"Hello, how are you?" I opened.

"I am fine, thanks, and you?"

"Fine, thanks," I said.

"Where are you from?" he asked.

"California. And you?"

He pointed at one of the villages in the valley below, and looked at me with his crazy eyes and a leer. I wondered why small talk about village roots was worthy of a leer, and noted to myself that yes, I must be talking to a crazy person.

I asked myself what kinds of people I had met in the past couple hours. A preteen boy who wanted to steal my sandals, a reluctant fry cook, and a crazy man. Not a rich community on which to rely for the evening. *Better move on, daylight's burning,* I thought to myself.

I hurriedly ate my toast, shouldered my pack, paid the fry cook, and scurried towards the door.

"Aren't you going to drink your tea?" the fry cook called out behind me.

"No, I've got to go. Thanks for everything," I said as I darted out of the restaurant towards the open road outside. I noticed that the crazy man had seated himself at my table. I gratefully breathed in the fresh air outside the restaurant. I felt more relieved with every additional meter I put between myself and the restaurant.

The restaurant had been perched at the top of one of the rollers, so now I was walking downhill. My speed increased, in part from the panic that had come to the surface in the final moments in that restaurant, and in part because my unnecessarily heavy pack was pulling me down the grade as I hurried.

About 10 minutes later I spotted a small hotel on the other side of the road. The signs outside highlighted that hot thermal spring water was pumped into the bathrooms for travel-weary customers to soak in at the end of the day. After my run-ins with the 12-year-old sandal-stealing boy from nowhere and the crazy man at the deserted restaurant, I was too skittish to camp outside that night. A bath in hot thermal spring water sounded great, so I pulled up to the hotel and asked them how much for a night.

SOMETHING'S WRONG

The next morning I pulled on my pack and walked out of the lobby of the Thermal Springs hotel. I started to cross the road to begin my day's walk, but stopped when I spied the hotel's breakfast buffet.

I had been in such a hurry to get back on the road that I was about to break one of my new cardinal rules: *Eat real food whenever possible.*

I eagerly wolfed down the cheese, bread, cucumbers, and tomatoes available at the buffet. I scarfed down a couple of glasses of orange juice, pulled on my pack again, and crossed the road.

I stopped at the shoulder on the other side of the road, pulled my camera and whiteboard out of the pack and wrote my daily dedication on the whiteboard. I photographed it, stuffed it back into my pack, and continued walking.

The scenery change that had begun to appear yesterday was nearly complete now. The lush flatlands of the Menderes River valley, where farm after farm had lined the road, had given way to gently undulating rolling hills, empty pastures of wild brown grass, and an occasional tree. My climb onto the Central Anatolia plateau had begun, and would last for about a week.

I had been walking only two or three minutes, taking in the new scenery and falling into the day's walking rhythm, when I felt a sudden stabbing pain in my right foot. I thought maybe there was a rock in my boot, so I stopped, pulled off my boot, held it upside down, and shook it to get rid of the rock.

Nothing came out. Figuring whatever rock I had picked up was gone now, I put my boot back on and put my weight back on the foot. A bolt of pain shot out of my foot and went up my leg. There was no rock. This was coming from inside my foot.

I walked a few more steps, hoping the pain would go away. It didn't. I walked a little further, taking extra care to watch my form and make sure I wasn't getting sloppy, but the pain became sharper. By the time I had covered another 100 meters, it was quite debilitating, an acute "you're not going to use this foot anymore" sort of pain.

Panic started to set in. I had walked over a thousand miles in the US in order to make sure this wouldn't happen in Turkey, and here it was happening.

I thought, *Boy, if this continues I won't be able to continue walking and I still have 95% of the country to cross. This is not the right time to find out I'm not going to be able to do it.*

But I limped on. Over the next few kilometers I tried to stay off the hard pavement by walking on a number of different surfaces. When there was dirt on the shoulder, for example, I walked there for a while. Coming to a construction zone, I walked for a while on the soft, newly-laid asphalt. The asphalt was sticky, and I could feel its heat through my boots, but at least it was soft. A little later I came upon a grass-covered median strip, and I walked on that for a while.

I stopped at a gasoline station midway through the day for a break. My foot was still hurting. The pain hadn't let up. I was in a full panic at that point, realizing that if the pain did not go away I would not be able to continue another day, and I was only about 5% of the way across a country I had promised, to myself and to others, to walk. I had even spent the last couple hours coming up with a Plan B, so I would be able to continue the walk even if I couldn't carry my pack anymore.

The gasoline station was in the middle of a construction zone, so there were no customers, just two attendants sitting in lawn chairs in front of the office, looking out at the empty road. Hiding my panic and my limp (or trying to, at least), I said hello and motioned to the store. One of the attendants jumped out of his chair and followed me into the store, where I bought a bottle of water and a bag of cookies. I figured I was one of the few customers that day, so I used the bathroom, said goodbye, and hobbled back to the road, trying to hide my limp as I went.

About an hour later, still limping, I came to a bend in the road. I recognized the bend from the map. The road was turning from straight east to southeast, the direction of the city of Denizli. There was little to no shoulder along the bend, just a steep drop-off, and to make the situation even more challenging, a guardrail curved around the bend. On one side of the guardrail, I would risk getting hit by cars. On the other side, I would risk falling off the drop-off.

Under normal circumstances, I would just take a deep breath, mutter a prayer, run through the section, and hope no cars showed up to hit me. But in my new state I couldn't run, and I still didn't want to get hit by a car, so I chose to hold tight to the guardrail and tried not to fall off the drop-off.

About an hour or two later I reached the village of Sarayköy. I stepped off onto a side road and walked a few blocks deeper into the village, looking for a mosque garden or some place to rest for a while. I found a covered garden area near a car mechanic's shop. A man about 35 years old was working in the shop and he came out to say hi. He invited me to sit down at a nearby picnic bench, protected under some wooden eaves from the late summer sun, and went back inside the shop to get a couple of glasses of cold water. I took a seat and waited for him to return.

It was hard to concentrate on anything except the shooting pain coming from my foot, but I tried to wipe any sign of worry off my face, so that when he came back he would see me relaxed and smiling.

He arrived with the cups of water and we sat there drinking our water and making small talk. After about 20 minutes he took his leave, apologizing for having to go back to work. I thanked him for the water and said all was fine and asked if I could sit there for a few more minutes. "Of course," he said.

I sat there hoping that either my foot would magically stop hurting, or that I would realize there was a Plan B that would make the problem irrelevant, but neither happened. So after a few minutes I pulled my pack on and limped back out to the main road. Visibility was clear, the road straight, so I initially estimated that it would be easy to cross. However, I found I still couldn't move fast enough to cross in the available window of about 30 seconds between passing cars. I could barely cross a deserted road through a quiet village. *This is bad,* I thought.

I finally managed to cross the road, and I walked another two kilometers to the center of the village, but then I stopped and thought, *I can't do this anymore.*

What was I going to do? I hadn't seen anyplace quiet and hospitable in this village where I could camp for the night. Plus, I was going to need to do some thinking and I was going to need to be alone for a little while to do it. A public place or staying in somebody's house was not going to work.

So I decided to catch a mini-bus back to the Thermal Springs hotel, where I had stayed the night before. I waved down a mini-bus, loaded my pack into the back, and rode back to the Thermal Springs hotel. The hotel owner welcomed me warmly, recognizing me from the night before, and quickly showed me to my room.

I had spent the day trying to put on a smiling public face and to hide my limp. I hadn't told a soul about my problem. Once I got up to my room I took off my pack, leaned it against the wall, and let the panic rush in. My walk had only just begun, and I could barely cross a street. In fact, I could no longer put any weight on my foot at all. I couldn't even walk across the room to get a bag of crackers and oranges I had set down on the desk, so I went without dinner.

It was late Saturday afternoon.

I gave myself a talk: *Okay, Matt, you can let things get as black as they need to go for the rest of the day. Just let your emotions run wild, don't worry about putting on a stoic public face anymore, just let the emotions flow now. But tomorrow morning you are going to have to wake up and solve the problem, because nobody else is here to solve it for you.*

I didn't know how I was going to solve the problem, but I decided I would have to take it on faith that I would.

It was pretty hot in the room, so I lay back on one of the beds and turned on the air conditioning. I put my feet up on the wall so the excess blood could drain from my feet and my legs. I tried to fall asleep but couldn't, so I just lay there with my feet propped against the wall and stared at the ceiling as the tears rolled down my cheeks.

Shortly after I realized it had grown dark outside, I hobbled into the bathroom and drew a hot mineral bath. *The hotel likes to brag about the healing powers of these hot thermal springs, maybe I should test them out,* I thought. I eased myself down into the warm, penetrating, cloudy-white water. I'm sure under any other circumstances it would have been quite relaxing, but I wasn't in the mood. The bathtub was lined with stone tile, and as I sat there naked, my foot throbbed against the unforgiving surface of the tile.

Realizing the bath was not going to make me feel any better, I stood up, dried off, hobbled back to bed, and quickly descended into a dark, dreamless sleep.

GOING BACK TO HORSUNLU

The next morning, I woke up knowing that I was going to have to do whatever it took to work my foot back into shape. So I hobbled downstairs to breakfast and decided to come up with a plan.

Before sitting down to eat, though, I walked a couple laps around the parking lot to test my foot without the load of the pack.

On my practice walks before coming to Turkey, I had made sure to walk barefoot about a mile every day, so even the tiny muscles in my foot would get exercise they didn't get when I wore shoes.

I had been wearing shoes every day during the walk now, and I knew from experience that when I stopped walking barefoot at least a little each day, those tiny muscles only lasted for about two weeks, so I suspected that the pain was caused by their atrophy and the fact that other parts of my foot would not be getting the same muscular support they were used to getting.

I figured that I would be able to work those small muscles back into shape if I could spend four or five days doing nothing but focusing on their recovery. That meant I would need a need a cheap and hospitable place to work, uninterrupted, for those four or five days. I thought of Horsunlu, where I had been a couple of days before. The people had been friendly and the public park had been a comfortable place to spend the night. Most of the villagers were at work during the day, so I would be able to work my foot during the day when no one was around to distract me. Horsunlu was probably my best bet.

When I finished eating breakfast I grabbed my pack from the lobby and hobbled across the street to catch the mini-bus back to Horsunlu, covering in just half an hour what had taken me a full day to walk.

As the bus pulled into Horsunlu I asked the driver to pull over at the village's traffic light. He got off the bus with me and went to the back and pulled out my backpack. I put it on and hobbled off the main highway and down the side road into Horsunlu.

The village was alive with festivity. It was weekly market day, and tents were set up alongside the road where shopkeepers sold items such as T-shirts, dried figs, spices, and cheap plastic kitchenware from China. I felt alone. People were milling around me everywhere having fun. I hobbled along desperately, full of self-pity, unsure of what I should do next.

As I passed the main tea garden, I spotted the familiar faces of people I'd met when in Horsunlu before. They called me over.

"Welcome back to Horsunlu!"

"Just couldn't resist us, huh?"

"We missed you!"

"Thank you," I replied as I pulled up a chair and joined them at the table. I waved the waiter over to bring me a cup of tea.

"What brings you back to Horsunlu so soon?" they wanted to know.

"Well, my foot hurts," I said, "and I need a few days to rest it up. Is it okay if I stay in the public park there?" I pointed over to the grassy park where I had stayed a couple of nights before.

"Sure, of course you can stay there again. We're happy to have you!"

I was very happy to be back in Horsunlu. I had seen these people only once before for one night, but I'd felt so welcome here that it quickly seemed a second home.

After finishing my tea, I picked up my pack, hobbled the 200 meters to the park, and set up camp under the same tree as before.

At the end of the day I was beginning to feel a little more confident that at least now I was in the right place, and tomorrow I would wake up and start working my foot back into shape.

HEALING MY FOOT

Once I got my tent set up in the park, the feeling of panic I had felt back in the hotel 36 hours earlier subsided, and now I calmly lay back in the familiar grass, my feet casually propped up against the familiar tree.

As the light fell, people came out of their houses to take evening strolls around the village. They began to notice that I was back. I suppose I was hard to miss: a foreigner, vaguely familiar now, his tent set up in the village's central park, reclining in the grass.

So about 20 times I had the following exchange:

Villager walks past the park, notices me, turns head towards me, stops walking, tilts head curiously.

"You're back!"

"Yes, I am."

"What brings you back?"

"My foot. I hurt it and I need a few days to heal it."

"So you'll be here a few days then?"

"Yes, looks like it."

"Welcome back. Geçmiş olsun."

"Thank you, much appreciated."

Tuesday, 11 September

After breakfast the villagers either climbed onto their tractors to go work in the fields or piled into the commuter train to commute to work in one of the nearby towns. I stayed behind to work on my foot.

I knew from my training before coming to Turkey that the first thing I needed to do was to diagnose the problem by walking barefoot. Walking barefoot gave me a level of precise feedback that was not available to me when shod. So I took off my shoes and emptied my brain so that my foot could tell me what it needed, instead of me telling my foot what I thought it needed.

I began walking barefoot on the stone pathways through the park, making a mental note of which muscles were giving me trouble and would need work in the next few days.

This diagnosis work took me about half an hour, and then I was ready to begin working those particular muscles back into shape. I limped to one end of the stone walkway and stared at the other end. The other end was a mere 50 feet away, but those 50 feet seemed as far away as the other end of the world. I took a deep breath, started with my left foot, and began walking. My right foot hurt every time I put my weight on it, which scared me, but I reminded myself that the point was not to be free of pain, the point was to rebuild the muscles in my foot so I would gradually feel less pain.

I limped to the other end, turned around, and repeated the process. *Stare at other end of walkway. Take deep breath and summon courage. Begin walking. Get to other end.*

I continued like that, walking back and forth, for about two hours. Once in awhile, one of the remaining villagers would walk by or watch me from a distance. I suppose mine was a puzzling presence — a stranger, tent set up in the park, Turkish barely good enough to explain what he was doing, walking barefoot back and forth, back and forth in the park.

At noon I took a lunch break, lying down on my back in the grass next to my tent, my feet propped up on the nearby tree to drain the blood and avoid any swelling. I munched on some cookies I had bought from the bakkal. One of the villagers had seen me walking my laps in the park and knew that I was healing my foot. She emerged from her front door, scurried across the street, and handed me a large block of ice before scurrying back into her home.

Thankful for the ice, I rested my right foot on it for a few minutes, and then stood up and walked back to the stone walkway to resume my work for the afternoon.

Shortly after lunch my foot felt good enough to begin walking longer laps around the park. On the other side of the park I spied a concrete amphitheater. The amphitheater was a mere 100 feet away but I had been so focused on my foot that morning that I hadn't noticed it. I decided that by the end of the day I wanted to be able to walk up and down the amphitheater steps.

Then the negative self-talk began:

You want to walk across the country, but you can't even climb up and down an amphitheater's steps.

You're never going to figure this out. Your walk is doomed.

I pushed the negative thoughts out of my mind:

That's just negative self-talk, don't listen to it, just concentrate on the next few feet in front of you. Take it one step at a time. No pun intended.

For most of the rest of the afternoon, I continued walking laps around the park. Walk a few laps. Rest on one of the park benches. Walk a few more laps. Rest on one of the park benches.

My impatient self and my methodical self began fighting each other:

This is ridiculous, you should be out conquering the world, my impatient self would say.

No, this is exactly what we need to be doing right now, my methodical self would chime back.

But this is ridiculous, you know it is, come on, admit it.

Whatever. This is what we need to do right now.

But, but…

That's right, calm down. There will be plenty of time to conquer the world later. Right now this is exactly what we need to do. Leave us alone, let us do our work.

For most of the rest of the afternoon, I continued alternating between walking laps around the park and resting on a park bench. I began eyeing the amphitheater stairs, knowing that my rendezvous with them was coming soon. They would be my test. Had all these laps around the park been doing me any good?

With about an hour to go before the villagers started returning home from work, and knowing that I would certainly be invited to a social gathering of some sort in the evening and wouldn't be alone in the park anymore, I decided that the test time had come. It was time for me to try the amphitheater stairs. I stood up from the park bench and walked over to the stairs. I eyed the top of the stairs. It was a small amphitheater, so there were only about 10 stairs, but again, the top end of those 10 stairs looked as far away as the edge of the universe.

I took a deep breath and stuck out my left foot. I lifted it up onto the first stair and put my weight on it. It felt fine. But of course it did. That wasn't the one I'd hurt.

I lifted my right foot onto the second stair and put my weight on it. A bolt of pain shot up my leg. I grimaced as I clumsily heaved myself up onto the second stair.

Uh oh, that wasn't good, I thought to myself.

I tried half of the stairs like that. Every time I put my weight on my right foot, the shooting pain went up my leg, and I grimaced.

Halfway up the set of stairs, I decided I would go back down and try again tomorrow. I turned around, but going down turned out to be harder than going up. The panic began to rise again.

I walked a few laps around the park, hoping to return to normal and to tamp down the panic. I returned to the park bench to rest, telling myself that I would learn how to walk the stairs tomorrow. Then I got up to walk a few more laps before going back to my tent to lie in the grass, prop up my feet against the tree, and wait for the villagers to come home.

When the farmers on their tractors and the office workers on their commuter train began to return, my friend Hüseyin, the one who, with his mother, had brought me the big platter of food the other night, stopped by and invited me to dinner at his house. His mother would be cooking.

"Of course," I said, already tasting her home cooking on my tongue. "What time?"

"We'll eat in about 30 minutes."

A half-hour later, I limped across the street to Hüseyin's house. I limped in part because my foot still hurt, but also because I wanted to keep my weight off it, noting that I had made some progress that day and didn't want to undo it.

Inside for dinner there were seven of us: Hüseyin, his wife, his mother, two of his sisters, his young nephew, and me. We spread a cloth out on the floor and ate village style, sitting cross-legged on the cloth, eating from communal trays of cold green beans in tomato sauce, carrot salad, and copious amounts of bread. After dinner, the women cleared the trays while Hüseyin attended to some domestic chores of his own, and then we re-congregated in the living room to digest the huge dinner with cup after cup of çay while watching the news.

After about an hour, Hüseyin said he needed to go visit a relative in the village and asked me if I wanted to stay and watch TV.

"No thanks," I told him, "much appreciated, but I think I'll go back to the park. Thank you so much for dinner, it was great."

Hüseyin and I both left the house. I crossed the street, and as I entered the park, the older men who had tried to convert me when I was there a few nights before spotted me, and, probably relieved to think that I was back for another religious conversion attempt, called me over to their table for some çay and God talk before bed.

Wednesday, 12 September

The next day, my Christianity still intact, I walked more laps around the park, and, many times, successfully climbed and descended the stairs. Things were looking up. I figured that tomorrow, my third full day in Horsunlu, I would tackle the dirt road outside the park, and that four days in Horsunlu would be enough (two of them had already passed). By then my foot would be good enough to resume the walk.

That evening, once again, Hüseyin invited me to dinner at his family's house. As we did the evening before, we sat village style, cross-legged on the floor, eating from communal platters.

After dinner and çay, however, instead of Hüseyin's running off to visit relatives, or my running off to participate in yet another attempted religious conversion, all nine of us (the seven from the night before, plus two additional ones) lounged back onto the pillows. I got to play my first game of Okey, the Turkish version of dominoes. I had only a vague notion of what I was doing, yet with a lot of help from my fellow players I managed to win a few games. I could barely recognize what a winning hand was, though, so for all I knew they were just being nice to me.

At one point, Hüseyin's cousin interrupted the game to bring out a shallow plastic tub and a clean cloth. He put my right foot in the tub and began to wash it with olive oil. He was aware that my right foot was hurting, and he wanted to do anything he could to help. I felt a little embarrassed and uncomfortable, having my foot cradled and washed, and I eyed the other family members to see the expressions on their faces. They seemed to approve of his activity, so I swallowed my embarrassment and allowed it to happen.

During the foot washing, Hüseyin got up to leave the room. I briefly thought he might not approve of the foot washing, but a few moments later he reentered the room with an armful of objects and walked over to me. He spread the objects out on the floor and took a seat next to me. He waited for his cousin to finish drying my foot, and then he asked me if I had heard of Rumi.

"Of course," I said. "Rumi was a great man."

Rumi was a 13th-century Persian poet and Sufi mystic buried in Konya, a city I would be walking through.

"Yes, he was. Have you read his poetry?" Hüseyin asked. He picked up one of the objects, a small book.

"Only a little. But I liked what I read."

Hüseyin handed me the book. It was a collection of Rumi's poems. I thumbed through it quickly. It was in Turkish, but I figured I could read it albeit slowly, it would be a good challenge for me.

"Take this book with you," Hüseyin said, "you can read it on the road."

"Thank you, thank you very much," I said.

Next Hüseyin picked up a large lead-and-glass lantern with an image of Rumi inside.

"This will make a great addition to your home after your walk," he said.

"Yes, it will," I agreed, eying it warily. Neither would I be able to carry a lantern made of lead and glass the rest of the way across Turkey, nor would I have a home to put it in when I finished.

I reached out to accept the gift and said, "It's so beautiful, but I am afraid it will break in my backpack. Is it okay if I leave it with you and pick it up after the walk?"

"Yes, of course," Hüseyin replied.

I knew I needed to lighten my load a bit, and saw an opportunity to leave some other stuff with him, too, "I also have some other things in my pack I'd like to leave with you and come back to pick up later, is that okay?"

"Sure," Hüseyin said, and he showed me to a storage room at the back of the house where I could leave the lantern and whatever else I'd like.

My logistical concerns taken care of, we resumed our game of Okey and drank some Turkish coffee.

About 9 p.m., I thanked his mother for dinner, took my leave, walked across the street back to my camp in the park, and curled up in my sleeping bag for a good night's sleep.

Thursday, 13 September

Thursday morning I woke up and waited until most of the village left for work again, and then I continued working my foot back into shape. I walked a few laps around the park to get warmed up, walked up and down the amphitheater stairs a few times to make sure the previous day's improvements were still intact, and then I ventured out onto the dirt road next to the park.

Though the soft dirt road made an excellent padding under my feet, the surface was a little uneven. But after a couple hours of walking laps, 300 meters out and 300 meters back, my foot adjusted to the unevenness. By lunchtime I was able to walk the laps with few problems. I was glad to see my foot was coming back into shape quickly and predictably. Another day of working it, I figured, and I would be ready to conquer the open road again.

FATIH AND FERIDUN

On Friday morning, my fourth morning in Horsunlu this time around, I woke up and got ready to begin another day of working my foot. I didn't know yet what I would do on that day, maybe start with some laps on the dirt road, and then graduate to walking out to the main road.

As I stood on the stone walkway trying to decide, Fatih, one of the villagers I had come to recognize, walked past. He spotted me and paused for a moment, "Come with me," he said.

"Where?" I asked.

"To my shop, of course."

"You mean, the one out on the main road?"

"Yes, of course," he laughed.

I briefly thought about how that would be skipping ahead a few steps in my self-imposed rehabilitation plan for the day. But the "always say yes" part of my personality won out.

"Sure, sounds good, let's go."

I walked, gingerly, with Fatih out to his shop on the main road. We took a seat in the shop's small, cramped office. I drank çay while Fatih returned some phone calls and Feridun, his assistant, looked over some papers.

Each time a customer poked his head into the office, I was introduced as an honored guest, and I told my story again. Yes, I was walking across the country. Yes, I was from America. Yes, I was walking alone.

Fatih had some business he needed to attend to elsewhere, so he left me with Feridun. I moved to a table outside in the yard. Feridun came over with a hammer and a paper bag filled with hazelnuts, and spread the nuts out on the table before me to keep me busy while he attended to the customers. I sat at the table breaking open the hazelnuts with the hammer and drinking çay while Feridun picked up a hose to water down the dusty yard in between helping customers who came in for bags of cement or bricks for their construction projects.

After a couple hours in the yard, Feridun's assistant Emin arrived and jumped into the passenger seat of a fully-loaded coal delivery truck. Feridun hopped into the driver's seat, fired up the engine, and drove the truck over to me.

"Hop in," Feridun called out to me.

"Where are we going?" I asked.

"Out for some coal deliveries."

I jumped into the delivery truck, squishing Emin to the center, and the three of us took off up the highway into the hills and surrounding villages to make the deliveries.

While we were making the deliveries, Feridun had a huge smile on his face. He waved hello to every car, truck, and tractor we passed, slowing down to hang out the window and chat with the drivers, one hand still on the steering wheel. Most people would see it as an afternoon delivering coal, but to Feridun it was apparently an opportunity to work the crowds.

We stopped to make a quick delivery at a corner market. I hopped out of the cab to buy a bottle of water. Feridun took the opportunity to make small talk with some of the other shop patrons and seemed to relish the opportunity to explain to them who the foreigner was.

Next we stopped at a house where four elderly people sat in the shade sorting figs. For some reason, one of the water mains was open and fresh, cool water was gushing out, flooding the street, the entrance to the yard, and part of the yard itself. Feridun was embarrassed. He wanted me as his guest to have as little interruption as possible. But I was happy to see all this abundance of clear, clean water. I took my shoes off and sloshed around through the mud and let the cool, clean water that was rushing over the cement ice and bathe my feet, one of which was still hurting kind of bad. I took a photo of my feet in the water.

At a later stop a woman was removing the pits from green olives and then stuffing the olives with red pimentos. While Feridun and Emin unloaded dozens of bags of coal, I climbed down from the truck's cab to watch the woman do her work. She used a scissors to cut pieces of a big pimento into little pieces. Then she would take one green olive out of one bucket, stuff a pimento piece into it, and put it into another bucket. All my life I had eaten stuffed olives, but it had never occurred to me to think about how they had been stuffed.

As much fun as the deliveries were, I am a homebody at heart, and I wanted to get back to the familiarity of my tent and the public park that had become my home. So I was happy when the last delivery was made and we stopped at a tea garden next to the highway, for one final tea before driving back to Horsunlu.

Not surprisingly, Feridun seemed to know almost everyone at the tea garden. He made his rounds, pressing the flesh while Emin disappeared to another location and I took a seat at one of the tables. One of Feridun's friends came to my table and pulled up a chair next to me.

"Hello, how are you?" he asked me in Turkish.

"Fine, thank you, and you?"

"Good, thank you. You're not from around here, are you?" he asked.

"That is correct, I am not from around here," I replied, "I am from

California."

"Is that in the United States?"

"Yes, it is. Have you been there?"

"No," he replied.

He peered into my eyes, searching for something. I wondered what.

"Is it true that Obama is interfering in Syria?" he asked.

"I don't know."

"Yes, Obama is interfering in Syria," he stated.

"That's good to know." A political conversation was about to start, and I didn't want to have any part in it, as my language skills weren't good enough to handle the nuances it would take.

He asked again: "Is it true that Obama is interfering in Syria?"

"I don't know, I'll ask him next time we have lunch."

He asked again: "Is it true that Obama is interfering in Syria?"

"I don't know," I replied, "It is absolutely true that you said he is." A phrase like this was at the limits of my Turkish, so I waited to see how badly I had messed it up.

The man looked at me, confused.

He asked again: "Is it true that Obama is interfering in Syria?"

"I don't know," I replied, again, "It is absolutely true that you said he is."

He paused, peered closer into my eyes, smiled, wagged his finger at me, and said, "You're not going to tell me, are you?"

"No," I replied, "I'm not."

He nodded. "Then let's drink some tea." He raised his glass to mine, smiled again, and said cheers.

We drank our tea and made tense small talk about the weather and the fig harvest. I commented on how beautiful the valley was, and how friendly the people had been.

Feridun, who had been walking around saying hello to everyone and shaking hands, came back over to our table. He tapped me on the shoulder.

"It's time to go. Let's go back to the truck."

I was relieved to have an excuse to duck away from my questioner. I followed Feridun back to the truck. Emin re-appeared, as if by magic, from wherever he had disappeared to. The three of us hopped into the cab. Feridun fired up the engine, and we pulled back out onto the main road and headed back to Horsunlu.

Scrunched into the cab with the two of them, looking out the window at the farms we passed, I wondered if Feridun's friend back at the tea garden had signaled to Feridun that he hadn't been pleased with me, but apparently all was okay. Feridun was as good-natured as he had been all day.

About 10 minutes later we arrived back at the cement yard in Horsunlu. It was getting late, and I wanted to get back to my tent in the park, so I thanked Feridun and Emin for a great day and took my leave. My right foot was still hurting a bit, so I limped the 5 or so blocks back to the park.

I had enjoyed my day with Feridun and Emin. While I limped back to the park, I congratulated myself on my day delivering coal in rural Turkey and how unusual I would probably seem to the people back home.

I'm one of the few, I am uniquely adventurous, I am one of a kind.

But then I thought of the self-satisfaction I had felt the week before, at breakfast on the second day of the walk, and how quickly my self-congratulatory bubble had been burst when the two Polish guys walked up to my table.

Don't break your arm patting yourself on the back, I cautioned myself, *you never know what's about to happen.*

I got back to my tent before the post-dinner crowd came out to the park for their evening socializing. It had been a long day, so I crawled into my sleeping bag and fell asleep without eating dinner. It had been an unplanned day, but a good one, and my foot was still hurting a bit, but I was itching to get back out on the road. I needed my beauty sleep.

Friday, 14 September

Friday morning I rose before dawn and knocked down my tent. I wrote a note to Hüseyin's family, posted it under their door, and walked out to the main road to catch the minibus back to Sarayköy to continue my walk into Denizli. My spirit had been restored, and though my foot still hurt, it had healed enough to carry my pack if I walked carefully.

THE WATERMELON GUYS

The day's walk was along a section of road with gently rolling hills, gradually climbing towards Denizli, a city halfway between the Menderes River valley and the Central Anatolia plateau. My right foot was still hurting a bit, not enough to limp, but enough to need to be careful with it. I welcomed the gradual uphill climb, because the slower pace meant I was moving my body slower, and so had extra time to pay attention to my form.

Midway through the morning, I felt like taking a little break. So I leaned against a rock near the shoulder. I set down my pack, opened it, and pulled out my iPhone to check my email. I saw an email from my friend Denise Waters, a teacher at an elementary school near Seattle. I had told her that I would welcome inquiries from her 4th-grade class. She had forwarded one of their questions to me:

"Why are you walking? Why don't you just take a bus?"

Good question, I thought. I'm not really sure. I looked out across the valley below for a moment, searching for that place deep down inside me that might have something to say. I tapped a reply into my phone:

Yours is an excellent question. Taking a bus would in fact allow me to see more of the country. Walking will limit my range. If something is a mere 60 miles out of my way, it is not a quick day trip. Sixty miles is an hour or two by car, but it is a week on foot.

The reason I want to walk is I want to challenge myself to be less afraid of the world. To be less afraid to admit I misunderstand something. To be less afraid to admit something is out of my control. It is difficult to admit those things, but much comes from doing so. After all, if I am busy insisting I understand something I don't, or trying to control something I can't, it is awfully hard to be open to creativity and inspiration.

I like to talk about these things, and I figure that if I am going to talk about them, I better practice them. Walking is me practicing them. It is me putting my life where my mouth is. It is me submitting to the world. When I walk, my speed is slow, and my range is limited. I have little choice but to accept the world as it exists in front of me. Because I am less mobile than the people around me, I have little choice but to submit to their way of life, to learn how to exist in the world they have created. There is no hopping in the car and escaping a problem.

If I ruffle someone's feathers, I have little choice but to remain present and participate in whatever unfolds.

Walking is a great way to see the country and meet its people, but I could see the country and meet its people by bus. Walking turns this trip into a personal pilgrimage, a way for me to practice submission to the world mile after mile, day after day, week after week, month after month.

I tapped "send," pulled my pack back on and walked back out to the road.

There wasn't much along this section of road, other than big rocks and fields of dry grass. It was as if the world had decided to either move to the more fertile valley below, or to the bustling city of Denizli above. No middle ground. So I walked for a couple hours by myself with nothing to interrupt me.

In the early afternoon I came upon a group of about 8 middle-aged men sitting in the shade of a large tarp they had raised by the side of the road. They were selling watermelons from the back of a rusty old pickup truck, and they waved me over to join them for çay and watermelon. I thought briefly about passing by with a quick hello, as I was eager to get to Denizli.

However, I decided to be friendly, so I called out "Hello" and crossed the road to sit down with them. Having been on the road for a couple of weeks, I had started to realize that part of my daily routine was going to be stopping by the side of the road and saying hi to people. I ducked under the tarp and reached out to shake hands with each of them.

They were peasant farmers from about 35 to 55 years old. They had stacked their watermelons high in the bed of the pickup truck and backed it under the tarp to shade the melons.

They had also set up a table and laid out slices of ripe, red, juicy-looking watermelons. I spotted an extra chair and took off my pack. While I pulled the chair up to the table one of the men set a glass of tea and a couple slices of watermelon on the table in front of me.

The tea was too hot to drink still, so I took a bite of the watermelon. I wiped the juice off my chin with my forearm.

"Where are you from?" they asked.

"California."

"Where are you going?"

"Well, first Denizli, but then Van."

"Are you walking?" they asked.

"Yes."

"By yourself?"

"Yes, just me."

They looked at each other and raised their eyebrows.

They turned back to me. One of them asked, "Why are you doing it?"

I paused for a bit but could not come up with a simple answer. I shook my head, chuckled foolishly, and replied, "I don't know."

I was learning that if I laughed at myself in an I-must-be-crazy sort of way while answering that, people would laugh with me and let it drop. But if I didn't, if I became serious and tried to explain in my limited Turkish vocabulary, the conversation would A) turn uncomfortably silent or, B) people would ask me if I worked for the CIA.

These men chuckled.

"You should write a book," one of them suggested.

"That's a good idea. Maybe I will."

"Will you mention us in the book?" one of the others asked.

"Yes, I'll be sure to do that."

After eating a few more slices of watermelon and making small talk about the beauty of the area and the friendliness of the people, I stood up, shook their hands again, and said goodbye. I shouldered my pack and walked out to the road to continue on.

I had drunk so much tea and eaten so much watermelon that I needed to go to the bathroom. I spotted a small roadside cafe up ahead on the other side of the road, and, when I reached it, asked the attendant if I could use the restroom. Our exchange was interrupted by an ear-splitting explosion from across the road right where I had been walking a few moments before. As we turned we saw a heavily loaded truck wobbling off the road onto the shoulder amidst a cloud of dust. Its front tire, which had blown out, was a flapping piece of rubber.

I thought, *Man, I'm glad I came over here to take a piss. That truck would have hit me.*

THE SECRET HANDSHAKE

About two hours later, with the sprawling edges of Denizli visible in the distance, I stopped at a gas station for a bottle of water and a snack. This was a well-equipped gas station, with an attached cafeteria and a covered outdoor seating area filled with wooden picnic tables, so I decided to eat more than the gas station convenience store junk I had originally intended. I called out a hello to the man behind the counter and ordered some toast and çay. The man said he would bring them out to me in a moment, and he motioned to the picnic tables, inviting me to take a seat at one of them for the wait.

I took a seat at the picnic tables and struck up a conversation with a couple men sitting at the table next to me. One of them said he was the owner of the station. He noticed my pack.

"Are you traveling by yourself?" he asked.

"Yes," I replied.

"Do you have a place to stay this evening?"

Wait a minute, I thought to myself, *no way, is it really going to be this easy?* For two weeks now I had been trying to figure out the secret handshake that was going to get me "in" at a gas station, and it seemed like no such secret handshake was necessary.

I held my breath as I answered. "No, I don't have a place to stay yet."

"Well, you should stay here."

Oh my god, I thought, *it's true, there is no secret handshake!* Apparently it was not only expected, but assumed, that I would camp overnight.

"I would be very happy to stay here!" I said. I tried to contain my excitement, thinking that if I looked too amazed the guy might get freaked out and rethink the invitation.

He pointed to a shady, quiet grassy area to the side of the station. I hadn't noticed it when I first walked up.

"Set up your tent there. You're my guest, feel free to clean up in the restrooms and have dinner at the cafeteria here. I need to leave soon, but we're open all night, the staff will take good care of you."

So I grabbed my pack and walked over to the grassy strip he had pointed to.

I set up my tent and laid out my sleeping bag. It was still a little light outside, too early for me to turn in for bed. I took out my iPhone and snapped a screenshot of the map that showed where I was that night and posted it to Facebook. I had gotten into the habit of doing this at the end of every day. I called it my daily "hey Mom, I'm not dead" blog post.

Within moments I got a Facebook message from Hakan, a Turk from İstanbul whom I had never met. He had been actively following my walk, but I hadn't been aware of that. Hakan had messaged me to say hello. He attached a screenshot of that same gas station where I was now camping. He had seen my "hey Mom, I'm not dead" blog post, quickly found my location on Google Maps, and, as quickly, found a photo of the gas station and sent it.

I felt momentarily disconcerted that someone I didn't know could track my location so quickly and easily, but then I remembered that that was the main point of posting my progress, and instead of freaking out at my lack of privacy I should seize the opportunity to make a new friend. So I messaged Hakan back that yes, he had found a photo of the correct station, and I was camped just to the right of the edge of the photo.

Then I lay back and nestled into my bag, satisfied with myself for having solved the gas station handshake question and graduating to a new level of hobo skills. As I drifted off to sleep I thought to myself that maybe it wasn't such a big deal, being invited to camp at a gas station. Apparently there was no secret handshake, no mysterious cult of hobo-ness, maybe the difficulty of it had all been in my head.

ROLLING INTO DENIZLI

Friday, 14 September

The next morning I woke up, broke camp, and walked over to the station's café for a breakfast of *menemen* (scrambled eggs, tomatoes, and green peppers) and bread. After breakfast I went back out onto the highway and walked into Denizli.

With a population of 500,000, Denizli seemed a huge metropolis compared to the tiny villages I had been walking through. I felt like a country hick. How quickly I had adapted to my surroundings the past two weeks. Even Aydın was a quaint little village compared to Denizli.

As I walked into Denizli, I felt under assault by a wall of noise. It seemed Denizli was one big construction site. Everywhere, jackhammers breaking cement and pile drivers drilling deep into the ground for god knows what. Traffic was heavy and drivers were busy honking their horns. Large trucks belched exhaust fumes as they lumbered by. I choked on the fumes.

My slowly-healing foot began to throb. My spirits had ended on such a high note yesterday, but now I was beginning to feel depressed, angry, and out of place. I projected this negativity onto the world around me. I imagined the truck drivers were laughing at me, a rube in from the countryside, sticking out like a sore thumb in the big bustling city.

I had been walking for a few hours with nothing to eat, so I was hungry. I stopped in for lunch at a roadside restaurant.

The restaurant was air conditioned inside, but I chose to sit outside on the patio because I was hot and sweaty. It was comfortable enough out on the patio. There were lots of plants, and I was sheltered from the sun and the noise and the dust. I began to relax, my bad mood and my anger at the world beginning to subside.

A young woman came out to serve me. I observed to myself that most of the servers I had run across in the past couple weeks had been men, and it was unusual to be served by a woman. This particular one was not only young, probably in her early 20s, but kind of cute too. She greeted me warmly as she handed me the menu, and while I ate she smiled at me and engaged me in a little flirty small talk.

By the end of lunch my mood had changed from *Man, everything really stinks here, I hate Denizli,* to *Ah, that pretty young woman smiled at me, life is good.*

As I finished lunch and shouldered my pack to go back out into the big bad city, I reflected on how little it had taken to change my mood from bad to good.

DENIZLI GAS STATION

In this better frame of mind I continued walking through Denizli. My gait was slowed by the pain in my foot, and by mid-afternoon I was only halfway through the city. I knew by the map that it was possible to make it all the way through the city by the end of the day, but the voice of self-doubt was yelling at me that I would never make it. I was determined to escape the noise and exhaust fumes, though. I didn't want to wake up to them in the morning. So I told the voice to shut up and let me walk in peace.

I got thirsty as I walked, and stopped to buy a bottle of cold water. Ahead was a shady park. I sat down on one of the park benches under a tree to cool off and slake my thirst.

While I rested I decided it would be a good time to catch up on some emails, so I pulled out my iPhone to check my email inbox. One of the emails was from my dad. He asked about some protests in the Muslim world regarding a YouTube movie denigrating Mohammed. The protests, he said, were centered around a town in Libya called Benghazi. He asked if I had seen or heard anything about this, or was experiencing any negative blowback or anti-American sentiment.

I thought back to the welcoming receptions I had received at the gas station the night before and in Horsunlu before that. I thought of the trays of food that people had been bringing me, the smiling faces and warm welcomes I had been getting for the past few weeks. I emailed him back that I was fine, and that no, I hadn't experienced any negative blowback or anti-American sentiment. I was walking alone through a part of the world many of my fellow Americans seemed to think was a boiling cauldron of anti-American sentiment, but the world they were reading about in the media and the one I was experiencing were completely different.

There were emails from other people too, but I didn't see anything urgent, and daylight was burning. I wanted to get out of Denizli, so I decided to respond to them later. But before I stood up and walked back out to the road I pulled out my pad of paper and penned the following comment to post on my blog later:

Offensive stuff

Some videos get made, some diplomats get killed, some people get all up in arms, etc. I'd like to weigh in on this, since I happen to be walking across a Muslim country, and then I'll return to our regularly-scheduled programming of me demonstrating that the world isn't something to be afraid of...

As an example, I'll use that case from a couple years ago where some pastor in Florida burned, or at least threatened to burn, some Korans. The details of this most recent case are different, but the song remains the same...

When a minister in Florida burns a Koran, how representative of your daily activities is that?

Are you running around hating Muslims, frothing at the mouth, spouting hate speech right and left? Probably not.

And how many of your friends and family are doing those things? Probably not many.

So if the Pakistani press's story about the Florida minister is not representative of the vast majority of human activity in the US, why do we think shots of a couple dozen Pakistanis up in arms means the whole Muslim world is angry?

Another question we often ask is, if Muslims really don't support anti-Western violence, why are they not organizing more anti-violence demonstrations?

The answer is in the answer to the question, why, when the pastor in Florida burns a Koran, do you not organize anti-anti-Muslim demonstrations?

The answer is probably that you are busy with your day-to-day life. You are busy getting the kids off to school. You are busy going to work. You are busy thinking about dinner and calling your husband to remind him to pick up a loaf of bread on his way home.

When a pastor in Florida burns a Koran, you don't think, oh my god, I need to organize a rally. You think, god, there are some crazies out there, and then you go back to what you were doing, because most of living is doing those things.

The same goes for those folks "over there." If you ever find yourself wondering why there aren't more "anti-anti-Western" demonstrations in the Muslim world, ask yourself why there aren't more "anti-anti-Muslim" demonstrations in yours, and you will have your answer.

You don't need to travel the world to understand it. You just need to take the same rules that govern life in the world right in front of you, and apply them elsewhere, too.

I closed my notebook, stuffed it into my pack, and walked back out to the main road. My foot hurt a little less after the rest.

A couple blocks from the park, I passed a gasoline station and noticed the attendants gathered for a break around a spindly folding table. They looked up at me and waved me over. I didn't plan to stop, since I had rested in the park just a few minutes before, so I pointed my eyes forward and put my head down, but one of the attendants ran out to the sidewalk to greet me anyway.

"Please, join us for tea," the attendant said.

"No," I smiled apologetically, "Sorry, I need to keep going."

"No, please, I insist."

Realizing there was no polite way to turn down the invitation, I smiled again and followed him back to the break table. The others were discussing a wedding they were going to over the weekend. They handed me an invitation and invited me to join them. Even though I was in a slightly better mood because of the friendly waitress at the restaurant at lunch, I was still feeling moody and I thought, *There's no way I'm going to this wedding, because it's tomorrow and I don't want to hang out here all day and I'm in a bad mood.*

But I smiled and took the invitation anyway because I didn't want to seem rude. I told them, "I'm not sure if I can make it but I'll see what I can do." Then I shook everybody's hands, said goodbye, and continued walking.

After walking for another hour, I recognized the signs of getting to the edge of the city. The buildings were starting to spread out, and traffic was growing less dense. But the shadows were growing long. It was time to look for a place to sleep. I was nervous because I hadn't quite made it out of the city yet.

However, emboldened by my new hobo skill of sleeping at gasoline stations, I began eyeing gasoline stations to see where I might spend the night. I stopped at one, sat down on a green plastic bucket turned upside down in the parking lot, and, as I chatted with the station owner, I looked around evaluating whether I wanted to stay there for the night. I had a feeling that this wasn't the one for me and I should continue on. So I said goodbye to the owner and continued on another five kilometers.

Just east of Denizli I approached another gas station. It looked a little run-down, but by then the prospects of finding a place to stay that night were getting pretty dim. The attendant smiled and greeted me when I went in. He introduced himself as Metin. Metin was working the mini-mart and told me that he was the nephew of the station owner. I saw a restaurant adjacent to the mini-mart and walked over to it. There were no other customers. However, a basketball game played noisily on the TV and an air conditioner blasted a stream of cool air into the room.

Metin followed me in and poured me a glass of cold water. I sat sipping my water and watching the game while the air conditioner blew refreshing cool air over me. Man, it just didn't get any better than this.

Except it did. I hadn't been sitting there for even 5 minutes when three young women who looked like they were in their early twenties walked in.

One of them, clearly the leader of the group, walked straight over to me. She stuck out her hand and introduced herself.

"Hi, I'm Ayşe."

I blinked a couple times, surprised and impressed by her directness, but I drank it in like a parched man who has just crossed the desert drinks in a tall glass of water. In two weeks on the road, not once had I experienced this kind of directness from a woman. I quickly rummaged through my brain, trying to remember how to keep my cool in such a situation.

I shook her hand and replied, "Hi, I'm Matt, nice to meet you."

"Where's your girlfriend?" she asked.

"My girlfriend?" I blinked again. I didn't know what she was referring to.

She described a news article she had read about me on the internet. The article had stated that I was walking for peace and my girlfriend was with me. I thought back to the first day of the walk in Kuşadası and how Joy Anna had been standing next to me when I was interviewed, and I realized that the paper must have misreported that she was my girlfriend.

Because Ayşe had read the news article, she knew where I was from, where I was going, and how long it would take me to get there. Like I had been with Hakan the day before, I was briefly taken aback that a complete stranger already knew so much about me, but then I remembered that was okay, and to relax and use the opportunity to make a friend.

"Excuse me, I need to go get my friends," Ayşe said.

"Okay, you do that," I answered.

Ayşe strode over to her friends at the cash register. She whispered something to them, they paid for their items, and then all three turned and strode back over to me. I swallowed hard.

Keep your cool, Matt, I reminded myself.

Her friends introduced themselves to me. One was also from Denizli. One was from İzmir. They took nearby seats, pulled out cigarettes, and, as they lit up, they asked me if I'd like one too.

"No thanks, I don't smoke."

"We didn't think so," the one from İzmir said.

We chatted and made small talk back and forth. They laughed, giggled, batted their eyelashes, and flipped their hair at me. I reminded myself that I was traveling alone, depended on the kindness of strangers, and needed to be careful that I didn't anger any boyfriends or family members, even though there were none around, so I struggled to stay as cool and aloof as I could. Plus, my language skills were not refined enough to participate in their witty banter, but I had the impression that that just made the exchange all the more fun for them.

I mentioned that someone had invited me to a wedding the next day. Ayşe asked me which wedding. I pulled out the wedding invitation I had gotten a couple of gas stations earlier. Ayşe grabbed it from me and read the names.

"Hey," she called out to Metin, who had been standing at the cash register across the room, "This is your village, do you know these people?"

Metin had been watching us intently from across the room. Now that he had been invited into the conversation, he came over. Ayşe handed him the invitation. Metin glanced at it.

"Yes, of course, the groom is a good friend of mine. I'll be going to this tomorrow."

Metin looked at me. "Would you like to come?" he asked me.

A few minutes before, I had been in a bad mood and had no plans of attending the wedding. But the light-hearted conversation with the flirty young women had changed my mood, and now I easily accepted the invitation.

"Sounds great, I'd love to," I replied, thinking for only a second how quickly my mood had changed, and how all it had taken was a few smiles and some hair tosses. *God, I'm so easy,* I thought to myself.

I told Metin that if I was going to stay an extra day to go to the wedding I would need a place to stay. "I have my tent, my backpack, and all the equipment I need," I said.

"Sure, you can stay right here at the gasoline station," he said.

The three young women said they needed to go, and asked if we could take some photos together first. I said, "Yes, of course! One by one or all together?"

One by one, they insisted. So I stood next to each one for a photo, and as I put my arm around the one who had introduced herself to me I remembered that I hadn't showered in a few days, and I wondered how bad I smelled. She didn't seem to mind though.

Then, as quickly as they had come, they departed. Metin went back to his work at the cash register.

I sat back down in front of the TV and tried to wipe the grin off my face. I was sitting in an air-conditioned room, I was watching a basketball game on TV, and I had just been flirted with by not one, not two, but three cute young women. I wondered what good deed I had done for the universe in order to deserve such a shower of riches from above.

Metin finished his work at the cash register and said goodbye for the evening, he would see me tomorrow and we would go to his village together. About an hour later, when darkness fell, I joined the gas station's night crew outside near the pumps for a bit more TV watching and some sunflower seed munching. When a customer would pull up, one of the attendants would jump up out of his chair, pump the gas, and then sit back down with us and grab another handful of sunflower seeds.

After a couple more hours of soap operas and countless handfuls of sunflower seeds, and as a nighttime news anchor explained to viewers that the West wanted to carve up Turkey and establish new borders throughout the Middle East, I crawled into my sleeping bag, which I had laid out on the tiled floor in the nearby office.

I was unable to block out the blaring noise of the TV, and I was descended upon by dozens of mosquitoes happy to be offered a feast of exposed flesh, and I had been too lazy to lay out my pad, so my sleeping bag lay directly on the hard tiled floor, but I was so tired that I fell asleep within minutes and slept peacefully through the night.

THE WEDDING

The next day, Saturday, Metin and I took a car to his village for the wedding. Our first stop was in another village to pick up beer and some snacks for later on in the evening.

Our second stop was Pamukkale, one of the most famous tourist sights in Turkey. Pamukkale means "cotton castle" and is known for its white limestone terraces, mineral baths, and natural pools of water. Metin asked if I would like to get out of the car and go inside.

I had lived in Turkey for a number of years and had seen many famous sights. But my job at the moment was to walk across the country and let that process change me — that involved walking and interacting with people and events as they unfolded in that process, not being sidetracked by sightseeing, as wondrously beautiful and ancient as the sightseeing places might be.

So I said to Metin, "No, let's just get out of the car and take a picture by the gate, so I can have a picture of myself at Pamukkale for the website."

Metin stopped the car and left it running. We both jumped out of the car and I handed him my camera. He took a photo of me standing against the fence with Pamukkale in the background. Then I took a picture of him standing next to the fence. We hopped back in the car.

We drove to his parents' house and sat with them outside in the garden. Theirs was a very clean, simple little village house with limited electricity and limited running water, but the garden was lush with lots of trees and a grape-leaf trellis. It was shady and comfortable. Metin's dad cut open a few different kinds of melon for the four of us to enjoy. After our snack we went inside and took afternoon naps before the wedding.

This wedding was very different from the dozens of İstanbul weddings I'd attended, which were one-shot deals, where all the components — drinking, socializing, eating, dancing, and of course the ceremony itself — were wrapped up into a single 4-6 hour event.

This village wedding was strung out over a couple of days. On the first night Metin and I attended a party called the *kına gecesi*, the application of henna onto the bride's hands and forearms. The event was open to all and was less a "hen party" than I'd thought it would be. It was more a dance party for the whole community.

The second event was the *mevlüt*, taking place on the second day, where guests are served lunch and a holy man gives a speech. I participated in the first part of this event but then had to leave early, since Metin had to be back at work in the city.

The third event, which Metin and I were unable to attend, was the *gelin alma*, the ritual claiming of the bride away from her family. I'd witnessed this at a few other weddings outside of İstanbul. It serves a purpose similar to the giving away of the bride in a Western wedding, but it's a little louder and more showy, involving plenty of music and a lot more people. Imagine a hundred people standing outside the bride's house banging on drums and blowing on flutes and demanding she come out.

The fourth event is the actual wedding ceremony.

My favorite of the two events Metin and I attended was the *kına gecesi*. At first, this event seemed clearly a night for women. Ninety-five percent of the people crowding the dance floor were women, and 95% of the people sitting in the rows of chairs surrounding the dance floor were women.

Most of the men in attendance stood toward the back, hanging out on the periphery, just watching and starting parties of their own, crowding around tables drinking and eating sunflower seeds.

As the night wore on the number of women in attendance shrunk, and the number of men grew. At one point I made the conscious decision to break a party-going rule I've maintained for decades, which is that the moment the men outnumber the women, leave, no matter what.

When the guns came out by the dozens, I broke another rule I have, which is stay away from parties with guns. But that night it was "When in Rome…"

At no point in the evening did I lack for social opportunities, even though I began the evening knowing only a few people. I couldn't walk more than a few feet without being called over to join one of the parties taking place within the party. Even after years in Turkey I am still amazed that all it takes to break the ice with a Turk is a smile, a hearty hello and a handshake, and a direct look in the eyes.

I'm not a big fan of hanging out with drunken men while they dance around shooting live ammo in crowded places, so by the time we left I was, shall we say, open to the idea of getting out of there.

A bunch of us loaded into the car and stopped off at the home of the groom's grandparents to pay our respects. Respects paid, we piled back into the car and headed out again.

We grabbed some more beers and drove up a dirt road high into the surrounding hills to engage in an activity treasured by young men in small towns around the world, including me: late-night drinking on some remote, deserted dirt road far from the nearest light source.

We even engaged in a competition to see who could scream the loudest for the longest time. I participated in this competition, of course, and in doing so I discovered within myself a talent for holding the same piercingly high note for a freakishly long period of time.

One of my displays of this talent was caught on video, I was told, and would soon be appearing on Facebook.

The previous record-holder and I bonded over our common talent, and in fact began calling each other *kanka*, a term of endearment translating loosely into "blood brother."

Throughout this entire second act for the evening I was entirely sober. Years ago I stopped drinking more than a few sips per evening, simply because heavy drinking makes me feel confused and disoriented.

I have, however, refined the skill of walking around with open bottle in hand, appearing to periodically take a swig just so as to not be a party-pooper. Drunk people are fun to hang out with, I just don't like being one of them.

A new kanka made and the local record for sustaining a single note at the top of one's lungs broken, I piled into the next car headed down the hill toward my bed.

It turned out I made my escape just in time — as we pulled away I heard the die-hards we left behind making plans to go for *işkembe*, a soup made from cow stomach. I am not a big fan of soup made from cow stomach.

ACCOSTED

Monday morning, the third week of the walk, I packed up my stuff and said goodbye to Metin and the gasoline station attendants. Then, as the sun rose from behind the hills, I walked to the main road out of town.

It was already hot and humid at 8 a.m., so after walking only half an hour I sat down in the shade under a tree, opened a bottle of water, took a big drink, and began eating a package of cookies — my breakfast.

Turkey's Prime Minister, Tayyip Erdoğan, was scheduled to visit Denizli that day. His motorcade from the airport would be traveling the road I was walking, so there was a lot of security out even in the early morning.

Three cops from the security detail came over to take their break with me, and we sat down at a nearby picnic table. They asked me about the lives of American cops. I am not a cop, I do not have any cops in my immediate family, and I don't have any close friends who are cops. So I was having a bit of a hard time accurately representing the lives of American cops. Most of what I knew about the lives of American cops came from the movies, and I told these cops that, but they didn't seem to mind.

"What is an American cop's salary?"

I took a wild guess.

"What is police academy like in America?"

I took another wild guess.

"How well does an American cop relate to the public compared to a Turkish cop?"

I was better equipped to field that question.

A call came over their radios summoning them back to work. They hurriedly finished their snacks, said a hasty goodbye to me, and scurried back to work. I stayed behind to finish my breakfast in a more leisurely fashion and enjoyed the silence.

A few minutes later I stood up, pulled my pack back on, and resumed walking out of town. I wasn't on the road for ten minutes when I heard a car driving up behind me on the shoulder, honking. I figured this was Turkey and cars drive on the wrong side of the road and honk their horns all the time, so I didn't even look back. But the car wouldn't go away. It kept following me and honking so I turned around to see what was going on.

It was Meltem, one of the three women I had met at the gasoline station Friday. She pulled on the emergency brake, jumped out of the car, and grabbed me by the arm.

"Here! Come with me!" she ordered, beginning to drag me by the arm to her car before I could say hello.

She stopped suddenly. "No, wait!" She tightened her grip on my arm and abruptly turned. Then she dragged me toward a market across the parking lot. "I need to get something," she said.

As we climbed some stairs towards the market, two cops taking a break in the shade laughed at us and said to Meltem, "You got yourself a foreigner!"

"He's not for me," Meltem said as she marched me past the cops into the market.

When it comes to relations between the genders, I am not known for being quick on the uptake. However, when she said those words to the cops I realized she was flying wingman for someone. I was the target. I'd just been acquired.

So we went into the store and she bought a pack of gum, all the while gripping my arm. Then she pulled me out of the store and to the passenger side of the car.

"Get in," she ordered. I reminded her of my backpack, so she let me take it off and stuff it into the back seat of her car.

"Let's go to the office," she said. "Ayşe is coming."

Ah, Ayşe. I had no problem with that.

We drove to Meltem's office, which was only a few hundred meters back down the road. It turns out her desk faced the road, and she had called Ayşe when she saw me walk past with my backpack. Ayşe had told her to go get me and then call her.

At the office, Meltem sat me down at a picnic table outside. A group of Meltem's male co-workers drifted out of their offices, gathered around, and began questioning me. But Ayşe raced up just then and parked her car and jumped out.

"It's too crowded here!" Meltem told her, waving her back. "Let's go to a restaurant." The three of us climbed into Meltem's car and drove a couple hundred meters to a nearby restaurant.

Meltem and Ayşe both seemed to know the waitstaff well. I took it they must be regulars there. The waiters seated us out on the patio at a table with a clean, white tablecloth under a thick, leafy green canopy of trees. I looked around and noticed that the restaurant was deserted except for the three of us. Two ducks swam by us in the stream below, a male and a female. They looked content. Meltem, Ayşe, and I ordered iced tea and some munchies. I had been interrupted while working, but I was liking the interruption.

Ayşe and Meltem asked me why I had stayed a few extra days in Denizli.

Had I met someone at the wedding? They began to banter between themselves. Maybe so. No, perhaps he stayed for one of us. Who did he stay for? He stayed for you. No, he stayed for you. No, he stayed for you. No, he stayed for you.

I thought, *Actually, I didn't stay for either of you. I was walking out of town when you stopped me.*

Meltem left the table for a few minutes, saying she needed to attend to some business. Ayşe and I shared a moment of awkward silence. I broke it by saying, "You know that woman I stayed for? She's you."

I felt ridiculous saying that, being that I had been walking out of town just an hour before. But Ayşe seemed to like it. She turned her face away from me, and I could see she was grinning from ear to ear.

Meltem came back to the table, and the three of us resumed making small talk. After a while I excused myself and went to the restroom. When I returned to the table I told them I would need to leave soon, I had some walking to do.

"Have dinner with us," they said.

"I would love to, but I have already been in Denizli for three nights. I need to walk."

"Stay in Denizli....One more night....What's one more night?...Have dinner with us."

I sat back down and thought. I needed to walk. I had to get my miles for the day. It was my job. But only a fool would turn down a dinner invitation from these two. Surely there must be a way to make this work, I thought.

"Okay," I said after some quick thinking. I told them I would leave my pack at the restaurant, walk my quota for the day, hop a bus back to Denizli, meet them for dinner, and then stay in Denizli one more night.

Our plans for the evening made, I stood up and walked over to the waiter to ask for the bill. He looked at me, and then he looked over at Meltem and Ayşe, who were gently shaking their heads and staring him down with cold, icy stares that seemed to say, "If you let this man pay, we will use a dull knife to remove your testicles." The waiter looked back at me, smiled sheepishly, and said, "Sorry, you are not going to pay for this one."

Meltem and Ayşe stood up and the three of us prepared to leave. "Let's meet back here at 8 p.m.," they proposed.

"No, 7 p.m.," I countered, thinking about having to get up early the next day to resume walking.

"No, 8 p.m."

"No, 7 p.m."

"*Ooof yaa,*" Ayşe said, rolling her eyes at me. "Okay, 7 p.m."

So I left my backpack at the restaurant and went back out to the main road to continue my walk out of Denizli.

The road east of Denizli was lined with granite mining and cutting operations. As such, that side of the city was unusually heavy with rock dust and quite industrial. The roads were clogged with trucks belching thick clouds of exhaust, as they had been when I first entered Denizli three days earlier. But this time I had a smile on my face and I could hear the birds singing.

I ended the walk for the day up on a plateau at a village called Kocabaş. It had one of the largest Turkish flags I had ever seen. I took a selfie of myself standing in front of that flag, and then I waved down a passing minibus and rode back to Denizli for dinner.

I arrived at the restaurant about 6 p.m. The waiters recognized me from earlier in the day and pointed me to a restroom where I could clean up. I spent the next half hour taking a sponge bath and trying to comb my hair as best I could.

A few minutes before 7 p.m., I asked the waiters if I could take a seat early and they escorted me to the same table where we'd eaten lunch. I sat drinking water and dipping bread into olive oil. Meltem and Ayşe arrived at 7:30, taking their seats and waving off the waiter's offer of menus.

About 5 minutes later, Meltem took a quick call on her cell phone, stood up, and said she needed to attend to an emergency at work and would need to leave the restaurant. As she got up to leave I couldn't help but admire her consistent and disciplined execution of a wingman's duties. If you looked up "wingman" in the dictionary, you would see a picture of Meltem.

Ayşe and I ordered dinner and made small talk. By the time the food came we were so busy talking we barely ate. At one point Ayşe reminded me to eat, my food was getting cold.

"I can eat anytime," I said. "Right now I am with you." The conversation continued. Both plates of food grew cold and were largely ignored.

The waiter knew a little English, and when the conversation moved on to more advanced subjects he was called in to translate. At first he would just translate a few sentences here and there as he walked by, but he gradually became a more permanent fixture at our table. He may as well have taken a seat. I did not like this development. I was not having dinner with the waiter, I was having dinner with Ayşe.

Come on Ayşe, I thought, *we have to get rid of this guy. Help me out here. This restaurant is your territory. Let's get rid of this guy.*

She did get rid of him, but not how I thought she would. "I know no English at all," she told him. Her face was tense and her eyes watered. "What do I do? I want to understand this man."

"Well then," the waiter said, "Talk to him. You will have to talk directly to him, not to me." He turned and left the table. Moments earlier I had wanted to push him off the ledge into the water below, anything to get him to leave, but now I wanted to thank him. I had badly wanted Ayşe to talk only to me, to look only at me. Now the waiter was leaving her no choice.

Ayşe turned to me, looked into my eyes, and we sat like that talking for almost two hours, not taking our eyes off each other. We barely acknowledged the waiter when he came back to clear our plates, or refill our water glasses, or ask us if we'd like to order dessert. It was one of the most challenging conversations of my life. I was not only struggling to keep her engaged with me in a language I barely knew, I was struggling to answer questions more personal than any I had ever had to answer before in English.

Ayşe was an unusually patient and determined conversational partner. As deep as I was digging to make the most of my Tarzan Turkish, she was digging as deeply to understand the awkward stranger sitting across the table from her. It had been a long time since anyone had bothered to discuss such personal subjects with me in any language, and if she was going to be patient and determined with me, I was going to be patient and determined with her.

At 11 p.m. Meltem returned. She tapped Ayşe on the shoulder. "We've got to go now," she said.

As we pushed back from the table, Ayşe asked me, "Where are you staying the night?"

I blinked, disoriented. *Oh shit, I usually would have taken care of that detail by now.*

I said, "At the gasoline station, I guess. They'll probably let me stay there another night."

We loaded into Meltem's car and took a back route to the gasoline station. Metin was there as well as some of his friends. I greeted them and asked if I could stay another night. "Of course," they said.

As I unloaded my backpack from the car, I began to hear the raucousness of a Turkish argument rising from inside the station. I hurried inside and found Ayşe and Meltem in heated disagreement with Metin and his friends. I understood some of the words, but there was something else going on that I didn't understand. I remembered, yet again, that the people around me had histories I was not aware of, and that sometimes, as restrained and polite and respectful as I tried to be, I would step on some toes. I suspected this had been one of those times.

Ayşe pulled me to the side as I entered the building and whispered, "Don't worry about it, everything will be okay."

I nodded back to her like I knew what was going on, but thought to myself, *No problem, I don't even understand what you guys are talking about, I just want to go to bed.*

They stopped their bickering, and Meltem and Ayşe and I said a hurried and awkward goodnight to each other. Then the two of them got back into Meltem's car. Meltem, flustered from the heated conversation they'd just had with Metin and his buddies, forgot to put the car in reverse and drove it straight into the side of the gasoline station. She jumped out of the car, and we inspected the damage, deciding it was not a big problem. Then Meltem and Ayşe got back in and drove away. I laid my sleeping bag out on the office floor for the third time in four nights and fell asleep.

FREE OF DENIZLI?

Tuesday, 18 September

Tuesday morning I awoke with a start to my cell phone alarm. I panicked. *Oh my god, I am still at this gas station! I should be making better progress. I am letting myself down and everyone back home, too. I came here to walk across the country, not to dine with pretty girls!*

Okay, okay, I quieted myself, *just wait a minute, all is not lost. I walked yesterday, and all I need to do to continue making forward progress is stand up, stuff my things into my backpack, and catch the bus back to where I left off yesterday. Everything's fine.*

I stood up and packed my bag and walked out to the shoulder to catch the bus. While I sat by the side of the road waiting for the bus I pulled a note from my pocket. I'd awakened in the middle of the night thinking of Ayşe and had written a note to her in English. I began translating it into Turkish so I could text it to her later. When the bus pulled up, I stuffed the partially-translated note into my pocket and boarded.

I rode the bus the 18 kilometers back to Kocabaş and stepped off where I'd taken the selfie under the giant Turkish flag. From there I resumed my walk.

About one kilometer ahead of me loomed an unusually large pedestrian overpass crossing the lightly-used highway. The only reason for its existence, it seemed, was for villagers from Kocabaş to cross the unused highway to their jobs at the local prison on the other side.

I set my sights on that overpass.

Get past that overpass, I told myself, *and you'll be out of the Denizli orbit and on to the next town.*

I knew I had to break the spell of Denizli, and I hoped forward momentum would do it.

My goal for the day was Bozkurt, a small town of about 12,000 people 27 kilometers east of Kocabaş, the first town I would reach when I finished the climb onto the Central Anatolia plateau. In my mind, getting onto the plateau would mark the end of the walk's first stage in the Menderes River valley. It would mean I had finished the beginning.

The day's climb followed a steep section of the highway through a sparsely-populated area. Sometimes I found myself walking past flat, wide expanses of tall, dry grasses and then suddenly I'd find myself in a section of rolling hills with groupings of oak trees and scrubby-looking shrubs. Like me, the land couldn't seem to make up its mind what it needed to be. When I would see the oak trees and shrubbery reminiscent of the walk into Denizli, I would feel the pull of Denizli tempting me backwards. When I would see the tall, dry grasses hinting at the plateau to come, I would feel a push forward.

I began to get hungry, but paused just before a lunch of *köfte ve pilav* (meatballs and rice) to pull the note from my pocket and type my text to Ayşe.

After lunch Ayşe called me back. I stopped walking to take the call. My phone Turkish is even more basic than my face-to-face Turkish, so the conversation was neither deep nor long. She had received my text message and was also apparently reeling from dinner the night before.

After our brief conversation I resumed walking and reflected on the past few days — Ayşe, Metin, and the others I had met in Denizli that weekend. I thought about the wedding. I chuckled about drinking in the hills with the guys after the wedding.

I wanted to hop a bus back to Denizli and settle down and spend the rest of my life there.

What craziness was that? Ayşe didn't speak English and I spoke Tarzan Turkish. We had different lives and I was old enough to be her father. I needed to break the spell of Denizli if I were going to do the job I'd set out to do.

My back muscles were aching from the climb, so I stopped and sat by the side of the road to rest for a while and to process the flood of images that had taken over my mind.

After a time, I was finally able to stand up and finish the climb to the top of the plateau.

The transition onto the plateau was quick and dramatic, like climbing up a long flight of stairs and stepping out onto a landing. In less than 100 meters I went from the climb, marked by scattered oak trees and short bridges over dry stream beds, into Bozkurt, a village perched on the edge of the plateau with grassy expanses as flat as boards. There were mountains off in the hazy distance, but the road directly in front of me was flat and straight now.

Hello plateau, nice to meet you. I'll be with you for a while now.

I stopped at the first truck stop in Bozkurt where I thought I might sleep. My head was still whirling with images. The truck stop was busy. It had multiple restaurants. There was plenty of grass but there were too many people and it was too close to the road. I needed quiet. As tired as I was, I walked further into Bozkurt.

I found a gasoline station, but the grounds were completely paved over and there was no place to pitch a tent. I called out to one of the attendants anyway, "I'm walking through. Is there a place I can camp? I have everything. I have my tent. I have my sleeping bag. Can I camp here for the night?"

He said, "No. There is probably no comfortable place here for you. You should probably move on."

Another half kilometer and on my third try, I found a gas station with a covered area and tall grass away from traffic. It had a restaurant. It had bathrooms. There were few people. It was perfect. I paused in front of the office, unprepared for the effort I knew it would take to converse in Turkish with the people inside.

The rational me said, *I'm going to need you to be mentally present for this conversation.*

The irrational me replied, *No, I don't want to be present. I want to stay in my dream world. I like the people back in Denizli, and I don't want to leave them.*

Rational me: *Sorry, but you're here now with these people and you're going to have to leave the others in Denizli in order to have this conversation.*

It was getting dark, and I knew the rational me would have to win the tug of war really fast if I were going to find a place to sleep that night. I shut down the voice whining to go back to Denizli and walked into the gasoline station office.

During the mercifully brief conversation with the station owner, I got clearance to set up camp and have dinner at the restaurant.

After dinner, as I nestled into my sleeping bag, I took a deep breath of the cool night air. At the higher altitude of the plateau the air was crisper and fresher than it had been in Denizli, and I was camping on green grass under the stars, not laid out on the floor in the office of a gasoline station breathing someone's second-hand cigarette smoke.

Before I went to sleep I calculated how far I had come. I had walked 242 kilometers, or 11.5% of the distance. I noticed that at some point earlier I had written in my notebook that if you can finish 10% of anything, and are determined to do whatever it takes to finish the project, you are highly likely to make it to the end. I asked myself if I was determined to do whatever it takes to finish the project. The answer was yes. I relaxed and snuggled further into my sleeping bag. Everything was going to be okay.

BOZKURT TO ÇARDAK

When I woke up the next morning my right foot was hurting something fierce, the anxiety was back, and I still wanted to go back to Denizli.

Get off the edge of the plateau, I told myself. *Get further down the road, you need to wade deeper into the pool, you need to replace this frame of mind with something else, anything else.*

I decided that all I needed to do that day was get to Çardak, a mere 5 miles down the road. If I could get to Çardak, I told myself, that would be enough for the day. In Çardak I could rest.

I packed up my tent and sleeping bag at 6:30 and thanked the gas station owner for letting me camp there that night. I told myself, *Before you leave Bozkurt, celebrate with a Turkish breakfast!* It was early, so there weren't a lot of places open. But there was one small three-table restaurant on my way out of town. I ordered the traditional Turkish breakfast of cucumbers, tomatoes, hard-boiled egg, cheese, black olives, honey, rose petal jam, and bread. It was a beautiful sunny morning. I had a comfortable seat on the outside patio. I ate every crumb off the plate, and all of the bread.

Before I shouldered my pack, I pulled my whiteboard and black pen out of my backpack and wrote a note dedicating the day to my mother. It was her birthday — 19 September. I held the sign out at arm's length, faced the morning sun, and snapped a picture.

The land ahead of me was flat and the road straight, and I could almost see Çardak from where I was standing.

Get to Çardak. Just get to Çardak, I muttered to myself. I sighed and began walking, once again.

Normally, I would have covered that distance in about ninety minutes, but because my foot was hurting so bad, I knew it would take me about four hours.

As I walked, I remembered Weebles. Weebles were small, plastic, egg-shaped, human figurines for toddlers. They were weighted at the bottom. You could knock a Weeble on its side, but it would pop back up, every single time.

When we were kids, my brother and I used to play with Weebles. Every Saturday morning we heard the jingle for Weebles on TV — "Weebles wobble but they don't fall down."

I hoped now I would turn out to be a Weeble.

My head began its spinning again. How had I become so lonely and so disoriented, so starved for human connection that dinner with a friendly young woman was enough to make me contemplate giving up everything?

It doesn't matter! Do the work anyway! said the Voice. I stopped walking long enough to type a blog post into my iPhone:

Discipline is not running a marathon. It is not losing 50 pounds. It is not walking across Turkey.

Discipline is running one mile, and then waking up the next day and running two miles, and then waking up the next day and running three miles.

Discipline is losing one pound, and then waking up the next day and losing the second pound, and then waking up the next day and losing the third pound.

Discipline is waking up knowing the entire day's walk could easily be covered by a car in 10 minutes, and then doing the work anyway. Discipline is being on the verge of tears because you've said goodbye to someone very important to you, and then doing the work anyway. Discipline is every day having a reason to not do the work, and then doing the work anyway.

Discipline is not the end result. It is how we get to the end result. Discipline, and its close relatives patience and faith.

I pressed send, pocketed my iPhone, and continued limping towards Çardak.

Çardak is a small town of about 3,000 people. As I had for about a week now, I tried to minimize my limp so that no one would worry or ask me if I was okay.

I poked my head into a cafe and asked where the center of town was. The owner of the cafe told me that I had another 500 meters to go. He may as well have said it was on the other side of the planet. I thought I would cry.

I asked him if there was a hotel in town. He said yes, I would find it in the village's main square. I couldn't miss it, he said. It had a big sign saying *Otel* (hotel).

I smiled as well as I could, said thank you, and tried not to snag myself on the bead curtain as I walked back out the door onto the street.

I walked deeper into the village and passed a tea garden on the left, full of people drinking their mid-morning tea. One of the groups at one of the tables spotted me over the stone fence, cheerily waved hello, and invited me to join them.

"I will come back later!" I called out. "First I have to find the center of town and get settled in. Is it this way?"

"Just a little further," one of the men encouraged me.

I was feeling scared and defensive, so I didn't trust their friendliness. Plus, because my foot was hurting so badly, "just a little further" sounded like a long way to me.

I found my way to the village's main square. There were a couple of restaurants, barbershops, corner markets, and the hotel. The hotel's exterior wasn't fancy, just a nondescript and unpainted municipal building stuffed into the corner of the square, but sure enough, there was a big sign outside saying *Otel*.

I crossed the square, hobbled up the steps into the hotel, and asked if they had any rooms available. They did, and they ushered me into one. The room was drafty, but it had a shower, and I hadn't taken one in ten days. "I'll see you soon," I said to the shower, "but I have some other business to take care of first." Then I crashed onto the bed and fell into a deep sleep.

I woke up to the phone ringing. It was Ayşe. She just wanted to say hello and make sure I was okay. "I'm fine," I told her. I said that I had enjoyed our dinner very much and missed her. We chatted for a few minutes. I told her Çardak was nice, but that I had only seen the inside of the hotel. We hung up. I took a shower, washed some clothes in the sink, and then fell back asleep.

After dark I woke up, pulled on my shoes, and wandered downstairs onto the square. *What day is it?* I wondered. *Is it tomorrow?* I was disoriented from the nap. Plus, it was 8 p.m. (I had slept through lunch), and I didn't like being out in a new town or village after dark. It was hard to gauge people and pick up on their social signals.

Most of the stores out on the square were closed, but I saw a light on at a *büfe* (snack bar). Two men, probably in their late twenties, sat at a table outside drinking tea. They waved me over, and I took a seat at their table.

"Do you have any food available?" I asked.

"Of course! We will find something and bring it out to you."

One of them went into the *büfe* and brought out a huge plate of rice for me. As I ate my rice the three of us made small talk and introduced ourselves. The one who brought me the rice was named Eren and he owned the *büfe*. The other guy introduced himself as Özgür.

During the conversation I noticed that Eren's eyes kept darting back and forth, glancing at me and then away. *Why is he doing that?* I wondered. *Does it mean he is not trustworthy?* Also, I sensed Eren and Özgür were signaling to each other with body language I couldn't figure out. It was dark. I was new. And, except for the three of us, the square was deserted. My "you don't understand the situation, get out of here" alarm started going off.

I gulped down the plate of rice and thanked Eren and Özgür for the food. They invited me to sit with them for a while and have a cup of tea. "No, thank you," I told them. "I'll be back, but I need to make a phone call first." Then I walked out of earshot, pulled out my phone, and called Ayşe.

She answered, "Hi! How are things in Çardak?"

I said, "I feel uncomfortable and the people seem strange."

"Then be careful, go back to your hotel room," Ayşe said.

That sounded like good advice.

I hung up and walked back to the table. By then it was about 9 p.m. I thanked Eren and Özgür for their hospitality and walked back across the square to the hotel.

Since I had slept all day I wasn't that tired, so I sat in my room and answered emails and wrote in my journal before falling asleep.

KILLING TIME IN ÇARDAK

The next morning when I woke up, I went back out onto the square and found Eren and Özgür at the büfe. They invited me to join them for breakfast.

I learned a little bit more about them then. I learned that they were very close friends and figured they had been passing private jokes between themselves the night before and nothing more. Also, I learned that Eren owned the bakkal across the street in addition to the büfe. I realized that his darting eyes the night before had probably just been him watching his store, which had been open but unstaffed. There was nothing to worry about, these guys were fine. After breakfast I went back to the hotel to take a nap.

I emerged from the hotel early in the afternoon, strolling out onto the center square and into the barbershop. It had been over a month since my last haircut, so it was past time for another one.

When the barber finished my haircut, I switched chairs and joined the other patrons for a cup of tea. As we talked over our tea, a man walked into the shop. He took a chair to wait for his haircut, spotted me, and asked if I was aware of the Greater Middle East Project.

The Project was a popular conspiracy theory to the effect that Western Europe and the United States wanted to redraw national borders in the Middle East. Erdoğan, the prime minister of Turkey, supposedly would be the emperor running an assortment of redrawn national entities which would include a smaller, carved up Turkey, a new state called Kurdistan, and other national entities, some of them loosely based on existing nations. Basically, the Project would reformat a large part of the world.

"Is this true or not?" he asked me.

His was a simple question, but my answer would not be. So I needed a few seconds to see if I could piece together a nuanced response in my Tarzan Turkish. I stalled for time.

"I don't know. You tell me. What do you think?"

"I asked you first. Is it true or not?"

Man, I thought, *I just wanted to come in here for a haircut, and then go back and take a nap. I didn't come in here to talk politics.* I usually tried to steer clear of political conversations anyway, especially when I was alone in Turkey.

He pressed, "Is it true or not?"

In my very bad Turkish I replied, "I understand what you are asking and I'm knowledgeable about the topic, but I can't have the conversation you would like to have because my Turkish isn't good enough."

Usually that's enough to end a conversation and for people to say *Well, we would love to talk about this topic with this foreigner but since his Turkish isn't good enough we will just have to stick with small talk.* And then the political conversation would end and we would talk about the weather.

But this guy would not back off. He was determined to talk about the Greater Middle East Project come hell or high water.

Finally, he asked me impatiently, "Does the Greater Middle East Project exist? Yes or no?"

I repeated, "My Turkish is not good enough for this conversation."

But the more I said it the harder he pressed me for answers, even on other points that I cared even less about.

I swallowed my last drop of tea, then stood up and started walking toward the door, shaking hands and saying goodbye to everybody, including the hostile questioner. I was so flustered, though, that I almost walked out without paying. But I remembered and stopped just as I began to step out the door. I looked over at the barber, tongue-tied. Now I couldn't even remember the Turkish for "How much?" a term I said dozens of times each day.

The barber looked at me and shrugged apologetically. He seemed to understand my frustration and how obnoxious his other customer was being. He said, "Don't worry about it, it's on the house." So I left and went back out on the square.

I crossed the square to say hi to Özgür and Eren. I was moving quickly from suspecting them to befriending both of them and their buddies too. They were a good group to know, because they had stores at the center of the village and they knew everyone. When Eren saw me he put down a plastic bin filled with bags of chips, smiled at me, and said, "Nice haircut."

"Thanks," I said. "I am going back to the hotel to take a nap now."

Özgür spoke up, "Come back this evening. We want you to meet The Mayor."

"The Mayor?"

"Well, actually, he's not the real mayor. We just call him that. His nickname is Şef. He used to run the local bank branch, but now he's retired."

"Okay, sounds good to me. I'll see you later this evening," I said as I turned towards the hotel.

Toward the end of the afternoon, when I woke up from my nap, I went back out onto the square and found Eren and Özgür sitting out on the curb in front of one of their stores eating sandwiches with a couple of their friends.

They offered me a sandwich. I thanked them and took the sandwich and started eating it, letting the breadcrumbs spill on the ground around me. Özgür got a broom and swept up the crumbs, telling me that spilling breadcrumbs was a sin. "Don't do it," he warned.

I noticed that they were not spilling their breadcrumbs, and I could not figure out how anyone could be so tidy when eating a sandwich made of crumbly bread. I certainly didn't have those kinds of eating habits, so apparently I was going through life offending God by spilling my breadcrumbs.

As we stood on the curb eating our sandwiches, Özgür piously sweeping up after me, Şef came by.

As it turned out, Şef was the village drunk. In his retirement he had taken to booze. Not just any booze, but a particular brand of rotgut.

Şef motioned at me to follow him. We walked into one of Eren's stores, where Şef bought a bottle of rotgut and picked up a couple of plastic cups. Then we crossed the street and carried a couple of chairs up a set of stairs onto a balcony overlooking the square.

We sat down and Şef poured a round of rotgut into our two plastic cups.

I'm not much of a drinker, and it was a horrible tasting rotgut. I took only enough of a sip to taste it on my lips. Şef, however, tipped his cup and slammed the rotgut back in two gulps. Then he set his cup on the ledge of the balcony and poured another.

I realized I would never keep up with Şef. He got drunker and drunker.

A group of pre-teen girls approached below the balcony, chatting and laughing together. Şef began making lewd gestures at them. I cringed as I sat in my chair not drinking the rotgut. Şef slammed back yet another cup and made more lewd gestures as the girls continued across the square. Then another group of pre-teen girls walked into the square and Şef made more incredibly lewd comments and gestures at them, too, while slamming back more and more rotgut. I got a bad taste in my mouth, and it wasn't due to the rotgut.

I got up to leave. This was not a good person to be with. I didn't want to be associated with this guy at all. Then I began to realize I'd been had. Eren and Özgür were playing a joke on me. I sat back down.

A group of also-drunk teenage boys strolled by. There is nothing more dangerous than a group of drunk teenage boys trying to prove to each other how tough they are. I must have been the greatest story in Çardak by then because they, like the man in the barbershop, started asking me about the Greater Middle East Project. They began speculating rowdily back and forth amongst themselves.

"He's probably a CIA operative!"

"No, he's a KGB officer!"

"No, Mossad!"

They agreed on Mossad, and from there on they referred to me as Mossad. In the spectrum of intelligence agencies, as I had been finding out in the past couple weeks, you start out as a CIA agent. Then, if you are a bad-ass you get promoted to KGB. If you are a real bad-ass you get promoted to being Mossad. When they began calling me Mossad I knew that even though they were drunk they were showing me respect and would not be throwing me off the balcony.

Getting thrown off balconies is for mere CIA officers.

They soon left to do whatever else drunken teenagers do. Şef finished the rotgut, walked me back to Eren and Özgür, and went home to sleep it off. By that time it was 10:30 p.m., so I said a quick goodbye to Eren and Özgür and went back to my hotel to wash off the dirty feeling of Şef in the shower's lukewarm water.

MORE ÇARDAK

Friday, 21 September

I began my second full day in Çardak using the hotel's slow internet connection to upload photos to my blog. Toward the middle of the day I ventured out into the square a few times to pick up supplies. On one of my sorties out into the square Eren and Özgür invited me to dinner at their büfe that evening. I accepted.

I never saw or met Eren's mother, but she'd cooked up an assortment of aromatic dishes which Eren brought to the büfe and set out on a table for our dinner. It was some of the best food I'd had in a long time — lentil soup, bread, rice. There was also çoban salata and a huge bowl of a reduced soup with ground beef, green peppers, tomatoes, and some spices.

After dinner five of Eren and Özgür's buddies (who I'd started calling the five guys), showed up. One of them barreled in on a motorcycle which he revved several times before shutting it off. They often hung out at the büfe, and they had taken it upon themselves to be my mentors and guides. Sure enough, tonight they had come for me.

"Mert (my name in Turkish)! Sit!" Motorcycle Man said, gesturing with his thumb to the back of his motorcycle. "It's time for you to take a tour of our village."

I hate riding on the back of a motorcycle. I feel like I'm going to die, and the fact that he was heavily drunk didn't increase my feeling of safety any.

It was dark, the road full of potholes, and there wasn't a helmet in sight. I figured God would just have to protect me, or, as the Turks would say, *Allah beni korur.* I suspected that before I touched that wire fence at the Turkey/Iran border I'd have many other opportunities to utter this phrase, just hoping for the best.

So I muttered, "Allah beni korur," and hopped on the back of the motorcycle and whizzed around town. Motorcycle Man showed me different places including Eren's and Özgür's apartments. Then he dropped me off back at the büfe.

I ended the day by going with Özgür and Eren to the village square for a cultural night with Turkish folk music and a light show. Basically everyone in the village was there, gathered on folding chairs in the center of the village square to see and be seen and to listen to the music and to hear the speakers. I watched for a bit, and then turned in at my hotel, feeling satisfied and at peace.

BOZAN

Saturday, 22 September

In the morning, early, before anyone was stirring in Çardak, I walked out to the main road and began that day's walk to Bozan, the next village. I'd made some good friends in Çardak and knew I'd want to come back.

I learned quickly that appearances on the plateau could be deceiving, especially when it came to estimating distances. The sky was big, the roads were straight, and the terrain was mostly flat with a few gentle rollers here and there. There was not much shelter.

When I spotted the village of Bozan ahead of me — my destination for the day — I thought I'd probably be there in 20 minutes. But the village, rather than coming closer, seemed to keep receding into the distance, and I walked two or three hours before I finally reached it.

Other than a place to rest, I didn't expect much from Bozan, which had a population of barely 100, but as I walked into the village I met a man crossing the highway. He greeted me, "Merhaba!"

His name was Yakub, and he was 28 years old. We shook hands. Yakub escorted me into the village to a tea house where he bought my tea and introduced me to a few other people.

Yakub was from Bozan but lived and worked in the nearby township of Dazkırı. He was an accountant for the township there. Yakub was married with one child, a son who recently celebrated his first birthday.

At the village's tea garden, Yakub and I met up with Yakub's older brother, and the three of us shared a couple glasses of tea and some get-to-know-you conversation. Yakub offered to show me inside the village mosque. So far, I'd only stayed outside in the mosque gardens where I could chat with people, wash up, sit in the shade, camp, etc, so I said yes, of course, I'd love to see inside the mosque. The three of us gulped down the rest of our tea and walked across the street towards the mosque.

"Take off your shoes," Yakub reminded me when we reached the door. My shoes weren't particularly dirty, but it was a standard show of respect expected at any mosque and most private homes in Turkey.

I pulled off my boots and stepped onto the thick layers of overlapping carpets inside. Yakub crossed the room to a table on the other side, where he pulled a Koran from a shelf. I walked over to his side of the room and peeked over his shoulder as he ran his finger along the page. One side of the page was Turkish, the other Arabic.

"Do you know both languages?" I asked.

"I know how to read Arabic, but not speak it. The Koran, in Arabic, is the unfiltered word of God, so we should all learn enough Arabic to read it."

"This next part is a song," Yakub continued, pointing back at the page. He began singing.

I tried to read along in Turkish, but with my limited Turkish I couldn't understand much. I just stood by and watched Yakub.

He was very passionate about whatever he was reading and singing. His voice cracked with emotion and his finger trembled slightly as he traced the words.

Yakub didn't try to convert me, he just wanted to share his reverence with me.

We can tell a lot about a person by listening to him talk about a subject that is important to him, regardless of what the subject is. How understanding of others is this person? How patient is he? Does he expect others to hold the same views, or is there room in his mind and heart for people who don't? In five minutes of worship, Yakub was telling me more about himself than he could in an hour of conversation.

After Yakub's mini demonstration of worship, as we exited the mosque, I mentioned to him and his brother that I should continue on to the next village. Yakub insisted that before I go, we should cross back over the highway and take advantage of a communal lunch that was being held in honor of a wedding taking place later that evening.

"We don't want you to walk on an empty stomach," Yakub said.

Good idea, I thought, *it's about time for lunch anyway.*

Lunch eaten, the three of us went back to the tea garden, shared a couple more cups of tea, exchanged Facebook addresses, and then went our separate ways.

I walked further down the road for about an hour, to a small village called Gökçek, found the mosque, and set up my tent in the mosque garden. Then I laid back in the grass to take a late afternoon nap.

This was one of my favorite mosque gardens so far. I was up out of the hot, humid valley below, so the air was crisp and fresh. The grass beneath me was soft and wispy. I stared up at the tall trees and the passing clouds and drifted in and out of a comfortable doze.

Shortly after dark, one of the villagers shook me from my nap and said to me, "Follow me, let's go have dinner."

I had no idea who this man was, nor was I very hungry, but I sprang to my feet and followed him across the street to his house. His wife greeted me at the door and asked me to sit down and have dinner with them. It wasn't a fancy dinner, just a few dishes of eggplant and some other vegetables they had prepared for their evening meal in their small village home. When we finished I crossed back to the stillness of the mosque garden, lay down in my tent and fell asleep again with a full stomach and a smile on my face.

DINAR

The next day I walked into the town of Dinar feeling lonely, uncomfortable, and out of place. I knew I needed some alone time to process something but I wasn't sure what, so instead of looking for a public place to stay, I checked into a hotel and went straight up to my room.

I felt a familiar pull. *Go back to Çardak. Just spend time there and give up the walk.* Part of me recognized how ridiculous that sentiment was. After all, Çardak was a small village of 3,000 people. I didn't even speak the language. I would be bored with the place in less than a week. But the siren call of Çardak was almost as strong as the siren call of Denizli had been a week or two ago. I longed for the comfort of Çardak. I wanted to bathe in its familiarity for the rest of eternity.

Amidst the noise, the cold, rational Voice whispered faintly to me, *Listen to me now, let me drive.*

So I pulled out a pen and wrote a blog post:

The Resistance
There's a book I love, absolutely love. I highly recommend it to just about anyone who will listen. It's called "The War of Art," by Steven Pressfield.

The book is a very quick, simple read. You never have to read it again, because the idea is so simple:

Whenever you try to do something worthwhile, the Resistance will do everything in its power to knock you off track. It will reason with you like a brilliant lawyer, or it will jam a gun in your face like a stick-up man, whatever it takes to throw you off track and put you back where you used to be.

The Resistance comes from inside you. It will never die. It will never go away. It is stronger than you are. Do not try to fight it. You will lose, and you will waste valuable time and energy that would have been better used getting your work done. So learn how to welcome the Resistance into the room, and continue working while it sits across the table from you, staring at you.

On this walk, the Resistance is with me at all times. Most of the time it appears in smaller ways, like yesterday morning in Gökçek, when I woke up and the air was so fresh and the grass was so soft I wondered if I could avoid walking for the day.

A couple of times, however, the Resistance hit me so hard I thought the walk would be over.

One of those times was when I hurt my foot a couple weeks ago. I don't think I'll ever forget the panic and black despair that washed over me on that day. But they were just the Resistance, come to distract me from the clear thinking I'd need to get myself back on track.

I stepped aside from them and spent the next few days nursing my foot back to health and chanting to myself, "calm down, just work the program."

This morning the Resistance came in one of its more common forms, that in which I wake up worrying that A. I'm not walking far enough, and B. I'm spending too much money.

So I checked yet again, and for the 3-1/2 weeks I've been on the road, I've been covering 55 miles per week (my goal is 55-60 miles per week), and I've been spending $13 per day (which is what I've budgeted).

Even with the downtime to nurse my foot, and some unexpected hotel stays, I am hitting both of my targets: walk 55-60 miles per week, and spend $13 per day.

So at least until the Resistance hits me again, probably sometime later today, I am feeling good. Out here on the road anything can happen, and it usually does, but as long as I hit those two targets, that anything is fine.

As I drifted off to sleep, I reminded myself of a key lesson I was learning:

Your emotions are going to fluctuate wildly on this trip, and they will be horribly inaccurate gauges of reality. So what you feel doesn't matter nearly as much as keeping those two key indicators on track.

KAPLANLI

The next morning, safe in the knowledge that my two key indicators were on track, I hopped the bus and went back to Çardak. I checked into the hotel I had stayed at a few days before and worked on emails and blog posts for the day. I waited until after dark for dinner, when I could sneak out to another market to buy a simple dinner of bread and yogurt.

The next morning I walked out onto the square, took good-bye photos with my Çardak buddies, and hopped the bus back to Dinar to resume my walk.

Tuesday, 25 September

In the late afternoon I arrived at my destination for the day, a village called Kaplanlı (pop. about 250). Kaplanlı was one kilometer off the main road, and I had to walk down a narrow gravel road to get there.

A few farmers passed by me as they walked toward the main road. I thought they might be walking to the nearest town to pick up supplies for dinner, as there probably was no bakkal in Kaplanlı due to its size. I waved hello to the two, half expecting them to stop me and ask what I was doing here, but they just waved back and continued walking as though foreigners carrying backpacks walked into their village every day. I continued walking too, the rest of the 500 meters into town.

As I walked into the village I could peer into people's backyards and see old crumbled storage sheds and mangy guard dogs and sometimes a single sheep tied on a rope to a pole. I was stunned by the poverty I saw. Also I was right about the village having no bakkal. However, I had eaten a large breakfast earlier and wasn't hungry, so it didn't matter.

As had become my standard procedure when entering a village, I found the mosque and sat outside on a bench waiting for some worshippers to exit.

I noticed a shady area off to the side of the mosque and stood to take a closer look. The ground was covered by a thick blanket of pine needles — a great place to pitch a tent. And since it was a mosque there would be bathrooms and a place to wash up. It had all the luxuries I would need.

A few worshippers came out of the mosque, and I introduced myself to them and asked if it was okay if I camped there in the garden. It turned out that one of the worshippers was the groundskeeper for the mosque. "Of course, it's fine for you to camp here," he said, as he introduced himself and a few of the other men.

I set up my camp at about 8:30, but since it was a little too early to go to sleep, I sat and rested on the wooden bench near the front door of the mosque rather than on the pine needles outside my tent. I chose the publicly-visible area because I didn't want to spook anyone by being a stranger who walks into their village from off the highway and then disappears into the darkness.

While I sat on the bench, a man from the village brought me a huge round tray filled with cheeses, olives, soup, meat, and plenty of bread, and set it on the bench beside me. I started to thank him, but he scurried away before I could get a full sentence out of my mouth. I looked down at the tray. It contained so much food I wondered if I could eat even half of it.

I ate as much as I could, and then stood up to help digest the meal, looking down at the remains and wondering, *Hmm! What do I do with the rest of this food?* I couldn't just leave it in the tray because I didn't want the villagers to think I wasn't satisfied with the meal they brought me. I decided to stuff it into some plastic bags I had been acquiring along the way and carry it out of the village. However, as I started stuffing the food into my pack, I realized it might attract mice during the night, so I prayed to God for forgiveness and surreptitiously flushed the food down the mosque toilets.

PEACE

The next morning, about forty-five minutes into that day's walk, I pulled off at a gas station for a morning break. I didn't need to stock up on supplies, having eaten so much the night before, and I had plenty of water. I just took a seat at one of the picnic tables in the back of the gas station to rest awhile.

Some travelers from Ankara drove up in their car and stopped. They noticed my pack and came over to introduce themselves. As we made small talk, I felt a longing to go with them. I thought about how they would travel in an hour the distance I would travel in a week. They were driving to a town I would arrive at in maybe three months. They owned cars and worked in offices. Theirs was a world where iPhones, chargers, electricity, and hotels were common. They enjoyed staying overnight in Hyatt Regencies.

I longed to go with them, but at the same time I realized, *No, I'm very happy to be here doing what I want to do.* I was at peace with the reality that all I had was what the next kilometer was going to look like when I walked it.

As they loaded back into their car and sped off, I knew I had broken the spell of Denizli and Çardak. I stood up, swung on my backpack, and started the steep descent into the town of Keçiborlu.

The road was narrow and the shoulder almost nonexistent. As I walked down the grade I tried not to get hit by the oncoming trucks as they labored up the hill toward me. As long as I was willing to breathe their exhaust fumes, I was safe.

Early in the afternoon I got to the bottom of the grade and entered the village of Keçiborlu. It would take another short day of walking to get to Isparta, the next major city. I double-checked the financial calculations that I had made in Dinar and decided to stay at a cheap motel in Keçiborlu.

Thursday, 27 September

The next morning I once again feasted on the traditional Turkish breakfast that came with the hotel room: the huge round platter with sliced cucumbers and tomatoes, olives, sausage, two kinds of cheese, a plate of bread, and this time, in the center of the tray, a fried egg rather than the usual boiled egg. I didn't care that the yolk was broken. I took a picture of the breakfast plate for my website.

Before starting my day's walk, I figured it was time to answer some more questions from my friend Denise's 4th-grade students near Seattle. I pulled out my iPhone to read their emailed questions and peck out my answers.

The next question was where did I get the hat I wore in so many of the photos they had seen. I wondered for a second, *What hat?* then realized they were asking about the dirty, crumpled-up, sweat-stained hat from Fowler Nursery in California I had been wearing since the first day of the walk. That hat had become as much a part of me as my boots.

The next question was about how I checked emails as I traveled. I used my old iPhone. That iPhone was my computer, my workhorse, and almost as much a part of me as the hat and the boots. I set it down on the table and took a photo of it I could post on my website too.

One of the students wanted to know why I ate so much junk food along the way. I chuckled, thinking, *Ah! When you're an adult you, too, will be able to eat as much junk food as you want.* But, wanting to be a responsible role model, I told her that many places along the walk were sparsely populated and I didn't have room in my pack to carry much food. I had to get what I could along the way at the gas stations. If I couldn't eat a nutritious non-junk-food meal, I told her, I would drink a carton of juice or just water and eat a roll of cookies that I could pick up at the gas stations. Whatever I could find to get me through to the next meal, that's what I ate. I told her that I made sure I ate at least 1.5 healthy meals a day. I had learned that this was what I needed to keep up my energy for the walk. If some days I would just eat one, then the next day I would make sure I ate two.

After finishing my breakfast and my emails to the kids, I pulled on my pack and went out to the road to start the walk for the day.

I traveled that whole day through mile after mile of parched, dry terrain where the mountains had been carved away by strip-mining. I was hoping to make it into Isparta but it was taking a little longer than I had planned, and by the time sunset was nearing I was still about 10 kilometers north of the city. I was quite hungry and thirsty. I hadn't seen a gas station or a restaurant all day and hadn't eaten since breakfast. As daylight dimmed, I trudged on through the barrenness looking for a place to at least shelter for the night, but I was finding only dry open land. And then, suddenly, up ahead at the top of a hill, I spied an oasis. Perched at the top of a hill was an OPET gasoline station that sat on a huge green lawn surrounded by large, well-irrigated trees.

Happily, I walked up the hill to the station.

The gas station attendants were very hospitable and welcoming and told me I could of course camp there on the lawn. They even turned off their automatic lawn sprinklers for the night so I wouldn't get wet. As I drank my carton of juice and ate my roll of cookies before dark, I sat next to my tent on the hill and gazed across the valley. Beyond one of the hills I could see Lake Eğirdir, where I would be in a couple of days.

HOTEL CALIFORNIA

Saturday, 29 September

In the morning I packed up, snapped the daily dedication photo, and resumed the walk into Isparta.

I entered the city around 10 a.m., had lunch, and decided to look for a hotel for one night before continuing to Lake Eğirdir.

While roaming the crowded sidewalks of the central part of the city, I felt lonely and out of place, paranoid that everyone was laughing at me. In the space of a month I had become most comfortable walking through small villages, arid deserts, and farm country, and now I was in a city of 192,000 people. I felt edgy and mistrustful of nearly everyone I saw, and I imagined I stood out, a hick from the countryside, lost in a city too big for himself.

I tried a few hotels, asking first about the price and then asking if I could see a room.

Finally, I found a relatively inexpensive one that was clean, well lit, and that had running water for showers. I decided to take advantage of the luxury and kicked off my shoes, lay down on the soft bed, and took a nap. I left the room only once that evening, for a short trip to get dinner. I spent most of my time following up on correspondence, particularly the growing stack of questions from the fourth graders.

Sunday, 30 September

The next morning, after greedily scarfing down the hotel's traditional Turkish breakfast, I began my walk towards Lake Eğirdir. I didn't think I could make it to the lake that day, because it was a 1½ day walk, and my foot was still hurting a bit.

As I was leaving Isparta I came upon a woman in her mid-50's who was walking to a nearby grocery store. I greeted her on the sidewalk. She said she was going to the store to buy items for her family's Sunday morning breakfast, and she asked if I needed anything from the store. I said, "No, thank you. I've just had a big breakfast."

"Would you like to come to my home to have breakfast with my family? We'd love to have you."

"Thank you," I said, "but I've just eaten a big breakfast at the hotel and I couldn't swallow another bite."

She continued into the grocery store and I continued walking down the street. A few moments later she caught up with me, carrying a bag full of groceries.

"Please, join us for breakfast," she said again.

"Thank you," I repeated, "but I've just eaten a big breakfast and I couldn't swallow another bite."

She opened her shopping bag and insisted I take something from it. I knew she was not going to leave me alone unless I took something, so I looked into her bag and chose a package of marshmallow cookies, not wanting to take items she needed for her family's breakfast. I wished her a very nice breakfast with her family and thanked her again for her kind offer and continued walking.

As I reached the edge of Isparta, a mini-bus, also headed out of town, pulled to the side of the road and stopped. A man jumped out of the bus. He ran over and introduced himself to me in English as Osman. He taught English, he told me, and he lived in Isparta. He was on his way to pick up some friends visiting from Poland. They would all pack into his mini-bus and ride to the lake for the day.

I told him I was heading to the lake also.

"Oh, would you like to ride with us?" he asked.

I declined and told him I would see him there but I knew I was unlikely to reach the lake that day. I did want to see him again, though, and meet his friends.

About three kilometers later I walked past a sun-baked couple driving back from their field on a tractor pulling a trailer full of watermelons. They waved hello and offered me a melon.

I tried to decline politely, telling them I wouldn't be able to carry a melon.

"You can carry it in your arms," they insisted.

I knew they weren't going to let me go without a melon. So I peered into their trailer, chose one of the smallest melons I could find, and cradled it in my arms like a baby. I thanked them for their hospitality and continued walking down the road carrying the melon.

I thought about ditching the melon by the side of the road, but I didn't want to be rude, even though no one would see me. So I continued carrying it. After about a quarter-mile my arm was growing tired and I thought, *I'm going to have to pay this one forward really fast.*

Most of the inter-city bus drivers recognized me, because they passed me on the road every day. When they saw me carrying a melon, several of them gestured at me, raising their palms to the sky while driving by and rolling their eyes as if saying, *What, now you're carrying watermelons, too?*

I just smiled and waved at them with my free arm and continued walking.

I stopped and arranged my watermelon in the grass by the side of the road, my bottle of water next to it, and took a still-life photo of them. About three kilometers later I found a gas station with one attendant and no customers. I said hello to the attendant and showed him my watermelon.

"Do you have a knife?" I asked. "Let's cut this watermelon open and we'll split it."

He excitedly went into the store and found a knife. We cut open the watermelon and sat out on one of the picnic tables eating the watermelon together. He asked me if I would take him back to the US with me.

I told him, "Yeah, next time I go back there why don't you go with me?"

But he seemed serious and wanted to get further into the details and asked when we would leave.

"Got a passport?" I asked.

He didn't have one. I told him he would probably need one, and the conversation about going abroad together ended quickly.

We finished the watermelon and I thanked him for his hospitality and he thanked me for the watermelon.

About two kilometers later I walked a stretch where the shoulder of the road plunged down into a steep 20-25 ft. drop-off so that it wouldn't be easy at all to clamber down off the shoulder if I had to. I passed a huge tomato garden below me and a family out harvesting them. They saw me walking above them and waved up at me to come down to join them.

Okay, I thought, *I have this really large backpack on. I can barely move as it is. There is no way I can just scramble down this steep embankment just so I can come and have tea and tomatoes with you.* I pretended I couldn't understand what they wanted and waved back at them and kept walking.

Pretty soon I heard little feet pounding the ground below. I turned and saw one of the boys in the family running alongside me down in the garden holding a plastic bag that had been stuffed with fresh red tomatoes. He was looking for a place to climb up. We finally, after about 500 meters, reached a driveway where he was able to climb up and meet me on the road and give me this gift.

I took the tomatoes from the panting boy, thanked him profusely, and turned and waved goodbye to the family. The boy turned and ran back to his family to continue with the tomato harvest.

Now I was walking down the road lugging a bag of tomatoes. The scent of the warm, ripe tomatoes caused me to salivate. I started devouring them, stuffing them into my mouth like popcorn, the juice running down my chin and soaking my t-shirt. I let the skins drop to the ground.

Meanwhile, the oncoming inter-city bus drivers laughed and pointed.

About five kilometers after I had finished all the tomatoes and stuffed the plastic bag into my pocket, I met another farmer who called to me from across the road and waved me over. This farmer was harvesting walnuts. We chatted for awhile, and I asked him if the trees were his.

He said, "Yes, and I'm harvesting walnuts. Would you like to take some with you?" Since the walnuts he had just harvested were still in the green husks, he went to his garage and brought out a plastic bag filled with freshly husked walnuts. I thanked him for the walnuts and continued on.

As I walked, I cracked some walnuts under my shoe and ate a few. The day was warm and I didn't have a whole lot of water and was extremely thirsty. After eating a few walnuts my dry mouth started to feel like it was full of cotton. I didn't want to be disrespectful or rude, but I needed to ditch the walnuts.

A few kilometers from his house I turned a bend in the road, and I threw the walnuts into a ditch and covered them with dirt. I stuffed the empty bag into my pocket along with the tomato bag.

About another hour or two after I met the walnut farmer I came to the town of Büyükgökçeli. I had marked Büyükgökçeli on the map as the town I would stay in, since that was where I would finish my 20 kilometers for the day. On the map it looked like a great place to stay, but up close it felt inhospitable. It wasn't a village where an indigenous population lived and made their homes like most villages I'd been through. It was a series of strip malls and gas stations for weekenders passing through on their way from Isparta to the lake.

I decided to continue on to the lake since it was only ten kilometers further, and staying at the lake would be a lot better than spending the night in this wide spot in the road. However, my foot had begun throbbing again, so I decided not to chance walking. I would ride the bus instead and come back to finish this leg of the walk in the morning. After finding a notable landmark that would be a clear marker of where to start the next day, I took off my pack, turned around, and faced the oncoming traffic to flag down a mini-bus into Eğirdir.

The bus was packed, standing room only. I did find a place for my pack and didn't have to wear it inside the bus. Since I'm over six feet tall, I stood with my neck bent and the back of my head crushed against the ceiling, so my view of the scenery on the drive to the lake was minimal, and I was unable to track the route we were taking. Mostly I saw the floor, and I took it on faith that we were headed in the right direction and that I would arrive at the lake as intended.

The bus did stop and drop me off in Eğirdir, a narrow little village nestled on a strip of land between a steep, rocky mountain on one side and the lake on the other. On the outskirts of the town of Eğirdir was an elite military training center for mountain commandos. The center of the town was filled with hotels and hostels for people fleeing the city on weekends.

I walked the last kilometer or so through the town looking for a place called Charly's Pansiyon. It had been recommended to me by a British woman who lived in the Antalya area near the Mediterranean coast. She had mapped out a number of historical walks for tourists, one of the most famous being the walk of St. Paul, which passes through Eğirdir village. One of her contacts in the village was a man who, along with his family, owns Charly's Pansiyon. His name is İbrahim. As are most of the hotels and hostels in the area, Charly's Pansiyon is located on a narrow peninsula that sticks out into the lake. By narrow I mean you can walk from one side of the peninsula to the other in three minutes. You can see the lake in both directions no matter where you stay.

The pension was in a beautiful setting right on the lake's shore. The first thing I did was walk out onto a large shady terrace that overlooked the lake. A cool, fresh breeze off the lake blew against my face as I took in the surroundings. In the center of the terrace sat a huge varnished wood-grain table. Smaller tables were scattered about under umbrellas.

İbrahim appeared and welcomed me, introducing himself and shaking my hand. I asked him if I could stay at the pension but pitch my tent and sleep outside. He said, "Of course you can! You are welcome to do that." The property, he said, ran down to the lake and I could sleep right next to the water if I wanted to.

Osman and his group happened to be staying at Charly's also. He and another teacher named Cem were hosting a group of teachers and non-profit organizers from Poland who were in Turkey doing a professional cultural exchange with professionals from the city of Isparta. They found me below at the lakeside setting up my tent and came over to invite me to join their group.

After I got my camp set up, I met them all upstairs on the deck of the pension. We sang and played guitar — two Turkish English teachers and I, along with six Polish travelers, all of us with the intentions of unifying the group with music, the language of the universe, though none of us knew the same songs. First, Cem and Osman took their turn on their guitars playing a song that only the two of them knew. Then the Polish people took their turn on guitar, playing one of their own songs that the rest of us didn't know. We went back and forth that way until we finally found common ground — "Hotel California." The whole world knows "Hotel California," or at least the chorus. So we drank beer and sang "Hotel California" over and over. Everyone joined in except Osman, who spent most of the time texting his girlfriend back in Isparta.

Finally, when I didn't want to sing "Hotel California" and drink beer anymore, I went down to the lake, sprawled out on my sleeping bag, and fell asleep, lulled by the refrain of "Hotel California" off in the distance and the lapping of the waves on the lake outside my tent.

CHARLY'S PANSIYON

I stayed at the pension for over a week, sleeping by the lake, taking showers with hot water every day, doing my laundry, and eating the traditional Turkish breakfast served on the deck. If it rained I had the option of sitting inside in the dining room, looking out the bay windows that surrounded the dining room.

One of the things I enjoyed the most at Charly's was the leisure of sitting on the deck listening to music with my headphones. Through the entire month of September I hadn't used my headphones. While walking it was important to be aware of my surroundings, and I couldn't unplug from my environment at all.

I did get an "earworm" that wouldn't go away for several days while at Eğirdir — America's "Horse With No Name." I don't like that song, but the lyrics came out of nowhere, and I let them in because they felt right.

I've been through the desert on a horse with no name
It felt good to be out of the rain
In the desert you can remember your name
'Cause there ain't no one for to give you no pain

During my stay I met a number of people passing through the pension, several of them British. One was a woman named Carla who stayed at the lake three or four months of the year. Carla had been coming to the lake for years, not as a guest, but paying her way doing odd jobs such as food prep (cutting up cucumbers, tomatoes, etc.), clearing the tables, making beds, and vacuuming. In return İbrahim allowed her to stay at the pension and eat for free. The rest of the year she would go back to her family in England. Like me, she spoke English and pidgin Turkish.

Another, a young woman in her late twenties, a born-again Christian missionary, was taking buses from one Turkish city to the other.

One day she joined me as I sat in the sun on the deck.

During our conversation she asked me, "What religion are you?"

I said my usual, "I'm a Christian, of course!"

She said, "Do you believe in God?"

I said, "Yes, I believe in God."

She asked, "Do you believe that Jesus was his divine son?"

I said, "No."

She said, "Well, then, you are most definitely not a Christian! And you should stop referring to yourself as one."

I was slightly bemused by that conversation and thought, *Well, if I stop referring to myself as Christian then what am I?* I was used to referring to myself as Christian because where I was walking you were either a Christian or a Muslim or a Jew. My Turkish was not good enough to explain to people what I'd have meant if I said that I was none of those things and that I was just "spiritual."

I'd had these kinds of conversations with the Muslims in almost every town along the way. I felt like I had been pummeled by a bully every time. The *"not only am I deeply religious, I am also right"* spiels were the same no matter whose mouth they came from.

There was another group who were regulars at the pension, and that was a group from an elite military training center for commandos a couple kilometers away. These were not your garden-variety infantry. They were in this area because of the mountains and the lake where they could train in different terrains. I was able to watch them jump out of helicopters when they practiced lake landings. There are also some high and craggy mountains around the lake that are covered with snow where they could train during the winter.

During the day, the travelers cleared out of the pension to take their day trips and the deck of the pension became a lake-view internet cafe for the commandos. They came in during leave hours in the afternoon to hang out on the balcony and drink tea or beer and check their Facebook and email their wives and girlfriends back home. Some of them must have had agreements with the pension owner, though, because apparently they had girls closer by who came in to join the commandos for a drink, and before you knew it couples were disappearing into the available rooms together.

The commandos had to be back on base about the time the foreign travelers came back from their day trips. So the pension had this 24-hour circulation of groups of different people I watched as they came and went.

Also during my days at Eğirdir, I did some walking around the town. There was a little square where I became a regular. As much as I enjoyed Charly's, I sometimes felt out of place surrounded by the foreign travelers there. I felt much more at home surrounded by the Turks in the village who spoke Turkish and ate Turkish foods like kaşarlı pide, a flat bread with cheese, for lunch.

One day as I sat in one of my favorite restaurants munching on my kaşarli pide, I was jolted out of my comfort while watching TV. This was the time the Syrian border was starting to become destabilized, and on TV the talking heads were discussing the Turkish parliament debate taking place that day on whether to authorize the Turkish government to make incursions across the border into

Syria. I knew I would be walking close to that border in a few weeks.

Another time I took a mini-bus into a nearby village to a farmers' market, the *Pınar Pazarı* (Spring Market). This was one of the biggest farmers' markets I'd ever seen and one of highlights of the area. I had trouble not grabbing handfuls of olives out of the tens of thousands of olives heaped colorfully on trays that were arranged down long tables, and I could barely resist sticking my fingers into the powdery red spices mounded in cloth sacks with their tops rolled back. There were fresh vegetables, fruits, butcher shops, restaurants, clothing for women, home goods — and tourists.

But most of the time I spent the week at the pension lounging on the patio, listening to music on my headphones, and answering more questions from the 4th-graders.

The other travelers didn't understand this. When they spotted me lolling around on the deck wearing my headphones during the day they would invite me on their day hikes. They were having the trips of their lives, following in the footsteps of St. Paul and soaking up the great history of the area. How could I just sit on the deck doing nothing?

The hotel staff and Carla and İbrahim would also come out and ask me, "Are you sure you don't want to do some of the activities?" "Are you sure you want to sit here all day and do nothing?" For me, though, this was my holiday from walking through the country visiting places, and all I wanted to do was sit on the deck and listen to music on the headphones, soak up the sun, and watch small whitecaps sparkle on the lake.

BREAKING FREE FROM HEAVEN

Monday and Tuesday, 8 and 9 October

I enjoyed the pension so much that several days when my week's vacation was finished, I would do a day's walk and come back by bus to the pension and spend the night. The next day I would take the bus back to where I ended the previous day, do a day of walking from there, then come back again to the pension by bus and spend the night.

I felt like I should be leaving Eğirdir behind, though. The old struggle was back — moving on from people I knew and from places where I felt at home. It wasn't that I thought it was wrong to enjoy the scenery, to sleep by the lake, to sit on the deck at Charly's, but that the resistance to staying in the present, meeting new people, dealing with new situations, was back, or maybe had never left. I found myself very uncomfortable with never having closure. Too many questions were opened but almost none were ever closed.

I had a job to do. The job was to walk across the country. It wasn't to get attached to things.

When I finally pushed myself out of the village of Eğirdir that Monday, I found the scenery on the eastern side of the lake amazing, much like northern Wenatchee along the Columbia River in Washington, country that was indeed home to me. As I walked down the narrow two-lane road above the lake I passed apple orchards and exquisite views of the lake. A huge apple harvest was in progress and many workers were out in the field picking apples.

I ate apples and drank tea with a family of farmers who waved at me to come join them on their break. Even after a month on the road, I still grappled with the tendency to stereotype people, and I imagined that a family of farmers would be uneducated and unfamiliar with urban life. As we drank our tea, I asked the family about themselves. One of the sons lived in Ankara, the capital of Turkey. He was a nurse. Another of the children, a university student, was home on break helping with the harvest. I appreciated their gentility and their pride in their family and their farm, and they were far from uneducated country folk. I was reminded, once again, that most of the time my stereotypes were wrong.

Most of the time that day I just walked, gazing out over the lake on one side and orchards on the other, then on up into the rocky bluffs beyond. The sky was crystal clear and the lake bright blue. I asked myself how I got so lucky. How had the universe chosen me to be the one to see this?

At one point I pulled off to the side of the road and turned to look back, somewhat yearningly, at where I'd been — where I'd slept by this lake listening to these waves outside my tent. There, perched on the ledge overlooking the lake, I felt very much at home.

Then, beginning to feel a bit like Lot's wife who morphed into a pillar of salt while turning to gaze back at home, I jumped up and started walking again.

Wednesday, 10 October

On the morning of 10 October, I finally packed up, boarded the dolmuş, and rode away from Charly's Pansiyon. At the Sarıidris turnoff I got off the dolmuş and started walking to Gelendost. Here the road began turning east away from the lake, and the scenery began to change from apple orchards to packing sheds and cold storage plants. There were still a few orchards but not as many.

I stopped and visited a few apple storage places and took pictures of their forklifts and packing areas for my dad. I began nearing the end of my miles for the day and thought I'd scout out the packing sheds for a place to stay. They seemed too busy with the harvest however, so I didn't want to bother them. Also, I wasn't seeing any gas stations along the way with grassy areas to camp in. I decided I'd probably have to find a cheap motel in Gelendost.

I'M A KILLER AND OBAMA'S A JEW

Thursday, 11 October

The next morning I walked out of Gelendost in the rain, which let up a few kilometers later as I entered a small village of about 1,500 people. On my left was a school where a bunch of little kids were outside doing their morning jumping jacks. A wave of excitement spread through the crowd as the kids spied a foreigner with a backpack coming their way. Calls of "hello, hello" began in heavily accented English.

Two girls ran out to the fence to greet me and invite me to join them for their exercises. I looked around for a teacher, but the children seemed unsupervised. Maybe the teacher had gone inside for a minute or two and would be returning, I thought. I decided to enter the schoolyard and find the teacher to see if I might offer my assistance by joining them all in some exercises or helping out in the classroom for a while as a novelty for the students.

The two girls gasped and began giggling when they saw that I was turning toward the schoolyard. Their classmates, jumping jacks forgotten, stampeded to the fence and ran alongside it, screaming and cheering as I neared the gate.

When I walked through the gate into the schoolyard, an older man, who introduced himself as the principal, intercepted me. He had come out into the yard to see what the commotion was all about.

He greeted me and said, "Why don't you come inside and we'll have a cup of tea." I knew he didn't want me to get the kids any more riled up than they already were.

I accepted his invitation, happy to avoid the tidal wave of excitement building amongst the students. The principal walked me up a flight of stairs to his office in the administration building and gestured for me to sit in a chair across the desk from him. A massive portrait of Atatürk rose high like a shrine on the wall behind him. Next to the portrait hung several framed Atatürk quotes. I was not surprised, since nearly all public offices and most private offices contained such shrines to Atatürk. Atatürk is the icon for secularism in Turkey.

Also, Atatürk has a reputation for being open to the outside world and for being an open-minded leader. So I thought, *If this principal worships Atatürk so much, then I'm probably on friendly ground here and he is probably fairly open-minded even though this is a smaller village.*

The principal initiated the small talk:

"Where are you going?"

"I am going to Van," I answered, "but first I will go through Konya. Have you been to Konya?"

"It is a nice city, but there are too many religious fundamentalists there."

He turned and pointed to the portrait of Atatürk. "Are you familiar with the works of Atatürk?" he asked.

"Yes, of course. He was a great man."

"Yes, he was. Where are you from?"

"I am from the USA."

"I don't like Americans. They are killers."

I hadn't been called a killer before. I bit my lip and reminded myself to be patient.

"What do you mean?" I asked.

"Well, they kill Palestinians, they kill Iraqis, they kill each other."

I didn't want to make any more of an enemy than I already had, so I tried to steer the conversation to more neutral subjects.

"So how far is Konya from here?" I asked.

Disregarding my attempt to steer the conversation to more neutral subjects, he continued his tirade against all things American or foreign.

Then, without skipping a beat, he mentioned that things were kind of difficult at the school right now.

"And why is that?" I asked.

He told me that he'd just lost his English teacher.

Gee, I wonder why, I thought to myself. But instead I just nodded and looked concerned.

"I want to continue language education for the students," he continued.

I did some quick mental calculations and thought *Well, I have some flexibility in my schedule.* I said, "Well, if you need a teacher I'd be happy to come back here and help out for a couple of weeks while you get a replacement."

He said, "Thank you very much for the offer, but you are not welcome at this school. You are American, and you would be a bad influence on the children. Besides, the community would not be happy with me for hiring a killer."

My offer of assistance refused, and having been told by this man that he did not like my kind, that we were haters and killers, I thanked him, wrapped up the conversation, and took my leave. Besides, it was starting to get noisy out in the hall, and a few of the children had started knocking on the door and trying to find excuses to come in. At that, the principal escorted me outside to the school gate and we said our goodbyes. I never got to play with the children.

I walked further into the village for about ten minutes and spotted a group of middle-aged men sitting at a teahouse across the street. They waved me over.

I crossed the street, said hello, and pulled off my pack. The men were busy discussing the plight of the world. When I sat down, the conversation turned to which recent US presidents were Jews.

"George W. Bush, was he a Jew?" they asked me.

"I'm not sure," I replied.

"Obama, he's definitely a Jew."

"Okay, if you say so," I replied. "I didn't know that."

"Clinton, though, he wasn't a Jew."

"Okay, good to know."

God, the people in this town are bigots, I thought to myself.

I had only been sitting for a few moments, but I was already finished with this conversation. I put down my tea, shook hands with the men, pulled on my pack, and walked toward the edge of the village. *Man, bigotry does not have a profile, I thought to myself. Young, old, secular, religious, educated, not educated, I have no idea when I meet a person what their views of the world are. And if I ever think bigotry does have a profile, I'm probably the one being bigoted.*

A few kilometers later, a farmer harvesting vegetables in his field called out to me. I walked over and shook his hand. He handed me a squash. I thanked him, walked back out to the road, and continued my walk, this time carrying a squash.

I didn't have a knife or any utensils, and there weren't any gas stations outside the villages in this area, so when I reached a bend in the road, I hid behind a tree and disposed of the squash.

BAHTIYAR

Toward the end of the day I approached the village of Bahtiyar. It was about ¾ mile off the main road and up a hill, so it would be a little extra walk.

One of the first things I ran into at the edge of the village was a middle school. Again the yard was filled with kids. But instead of innocent second graders, a mob of 12-year-old boys ran over to meet me. I don't particularly like being surrounded by large groups of pre-teen boys. They are often the most unpredictable of groups. I never know whether they have learned manners yet or not.

However, this group was very friendly. So after a couple of minutes of walking amongst them my paranoia began to relax. I asked the boys if there was a bakkal in the village. They said yes, but it was up the hill a bit in the center of the village. They were happy to escort me there. As we walked they eyed my pockets and my pack, and I started to feel nervous, exposed and vulnerable, but I told myself that they were just curious, not greedy or covetous like the two kids back in Germencik. I reminded myself how wrong the school principal had been about me that morning, and how I had wanted him to give me the benefit of the doubt, so I would need to do the same for these boys now. As we walked, I let them pull in tighter and continue eyeing my pockets and pack.

The boys led me up the hill to the village center where there was a bakkal and a *kahvehanesi* (coffee house). Before I could make it to the bakkal, though, the village elders waved me into the kahvehanesi.

They waved the kids away, and I walked up a small flight of stairs and sat on the porch with them. One of them was the father of the muhtar, so I silently thanked the boys for bringing me to the right place.

The village elders invited me to take off my pack and sit down and have some tea with them. I was physically very tired from the day's walk and emotionally drained from the morning's social activities, but I smiled and did as I was told.

They asked me where I was from, where I was going, why I was walking, etc. I asked them a bit about the village. They told me its population was about 1,000. That's about what I had figured, since I had spotted two bakkals.

They asked where I stayed on my trip, and I told them — gas stations, mosque gardens, public parks, wherever I could find a spot. They volunteered that I should stay there in the village that night. I was happy to have an important order of business already taken care of, and it was barely 4 p.m.!

After a bit more small talk I asked if I could rest a bit. They said of course, and showed me to a table inside the kahvehanesi. I thanked them and sat down, but what I really wanted was a quiet place where I could lie down for a while and close my eyes.

A few minutes later I got my wish when a young man in his late 20s named Mehmet came over to my table. Mehmet and I had met a few minutes earlier when I was sitting out on the porch. Mehmet told me to come with him, I could rest at his house and then have dinner before coming back to the village. Mehmet and I left the kahvehanesi, the two of us walking down the road towards the edge of the village. I had only met Mehmet a few minutes before, but on this walk I often followed strangers into unfamiliar situations I barely understood. When I got nervous I reminded myself of two things: one, that the best experiences I've had came from situations I didn't understand, and two, that beggars can't be choosers.

While we were walking, Mehmet volunteered that he had gotten married a mere month before.

I asked him how he met his wife. Since it was a small village, I supposed he would tell me she was from the village too.

"I met her on Facebook," Mehmet said. "She is from Turkey, but she goes to school in France."

"Interesting. What does she study?"

Mehmet ignored my question. "I plan to move to France soon too," he said. "I currently work as a sous chef in Antalya, and I can probably continue that kind of work in France, too."

Mehmet's home was about one kilometer (one-half mile) beyond the tea house, at the edge of the village. His front yard, which was packed dirt, contained a little wooden shed with some farming tools in it. A goat stood tethered to a tree by a rope around its neck.

Like the houses in most Turkish villages, Mehmet's was made of cement and unpainted. It would be considered rustic by urban standards, but was quite normal for a small village. It didn't really look like a home until you got inside the living area.

I took off my shoes when we got inside. Mehmet mentioned that his father had passed away, so now it was just him, his wife, and his mom in the house. Mehmet said a few words to a woman in one of the other rooms.

"Who is that?" I asked.

"That's my wife," Mehmet told me.

I had assumed she would be in France, and Mehmet probably noticed the quizzical look on my face.

"She's home from school on break," he continued. We walked through the living area and up the stairs to the guest bedroom.

"We are preparing dinner down in the kitchen, so why don't you lie down and take a little rest here," he said.

I thanked him and lay down on the bed. The room was quiet and the bed comfortable, but there was no heat in that part of the house. Since I was still sweaty from walking with my pack all day, I quickly became cold. But still it felt very good to be lying on that bed in a quiet room.

After about twenty minutes Mehmet came back up to escort me downstairs for dinner in the living quarters. The living quarters were heated, the walls painted, and the furniture smartly upholstered. My stomach began rumbling when I smelled the aroma coming from whatever his wife was cooking. Mehmet and I sat in the living room watching TV in our socks.

Soon his wife came in and set a big tray of food on the floor. The three of us sat on the floor around the tray and ate dinner rural Turkish style.

Mehmet mentioned that he and his wife were big fans of Nutella, and he pointed to a big jar of the stuff sitting in the center of the tray. We had a Nutella-dipped dinner, smothered everything in Nutella, even the pickles.

I wanted to plow into that food as if there was no tomorrow, since I hadn't eaten since breakfast the previous morning. But I tried to show restraint, watching my hosts closely so I could match their pace and not eat all the food myself.

After dinner Mehmet's wife cleared the tray while Mehmet and I sat in the living room digesting our food, drinking tea, and watching TV. I wasn't sure whether I was going to stay the night at that house or not, and I didn't ask. I had learned that inhabitants of these small villages, especially the farmers, didn't try to control things as much as I did. If I started asking specific questions like, "Where am I going to stay? What are we going to do next?" they usually just shrugged their shoulders and said, "Oh, I don't know, we'll see." I was learning that this didn't mean they weren't going to take care of me, I just needed to relax and trust that everything would be okay.

A few minutes later, during one of the commercials, Mehmet stood up abruptly and said, "Let's go back to the village." I stood up and asked if I should bring my pack and he said, "Yes, bring your pack with you." We put our shoes on and I put my pack back on. I said goodbye to his wife and thanked her for the dinner. Then he and I walked back into town to the kahvehanesi.

At the kahvehanesi the big event of the evening was back-to-back episodes of *Kurtlar Vadisi* ("Valley of the Wolves"), a popular Turkish action television show, essentially a Chuck Norris-style shoot-em-up where the tough-guy star chases after the bad guys and periodically knocks his less-disciplined underlings into line.

Before the start of the shows, Mehmet and I watched a few backgammon games and he and the others introduced me around to the people I didn't know yet. Mehmet mentioned to me that the US was trying to push Turkey into war with Syria, but something in my face must have said I didn't want to talk politics, and he immediately dropped the subject without saying another word.

The TV shows started and we all gathered around the screen. Near the end of the first episode, the village muhtar decided it was time to supply me with a home for the evening. He walked over to my table and introduced himself and, after making sure my passport and visa were all in order, he told me to come with him. I said goodbye to everyone and thanked them for their hospitality and left the teahouse with the muhtar. He took me next door to the administrative building where they had a spare room they had planned to put me in for the night. Before showing me to my room, the muhtar needed to take care of a little administrative business with one of the other residents, a villager who was buying a piece of property and needed to register his deed.

I sat in the muhtar's office while he did his paperwork, and when he finished he signaled for me to follow him.

We went out to the guest room where they planned to put me up for the night. It was a little on the dingy side with a couch that was a little too grimy to sit on and a rug that was a little too greasy to touch. A dim light bulb dangled from the ceiling.

Beggars can't be choosers, I reminded myself, as I smiled and thanked the muhtar for his hospitality. I set up my tent, so there would be some fabric between me and the rug, then used the nearby outhouse and turned in for the night.

A KOREAN?

The next day I woke up early, packed up my stuff, and took a look around the room. Eight hours ago I hadn't wanted to touch the floor or sit on the couch, but that dark, dingy place had become a safe home to me in a very short time. I recognized the feeling, sighed, and pulled on my pack anyway.

The muhtar was not yet up. The administrative building was deserted, as was the kahvehanesi I'd been in the night before. Across the street, however, was a teahouse filled with the village's retired farmers who now worked at solving world problems over countless early morning cups of tea. I walked over to them to say goodbye and they wouldn't let me go without sitting down and joining them for tea and simit.

After I had breakfast and chatted with them a bit I took a picture of myself with them and walked back out to the main road.

East of Bahtiyar, the terrain was much different from that of the previous days. The hilly apple growing region that reminded me of eastern Washington had given way to sparsely populated, wide-open land better for sheep grazing.

After a few kilometers I felt my mood begin to plummet for no identifiable reason. I thought back to previous weeks when I'd walked through barren, wide-open lands similar to this and remembered the mood swings I'd experienced then, as well. I'd start feeling depressed, exposed, isolated, and vulnerable. I wondered if changes of scenery were influencing my emotions, or if I were just seeing a pattern where one didn't really exist.

I finally forced myself to give up on that debate, telling myself, *You'll never be able to figure that out. Just shut up and walk.*

A few hours later, I began going through an even drier, more deserted area. I'd long since run out of food and water. I hadn't seen a car for miles, and there wasn't a building or person in sight. Suddenly a cyclist on a mountain bike sped up behind me. I hadn't seen or heard him coming even though the terrain was wide open and all was silent. He was pedaling strangely fast for an uphill grade, using one of his lowest gears. He looked Korean. He carried no baggage on his bicycle, so he had no tent or sleeping bag, and I had seen no tourists or cycling groups around, so there would be no nearby sag wagon carrying his equipment. No, this was just a lone Korean traveler out here in the barrens carrying nothing. He didn't say hello or acknowledge me in any way. We made no eye contact.

Recognizing that I might be in one of my hypoglycemic fogs and not completely coherent, I told myself that maybe the Korean bicyclist hadn't been real, maybe I had hallucinated him. But then I remembered the Polish guys from the second day, and how shocked I had been to realize there were others out there, and I thought, *Well, maybe he was real.*

But then I told myself, again, *You won't be able to figure that out, either. Just shut up and walk.*

I finally saw a gas station ahead and went straight for the market, trying not to look too desperately crazed as I eyeballed the shelves filled with crackers and cookies. I wanted to dive in and devour everything in sight. After buying some snacks, I went outside to a little gazebo to sit in the shade and drink my water and eat my snacks.

I eagerly made small talk with a couple of attendants while I ate, the only people I'd seen all day except for the retired farmers in Bahtiyar and maybe a Korean on a bicycle.

The attendants invited me to stay at the station for the night, but it was only 3:30 in the afternoon, a little too early. I finished my snacks, pulled my pack back on, and walked back out to the main road.

I briefly thought back to the beginning of the walk, when I wondered what secret handshake the Poles were using to get invitations to sleep at gas stations. Now I was turning down invitations. There was no secret handshake.

When I got to Şarkikaraağaç, my destination for the day, I walked straight to the city center and hopped a bus back to Lake Eğirdir. After the strangeness of the previous days, I needed a weekend of relaxing by the lake, listening to the waves lap against the rocks, feeling the breeze from the lake blow across my face. I wanted to hear the noise of the tourists traipsing in and out. I wanted to hear the soldiers' coarse laughter as they joked with the women. Most of all I wanted to sit on the deck and do nothing.

ABANDONED PEAR ORCHARD

Monday, 15 October

Bright and early Monday morning, 15 October, I took a bus from the lake back to Şarkikaraağaç and began walking again.

I'd gotten a late start. After a few hours it began to get dark, and I realized I wasn't going to make it to Kireli, the village I'd hoped to reach that day.

I thought to myself, *I've stayed in many places so far, but I haven't camped, uninvited, on private land yet, and that's an important hobo skill, so I should learn it sometime, and now is as good a time as any.*

So I started eyeballing the land immediately to the sides of the road.

Off to the right was a large flat field planted with ground crops of wheat and barley. *Nope,* I thought, *no good, nothing to hide me from drivers passing by on the road.*

On the left side I saw a dense row of tall poplar trees used as a windbreak protecting an abandoned pear orchard. There were tractors working the adjacent fields, but none in the pear orchard, and the poplars would hide me from anyone traveling on the road.

I still felt a little fearful, not so much of robbers or some other bad guys, but mainly that the farmers might see me camping on the property unannounced, and might not be welcoming. But I figured, *Well, you're going to have to get over this sometime. May as well do it now.*

I pushed through the brush underneath the poplars and sat down out of sight of the road. The nearby farmers would be able to see me though, so I stayed motionless so as not to attract their attention. I sat like that for a little over an hour, until the last tractor had left for the evening, and then I set up my camp in the falling darkness.

Once camp was set up, there was nothing else to do and it was cold outside, so I lay in my bag. Since it was my first night sleeping on private property, I was kind of paranoid that someone was going to notice me there or that the police would come by. No one bothered me though, and I fell into a deep sleep.

BEELINE FOR BEYŞEHIR

Tuesday, 16 October

Waking in the morning with a gentle breeze on my face, I lay in my sleeping bag for a long time, watching pear leaves shimmer in the early light. All was quiet except for the breeze and the occasional roar of a truck passing on the road. However, I did not like waking up with the feeling that I needed to get out of there before I was discovered.

I reluctantly crawled out of my sleeping bag and took a photo of my tent in the pear orchard. Then I broke camp and walked out to the road where I snapped my daily dedication photo and wrote: "Today is for the village of Horsunlu — a place I never lacked for a place to stay, food to eat, and people to watch over me."

As I walked, I reflected on what had happened to me in the pear orchard between going to bed feeling fearful the night before and waking up not wanting to get out of bed the next morning — in fact, lying nestled in my bag thinking, *Oh my God! This place is so beautiful and comfortable I'd like to come back here and stay awhile!*

Absolutely nothing had happened, except that eight hours had passed and I had survived. Is that what home is? I wondered. A place where you can be for eight hours without dying or being harmed? Can you start feeling that way anywhere if you are there for eight hours and survive?

I walked the couple of kilometers into Kireli and ate breakfast. I hadn't eaten since breakfast the day before except for a few rolls of gasoline station cookies, so I relished a breakfast of *sucuklu yumurta* (eggs fried over easy with sausage mixed in) sopped up with slices of bread. It felt good to get some food in my stomach.

The area where I was walking was still sparsely populated and there was very little road traffic. I was walking through another cultivation area — wheat, barley, turnips — and off in the distance there were large tractors, combines, and equipment out tilling the land, getting it ready for next year's crops. But there was no one nearby to say hello to. The farmers off in the distance were too far away to even wave at.

Usually on the highways I saw minibuses and cars traveling between the villages. And often along the way when someone did pass they would call out to me and ask if I needed a ride somewhere. But here I would walk for 30 minutes at a time without seeing a car.

After a few hours I came upon a rest stop/cafe where I stopped for a bowl of soup.

There was only one patron there besides myself. I saw row after row of stainless steel chafing dishes, but no food. I asked the lone attendant if they were open. He looked at me with surprise, perhaps not expecting any patrons that day.

"I think there's some soup in back, let me check," he said.

He found some soup, heated it up for me, and found some bread to go with it.

As I sat out on the patio dipping the bread into the soup and drinking my tea, a retired turnip farmer walked up to my table.

"May I sit down?" he asked.

"Yes, of course." I motioned to the empty chair across from me.

We made the usual small talk: Hi, how's it going? Do you live around here? What are you doing? Where are you going?

Then, as casually as he had commented on the weather and had asked me where I was from, he said, "Are you Muslim?"

"No, I am not."

"Too bad," he said. "If you were, you could stay here."

I thought, *First, it's barely noon, and I didn't ask. Second, if you were a good Muslim, you wouldn't apply that test.*

But instead, I just took the last sip of my tea and said, "Ah."

My lunch finished, I stood up, wished the farmer a good day, pulled on my pack, and walked back out to the road.

As I walked, I scanned the terrain in front of me. There were very few trees and even fewer bushes, just mile after mile of turnip fields. Dirt and more dirt, on and on. Even the farmers driving faraway combines were gone.

My spirits felt as barren as the land in front of me. Negative thoughts rushed in to fill the void. Since the beginning of the walk, Turks had been telling me that I would find people less welcoming as I moved east. At the moment they seemed to be right.

I thought of the retired turnip farmer at lunch, and how he had rejected me.

The self-doubt dug deep. I started wondering, *Why am I doing this? It's pretty pointless. I have only one or two significant experiences each week. Why am I spending three days walking on the side of the road, sleeping in gas stations and pear orchards, to get each one?*

I began rebelling against my own golden rule for the walk: Do not judge, not even yourself. Just observe. Stay present.

No, I thought, *I don't want to be present, I don't want to get out of my own mind. It's comfortable in here. I want to stay in here for a while.*

My opposition voice countered:

No.

You cannot stay in your mind. You have to come out and be present.

In the past few days you have been turned down exactly once for your religious beliefs (or lack thereof), but have been offered places to stay four times.

Yes, people told you it would be dangerous here, that the locals would not be welcoming. But that is not what is happening. So snap to. Stay present.

If that guy had been listening to what God told him, and not to what others had told him God told him, he wouldn't have considered your religious background relevant to your need for shelter.

I laughed out loud, relieved to see the opposition winning. I relaxed, confident that I was not about to find myself in the middle of a foreign land, believing myself to be engaged in a wrong-headed and fruitless pursuit.

Still, a nagging sense of discomfort had begun to settle in, and I felt the drive to walk further and faster than necessary, to hurry through this area as much as possible.

About two hours after my encounter with the retired turnip farmer, I walked by a family harvesting turnips in a field about 50 meters from the roadside. Feeling the unexplained push to make good time, I kept my head down and tried to walk past. But the father was jumping up and down, waving at me as if meeting me was the single most important thing in his life at that moment. I begrudgingly raised my head to make eye contact and wave back.

The father motioned me over and eagerly introduced himself. His name was Mustafa. He introduced me to his wife, their grown son, and his grandsons Selçuk, whom he was holding in his arms, and Mustafa. The whole family was taking a break from the harvest and having tea as I walked by. They motioned to me to take a break with them.

I pulled off my pack and, since there were no shade trees for miles, took a seat in the sun.

I drank the first cup of tea, and then rose to leave, but they insisted I stay for another one. After the second one I rose to leave again, but they insisted I stay for a third. After the third glass of tea, I rose again and insisted that I really must go. They relented, but asked if we could take some photos together before I left. After a couple photos I pulled on my pack and walked back out to the road to continue my walk, leaving the family behind to return to their harvest.

While drinking tea with the family, I had started having a premonition that I should walk all the way to the city of Beyşehir that day. Beyşehir was at the southern edge of the lake, and hadn't begun to appear in front of me yet. But by the time I got back out to the road, the casual, fleeting thought of "I should go to Beyşehir today" had turned into an urgent drive I could neither explain nor ignore, so I sped up.

It wasn't easy trying to speed along this section, as the road surface was rough and the rocks in the pavement were sharp. I mused that when you are driving in a car, the shape of the road's rocks is almost insignificant, but it is very relevant when you are walking.

After two more hours of walking, I noticed that the sun was hanging low in the sky, and my feet were hurting from hours of walking on the sharp rocks. I saw Beyşehir in the distance and estimated that it was an hour away. An hour later it still looked an hour away. *Is it possible,* I asked myself, *for a whole city to pick up and recede into the distance?* I thought back to my first days on the plateau, when I was still getting used to the new scale of things. This was even worse!

Shortly after the sun disappeared behind the mountains, I reached the edge of Beyşehir. The city's population was only about 40,000, but with my new standards a city like that seemed large and sprawling like New York used to seem. Walking through the industrial suburbs seemed to take hours. I grew nervous as the sky grew darker, and my hips and back, unaccustomed to the day's extra miles, began to cramp. My feet ached from the afternoon of walking on sharp rocks, and more and more of the cars were using their headlights.

A large truck pulled to a stop alongside me. Four crew members, apparently construction workers just off their shift, sat crammed into the cab. They seemed really excited to see me. They opened the door and one of the crew hopped out and hurried over to me with a bag of red apples. He handed me the bag, gave me a quick handshake, and then hurried back to the truck.

I continued into the city, eating apples in the dark.

I walked up to the first relatively cheap motel I saw and asked if they had any rooms available. They were closed for renovation, but the owner began to call around to find a place for me. Because of the upcoming holiday, Kurban bayram, most of the hotels were already full.

Finally, he found one with an available room, the *Oğretmen Evi* (Teacher's House). I told him I wasn't a teacher and asked if that would be a problem. He shook his head and said he didn't think so, but it was across town, would I like a ride over there? I could barely stand, and wanted to cry, my hips and back still cramping from the day's double walk. "Yes, thank you," I said to the offer.

CRAMPS

I woke up the next morning with the sun streaming into my room. I got out of bed to check out my surroundings since, when I arrived the night before, I was too tired to do anything but go directly to bed. The manager had apologized that he was short on available rooms and asked if I'd be okay with upgrading to a suite at the regular dorm room price, so I knew I was in a big room, I just didn't know how big. It was a suite larger than any house or apartment I had ever lived in. It had beds I wouldn't need to use, and couches I'd probably never sit in. And to think that a mere 24 hours earlier I had woken up in the dirt in an abandoned pear orchard!

I walked over to the balcony doors and flung them open to let the breeze from Lake Beyşehir blow over my face. My room looked out to the west over the lake, and I could see the hills on the other side.

I began to get dressed to go downstairs for the hotel breakfast. I was starved. After breakfast I planned to go out and scout around for some supplies, and then I would hurry back and relax in the room and take in the surrounding scenery while handling some administrative details — emails, photos, and the like.

But suddenly I doubled over. A piercing cramp gripped my abdomen. I had felt these cramps every couple years since my mid-20s, and I knew I would be completely disabled on the floor for three or four days. It was a good thing I'd followed the premonition that I should walk two days' journey in one day and get to Beyşehir early. I definitely wouldn't want to have these cramps while on the road. I'd probably be lying on my back in the dirt somewhere.

So, though I had one of the most amazing locations of any hotel, I spent most of those four days in Beyşehir writhing on my back on the floor, looking up at the ceiling, groaning. The staff at the hotel were very good to me during this time, taking pity on the strange tall American who had thought he'd walk across their country, and now, just over a quarter of the way through, lay flat on his back on the floor of his suite groaning day after day. They brought me food and drink when they could and drove me to the pharmacy so I could get medication.

I was at a low point. I was ready to quit and do something else. My online followers began writing me after a day or two wondering where I was. They told me where they were and what they were doing. One was doing a spoken-word performance. My dad was planting a garden in his backyard. My brother and his wife were going to have a baby. What was I doing? Lying on the floor hoping my insides would get moving again, so I could get rid of whatever was causing this cramp. I hadn't even been able to get to the window to enjoy the sunset over the lake.

Not only was I in pain, I was lonely, despondent, and bored with myself. I always got bored with myself. I had had a good job in Seattle. I got bored with that and quit. I had bought a house in Seattle. I got bored with it and sold it. I was 42, and I'd done a lot of things. But I'd gotten bored with a lot of things. I'd quit a lot of things. Now I was seeing the things other people got when they pushed through the boredom, and I wanted those things too.

I needed help!

I emailed Rory Stewart, a Scottish author who wrote *The Places in Between*, about his trek across Iran, Afghanistan, and Pakistan. He had been one of my inspirations for doing this walk across Turkey. I asked him what he did during his low moments. He emailed me back right away that day, saying, "During my low moments I found it was important to concentrate on the spaces in between my breaths. Breathe out and then breathe in. Then live in that space. Think of nothing else. Just concentrate on those spaces and let time pass. The bad feelings will pass." This is what he recommended for me.

My breath was very shallow because of the cramps, so I was taking a lot of breaths and had a lot of spaces to live in. I lay on my back for about three days and each day let the staff know at the reception desk that I was going to stay one more day.

I used to think it would be a fascinating thing to walk across an entire country. I had followers who thought it was a fascinating thing I was doing, walking across an entire country. Turkey, nonetheless! Not just the US, or England, but Turkey. Behind the scenes, though, it was really boring. I walked, and I looked for places to sleep. Today I was waiting for my bowels to move.

I had 74% of the walk left to go. What would I find there? Now, in the spaces between my breaths, I knew that my job — my mission — was to overcome my nature, and to engage in something so boring and tedious that I couldn't help but want to quit, and to finish it anyway.

I vowed that when these cramps passed in a few days, I would push through whatever boredom came after that, and finish what I had started.

On my fourth full day in Beyşehir I began feeling better and didn't have cramps for the whole day. I figured that the next day I would start walking again. So I went into town to do some exploring and pick up some winter clothes. It was starting to get pretty cold.

I walked around in some of the markets and found a sweater and a scarf that I could use and then walked around the markets again. I saw a stall with thermal underwear and stopped to buy some. I was ready to leave that market and then found a wool hat. I figured that might just be the most important purchase I'd made that day. I was ready to continue my walk the next day.

All that day I felt the now-familiar uncertainty, wanting to hang on to the comfort I'd had the last few nights and would be having this one last night, followed by the dread of not knowing where I would sleep the night after that. Then again, I had a huge project I needed to get done, so I was going to need to face that dread. The pole between the two was ever-present, even when I was laid up and unable to walk.

So I finished my time in Beyşehir, not a bad place to have fallen sick. It had some friendly, helpful people. There was food nearby. I was staying in a large suite with a beautiful view. And that evening I did get to watch the sunset. But it was time to move on.

MOVE ON

After four days at the hotel in Beyşehir I was eager to get moving again. I felt the familiar pang of leaving behind what had become comfortable and familiar. However, I was starting to realize that the feeling was not going to go away, and that rather than trying to make it do so I needed to find it within myself to keep moving forward anyway. I pulled on my pack, said goodbye to the hotel staff, and hit the road.

The day's walk to Sarıköy went pretty quickly, as there were no places along the way to stop and rest, have a cup of tea or chat with the locals so I rolled into Sarıköy more than an hour earlier than expected and looked forward to a relaxed search for a place to stay that night.

The village was set back from the main road a few hundred meters, so I asked a family down at the main road if the village had a bakkal. I asked in part because I was looking for food and water, but also because I preferred to let the locals direct me into a village that was off the main road, rather than entering the village on my own without permission.

The answer to my question was "No, there is no bakkal. We buy everything at the çarşı." Çarşı is a broad word meaning market, or bazaar, or sometimes even the commercial center of a town. It's one of those words that means a great deal to the locals, and absolutely nothing to anyone else. So "we buy everything at the çarşı" was not helpful information for me.

Since this was a small village, maybe only a few hundred people, I thought maybe there really was no bakkal, but I asked again: Is there a bakkal? I added that I was just looking for water and a little food. I held up my empty water bottle, thinking maybe they'd offer to fill my bottle or hand me a piece of fruit or something.

No such luck, but this time the older woman in the group spoke up and said that there was, in fact, a bakkal but it was closed and would not open for another hour and a half.

This was unusual. There were times I'd walked into a particularly small village in which the one bakkal was not open all day. But whenever that had happened, another villager, usually a young boy, ran over to pull the bakkal owner back to work.

The woman pointed to the center of the village, off the main road and up the hill a few blocks, so I started walking up that way. I stopped at the mosque to rest up a bit and wait until the bakkal opened. After only 20 minutes hanging out at the mosque, I decided to walk up to the bakkal anyway.

I shouldered my pack and walked out onto the street, almost getting knocked over by a small boy and girl chasing each other around the village. They stopped dead in their tracks, mouths wide open, staring up at the giant humpbacked stranger walking through their village. Some older boys nearby laughed at the little kids' shocked expressions. I greeted the older boys and asked if there was a bakkal nearby. They said, "Of course, there's one just up the street, follow us."

We got to the bakkal, which was open and had been all day. It was attended by a 35-year-old man named Fatih. I asked Fatih if there was any water, a softball question if ever there was one — I have never seen a bakkal that did not sell water. When I asked, Fatih said no, we don't sell any water, we all get our water from the town's fountains.

I bought a loaf of bread and a small carton of yogurt and asked Fatih if there was a place I could sit and eat. He pulled a carton of sugar cubes out from under one of the shelves, dusted it off, and indicated I could sit on it. I did so, and, after offering Fatih some of my white bread and yogurt (which he politely declined), I dug into my lunch.

While I ate I asked Fatih about life in the village. He was from the village, the only child of his family left after all his other brothers and sisters had moved away to the nearby cities. He was married, had a couple kids, and was looking forward to celebrating the upcoming holiday, Kurban bayram, with friends and family. I asked him some questions about slaughtering the sheep for the holiday, but I couldn't understand his accent very well and so had no idea what he said when we talked about anything but the most familiar and well-worn subjects.

Fatih told me numerous times he liked village life, that it was quiet and relaxed, not noisy and stressful like life in the cities. I asked him how business was at the bakkal. He said the bakkal wasn't doing very well. I was not surprised, given that some of his fellow villagers were barely acknowledging it existed, and when they did they thought it was closed when actually it wasn't.

When I finished my loaf of bread and carton of yogurt, Fatih cut off a piece of homemade *helva* (a sugary paste eaten for dessert) stored in the glass counter and gave it to me. I savored it and wished for more but didn't want to be greedy.

At this point I usually went for "the ask," that time in the conversation when I directly asked if there was a place in town where I could camp for the night. Everything was in my pack, I would say. Tent, sleeping bag, everything. All I needed was a place to lay it out — a mosque garden, an empty room, whatever.

Fatih said, "No, unfortunately, probably not here in this village. We are too small. Our mosque does not have a garden, and there is no school or park." Fatih suggested I walk up the road a few kilometers, where I would find a gas station and a rest area to camp in.

When people said no to me, the most common thing they cited was their village's lack of facilities. I wanted to counter that if they had seen some of the places I had considered acceptable places to sleep, they'd be amazed. A hard tile floor in the corner of a gas station's office. A spare, unlit storage room. A dirty orchard on the side of the road.

But by now I realized that none of this information would change what they had to say. They were not saying no because of the reasons they gave, they were saying no because of something else, and that something else quite likely had absolutely nothing to do with me.

In the earlier days of this trip I thought the results of my requests for a place to stay were driven by my approach: in the way I asked, in who I asked. When I began to realize the results had little to do with me, I thought maybe they had to do with the venue — was there a patch of grass somewhere, for example? But for every place that had turned me away for not having a patch of grass, a place without a patch of grass had welcomed me warmly.

Then I thought maybe it was the size of the village. Maybe a village that couldn't support a bakkal couldn't support visitors. But for every tiny village that couldn't support a bakkal and had turned me away, there was another tiny village that couldn't support a bakkal and had taken me in.

Every time I thought I was starting to detect a pattern, I realized there was also data to refute it.

At the beginning of each day, I didn't know what the end of the day would hold in store for me. In fact, at 3 p.m., when I typically walked into that day's intended destination village, I had no idea what kind of reception I would get. I had been shown to the imam's living room. I had been shown to the town's vehicle maintenance yard. I had been shown to the mayor's office. I had been shown to the mosque garden. I had been shown to the hard-tiled floor of a gas station's office. I had been shown to a cheap hotel. And sometimes, once or twice a week, I was kindly shown the exit. And almost none of it had anything to do with me.

I stood up, thanked Fatih for the chat, pulled on my pack, and walked back out to the main road so I could cover those next few kilometers before dark. When I arrived at the station Fatih had mentioned, I looked around, decided I didn't like it, saw that I had about 45 minutes left before the sun sank behind the hills, and continued around the bend where I could look for a campsite off the side of the road. I wanted to breathe the crisp air and look at the stars as I fell asleep.

GOD, I'M SUCH A HICK

Wednesday, 24 October

As I began walking the next morning, some guys at a small paint store across the road called me over to join them for tea. The tea wasn't ready yet, but the company was great, especially since I hadn't visited with anyone since Fatih at the bakkal in Sarıköy.

The road that day was bumper to bumper with holiday traffic leaving Konya for Lake Beyşehir for the four-day Kurban bayram holiday. The road was under construction, but the construction crew was off for the holiday. So I was privileged to have to myself a quiet dirt lane to the side of the main road as I headed toward Konya. No worries about getting hit by trucks or having to jump off shoulders every few minutes.

The terrain was still flat and barren, no village, no people to talk to. By evening, when I looked for a place to camp for the night the road was running through a river bottom that was drainage for Lake Beyşehir. I found a place to camp down an embankment, sheltered by rocks and trees.

That night, when Nature called, I got out of my tent and stood shivering in the cold night air three feet from my tent. It was not dark at all. The sky was perfectly clear and full of stars. The moon lit up the hills, the trees, the rocks. Every single blade of grass glistened in the light. I could almost make out the patterns in the bark of the trees on the ridge above me. I was standing in my own personal amphitheater. Could something so beautiful be had by merely showing up?

Thursday, 25 October (first day of Kurban bayram)

I awoke to Kurban bayram (Feast of the Sacrifice), perhaps the holiest of the religious holidays in Turkey. The holiday would run for four days, Thursday through Sunday. In Arabic Kurban bayram is known as "Eid al-Adha."

The traditional way to celebrate Kurban bayram is to sacrifice an animal, like a sheep or a cow, keeping 1/3 of the meat for one's own family, giving 1/3 of the meat to relatives, friends, and neighbors, and giving 1/3 of the meat to the poor and needy.

Even in big cities like İstanbul, some people still sacrifice an animal. The weeks before Kurban bayram see empty lots suddenly fill with sheep that families can pick out. Even outside the Carrefour (French equivalent of Walmart) across the street from where I'd lived in İstanbul, I stepped over blood running through the cracks in the sidewalk on the first day of Kurban bayram.

However, in most cities in Turkey the slaughtering of livestock has given way to cash donations to charities. For example, almost every other ad on TV the week before Kurban bayram is from a charity like the Turkish Red Crescent (the Turkish version of the Red Cross) asking for money for this or that cause.

Kurban bayram celebrates the story of Abraham and how he was so devoted to God he almost sacrificed his own son before God stopped Abraham and told him, "I'm just testing you! Here, sacrifice this ram instead."

This was one of my favorite stories as a kid reading the Bible in Sunday School, and I was surprised when I realized that Muslims, on their holiest of holidays, celebrate the same story. That was one of my favorite "the differences aren't nearly as significant as we think they are" anecdotes.

There are differences in the stories between the religions (which son was nearly sacrificed, etc), but in my opinion arguing over those differences is petty, internecine fighting we should "soldier up" and get over, because the point is that the three Abrahamic religions (Judaism, Christianity, Islam) celebrate pretty much the same story.

After I broke camp that morning I took my usual dedication photo, dedicating the day's walk to my Polish doppelgangers, Piotr and Derek, whose spirits had been with me even though I hadn't seen them since the second day of the walk. I had been musing about how their hobo skills had inspired me and encouraged me to learn the skills I needed. I wasn't the same person I was back when I met them two months before. I wondered how they would see me now. I wondered how they were different from when I had met them.

I thought there might not be much traffic that day, since it was Kurban bayram. I began my walk ascending Hanönü Pass, elevation 5,118 feet (1,560 meters). As I reached the top of the pass, big, dark rain clouds rolled in right behind me. At three kilometers into the descent I found a small grove of about six or eight tall trees that I could camp under for shelter from the rain. Under these trees I would be marginally hidden from traffic on the road and from the owners of the land who, because of the holiday, were probably gone anyway.

There was no place along the way where I could get food though. It was sparsely populated and the few gasoline stations or cafes I saw were closed because of the holiday. Fortunately, I had stocked up on cookies and water.

I set up camp under the grove of trees and turned in about 6:30 p.m. since it had started raining and there was nothing else to do.

Friday, 26 October

The next morning there wasn't a cloud in the sky. Before packing up I sat and watched the sunrise. This had been one of my favorite campsites so far, mostly because it had been so quiet during the night, only about one car on the road every ten minutes, and I was able to sleep well.

I had seen on the map that I was headed for a lake called Altınapa that day. I figured I would end the day at the lake and camp there for the night, continuing into Konya the next day. But when I got to Altınapa I found it was a work-only reservoir supplying water to the city of Konya (approximate population 1 million). The lake was surrounded by a barbed wire fence.

I decided that I'd better try to get to Konya in one day rather than the two I had planned. To continue the descent into Konya I had to climb back out of the Altınapa basin. The climb was on a traffic-friendly road — two lanes in each direction. But it was very steep with no shoulder on the side where I walked. So I had a choice. Either cross the road and walk up the hill on the other side with my back to the traffic, breathing the exhaust fumes of slow trucks as they labored past me up the hill, or walk facing the traffic on the side with no shoulder. There was a guardrail on that side with a twelve-inch ledge I could walk on, but the ledge dropped off into a canyon. I chose to walk on the ledge. Then I climbed precariously uphill, one foot in front of the other, holding desperately to the guardrail on the ledge while balancing with my backpack. On one side, the on-coming traffic screamed past me down toward the lake, and on the other side a steep ravine threatened to swallow me. Also, I was tired and thirsty and hadn't eaten real food for a couple of days. But there was no way I could stop.

While I balanced along that ledge, I thought of this one woman who was following my walk on Facebook, ecstatic for me that I had seven months of walking across this beautiful country that she had vacationed in. Hers was the Turkey of Blue Tour cruises, beautiful bays, crystal clear water, snorkeling, beautiful mountains, İzmir, ancient churches and mosques. And here I was hot, sweaty, starved, and thirsty, trying not to lose my balance while treading on a precipice at the edge of a busy highway. I was very cranky about then and wanted to shout at her, *Woman, you do not understand. I am not on vacation here. My experience of Turkey is completely different from anything you imagine!*

Finally I did make it to the top of the ridge. The shoulder began to widen out a little, and I started to calm down as I crested the ridge and began a wide descent into Konya.

Toward the end of the descent I rounded a curve, and a view of the city of Konya opened up before me. The sight of this city that contained a population of one million people overwhelmed me. I used to think a city of this size was just one small part of a larger city. Now a million was a sprawling megalopolis. I had become such a hick!

By the time I entered Konya I felt I could go no further until I found some water and hopefully some food. I also had an urgent need for a bathroom, since for most of that day it had not been appropriate to pull off the road and use the nearest tree.

I stopped at the very first fountain I could find and filled up my water bottle. Then I rested a bit, sitting on my backpack and drinking my water. I had reached Konya and the walk was one-third over. While I was sitting on my pack drinking my water, a car stopped by the side of the road and a family got out. One of them was holding a plastic bag, and they began rummaging through their trunk for whatever food they could find. They came over to where I sat, greeted me with smiles, and handed me the plastic bag now filled with the only food they had found in their trunk: semi-rotten fruit. It was the first food I'd seen in a few days, so I rummaged through that bag and ate every morsel of whatever I could find that was not completely rotten. That fruit — God bless them! — got me far enough into the city to find some more substantial fare.

I walked further into town and found a mosque where I could use the bathroom. Then I found a bakkal where I stocked up on some snacks and hopped a bus to the city center's Öğretmen Evi, where I got myself a private room with shared shower.

I stripped off my clothes, wrapped myself in a towel, and took a long, hot shower, my first shower since Beyşehir. The hot water cascading down over me made me feel happy.

I didn't know how really bad I'd smelled until I walked back into my room. It was horrible. It smelled like a wet yeti in there. I'd been stuffing my sweat-soaked, rain-soaked wool clothes and underwear back into my backpack, where they had had days to heat themselves up and begin stinking.

Konya, the home of Rumi and the whirling dervishes and many other famous spots, is both a religious and tourist center of the Middle East. I had planned to spend a couple of days touring the city. But that is not what happened. As soon as I smelled that backpack and its contents I picked up my phone and called a friend in İstanbul.

"Hey," I said to her. "I'm coming to İstanbul tomorrow. Are you there? I would like to come and visit." I did need to go to İstanbul anyway to get paperwork started for my visa. I might as well go a little early and do some laundry.

She said she was there and that that was fine.

I hung up the phone. Now I was clean and my city clothes were reasonably clean too, though my backpack still smelled like hell. I walked out into the city to finally get myself some real food at about 7:30 p.m. I was really going to feast. But I found every place closed for the religious holiday, not just the restaurants but the markets were closed too. I walked around for awhile and finally found one market that was open. They didn't have much food left, but I found some salami, a carton of yogurt and a loaf of white bread and paid for it, feeling like I had food fit for a king. Then I walked back to the Öğretmen Evi, sat cross-legged on my bed, and stuffed myself with salami, using pieces of bread to scoop the yogurt out of the carton.

STARTING VACATION

Saturday, 27 October

The next day I spent about two hours visiting the tomb of Rumi before hopping the bus to Ankara and İstanbul to take care of some visa and other business and in the meantime clean up my smelly belongings.

On the bus out of Konya, seeing the countryside, it didn't take me long to get back in touch with how much I loved walking across the country, to want to turn around and go back and walk again the next day. I don't think we were three miles down the road before I began smiling and laughing to myself, imagining myself walking along the shoulder, thinking about how much I loved traipsing down the road waving at people as they drove by. I didn't know what it was, there was just something about walking and being homeless that had begun to possess me.

YOUR WALK IS POINTLESS

Tuesday, 13 November

Two weeks later I was back in Konya to resume the walk. I would have only one week before I had to return to İstanbul to pick up my new residency permit, and I wanted to get some miles in.

I was stiff after having been off for a couple of weeks, so I began the day with some extra stretching. Then I pulled out my increasingly ratty whiteboard and dedicated that day's walk to my friend Christian, who had met me for sightseeing during my time off. I'd felt inspired after spending time with him and happy that somebody understood that when I was walking I was not on vacation, I was at work. This walk was my job. Christian had understood that even before I opened my mouth to articulate it, and I was grateful for that. On the dedication board by his name I wrote, "Get the work done."

As I walked to the edge of Konya, I got lost, taking a wrong turn and found myself at the eastern edge of town when I had wanted the southern edge. I thought back to the 4th graders in Denise Waters' class, and how one of them had asked me if I got lost often. I was a third of the way across the country, and this was my first time getting lost. It's hard to get lost when you are walking straight across a country.

When I finally got my bearings and started down the right road, I spotted a carpet salesman standing in the doorway of his store with his arms folded, watching me and grinning.

I said hello and introduced myself in Turkish. We shook hands and he introduced himself in English. He was still grinning, and I wondered what was so funny.

He asked me about my walk and why I was doing it. As usual, I had trouble explaining the why in Turkish, so I switched to English. But I couldn't explain it in English, either.

"Your walk is pointless, it is a waste of time," he said.

Wow, you are very forward, aren't you? Do you always speak to strangers this way? I couldn't explain the deep reason for doing what I was doing, but I did not want to agree that I had sacrificed so much for nothing.

I bit my lip. "Perhaps it is," I said. "I guess it is about as pointless as selling carpets."

Be careful Matt, don't get dragged into that conversation. For months I had tried to steer clear of feeling I needed to answer the "why" question. The drive to answer that question was strong, and I wanted to learn how to keep from feeling I needed to justify myself. So, I waved goodbye and told him I needed to keep walking.

As I walked through the south side of Konya, an area filled with car repair and cattle feed shops, I stopped for lunch and ordered *fasulye ve pilav* (beans and rice). A very friendly man stopped by my table.

"I know who you are," he said with a wide grin. "I saw you last night on our news channel." He introduced himself as Ali and asked if he could join me.

"Of course," I said and motioned for him to sit down. Ali, I learned, owned a motorcycle repair shop. He had two kids — a boy and a girl — and a cousin who was a teacher in the USA.

It became obvious that Ali had made it his mission to take me to tea after lunch and introduce me around the neighborhood.

One of Ali's friends in the neighborhood was Hikmet Usta (usta means "craftsman" and is often used as a title of respect for a professional who works with his hands). Hikmet was a mechanic at a car shop next door to Ali's motorcycle repair shop.

Hikmet insisted that I have tea with him and the cluster of mechanics in that particular neighborhood. I had to stop at three cups of tea, though Hikmet begged me to stay longer — I still had a long, long way to walk that day.

As I left Konya, headed south, the terrain was flat, almost treeless. I saw very few places to camp.

I pulled into a village called Çarıklar, about 25 kilometers south of Konya, at 4 p.m. It was starting to get dark. I figured that if I couldn't make it work in Çarıklar I'd hop a bus back to Konya and stay in Konya.

SLEEPING IN A KORAN SCHOOL

As I entered Çarıklar I greeted a young man coming out of one of the houses. We chatted for a moment, and then I asked him if there was anyone at the mosque a couple hundred meters down the road towards the village. He said that if there wasn't, there were a couple more mosques in the village proper (a couple kilometers further off the highway), and I could try there, too. The imam, he said, would be very helpful. I asked him what the imam's name was. He said he didn't know who the imam was.

I walked to the first mosque. It had a huge garden with multiple places to camp. I stood near the door and waited for someone to show up. It was getting colder, though, and darker, so after twenty minutes I decided to try one of the houses at the back of the lot and see if anyone was home.

Someone was home. A young girl answered the door while an older woman wearing a scarf over her head, her mother, I figured, hovered in the background drying her hands on a dish towel. She appeared to be preparing dinner. There was no man of the house in sight. I knew the answer would be no before I even opened my mouth.

I told the woman that I had been walking and that I was looking for a place to camp for the night. I wondered if I could camp in their garden. She told me no, that would not be possible.

I continued the kilometer or two into the village proper. The village had two bakkals so I estimated the population was around 1,000.

It was dark out by then, and I could not see much. I stepped into one of the bakkals. It was very busy, teeming with children out of school for the day buying candy and adults just off work coming in for bread and other household goods.

"Hello," I called out.

"'Hello," answered a teenager behind the counter. "How can I help you?"

I told him what I was doing, and that I was looking for a place to camp for the night. I asked if there was a place nearby where I could camp.

By then some of the adults had gathered around. They and the teenager began commenting on how cold it was getting at night. I assured them it would be no problem, that in my backpack I had everything I needed for cold-weather camping.

They began chatting amongst themselves, but since I was having a hard time with the Konya accent, I couldn't understand what they were saying.

I asked the teenager again, "Is there a place I could camp nearby?

"They are looking for a place for you," he said.

That was almost always a good sign. I'd learned by then that when a group of adults said they were looking for a place, it meant they had taken upon themselves the responsibility of finding a place for me to stay, and that if I were just patient, they would find one. In fact, the places they found tended to be better than the ones I would be satisfied with. At the end of the day, I just wanted a flat spot hidden from the prying eyes of unknown strangers. If that meant a grove of trees outside in the cold, that was perfectly fine with me. But when people told me they were looking for a place, it usually meant they were looking for a sheltered spot indoors.

I sat down in the bakkal amidst the hubbub of people coming and going. A few of them chatted with me for a bit, others just bought their stuff and left in a hurry.

After about an hour, the teenager's father came in and took over the post behind the counter. He and his son had a brief conversation, which I gathered was about my situation, as they kept glancing over at me. The father said something and the teenager grabbed some keys from the wall and told me to follow him.

I grabbed my pack and followed him to a building across the street. He unlocked the door, pushed into the first room, and began rearranging some benches to create a path to the second room. This was a school for Koran classes, but the classrooms hadn't been used in a year or so, and the rooms were cluttered and dusty.

The first room had a cement floor, but the second room's floor was carpeted. One of the other teenagers who had come in behind us laid out some additional carpets.

"So it will be comfortable and soft," he said, patting the floor.

A few other teenagers who had followed us in grabbed a large trash bag and covered up a broken window.

The teenagers asked if I would be okay there. I told them this would be great, and I thanked them profusely. They asked if I was hungry or thirsty. I assured them I had already eaten and that I'd had plenty to drink. I told them when I would be leaving in the morning. The first teenager said the bakkal would be open at that time, just stop by and say goodbye and leave the keys. They wished me goodnight, handed me the keys, and closed the door behind them. By that time it was about 6:30 p.m.

There was no light in the second room, but there was indirect light from the first room. I set up my tent, took care of some other housekeeping details, and stretched my legs and feet. By that time it was about 7 p.m. It was dark, and I was cold and extremely tired from the day's walk. Since I had nothing else to do I turned in early.

About 7:30 p.m. I heard a loud banging on the front door. I got up to answer. An older man wanted to find out who I was, and who had told me it was okay to stay there. That happened quite often — a village might be small, but communication was not instantaneous or tight. He was easily satisfied, and I closed the door (leaving it open a crack, though) and went back to my tent.

About 8 p.m. the teenager from the bakkal and one of his friends came to check on me. They made sure I was comfortable and not in need of anything, and then they took their leave.

I stayed up until about 9 p.m. and then fell asleep.

Wednesday, 14 November

At 7 in the morning, I packed up my stuff, wrote a thank you note, and walked across the street to return the keys and say goodbye.

Mehmet Bey, the village mayor, was there to greet me. We chatted for a bit and exchanged phone numbers. I asked him the village's population. He said 1,200. I congratulated myself for seeing reality yet again support my "one bakkal per 500 people" theory.

Mehmet Bey asked me what religion I was. At first he had thought I was Muslim, because in my thank you note I used a phrase people said to me often, "Allah sizi korur" (God protects you). I told him I was not Muslim. He suggested that I convert. I thanked him for his suggestion and said we all love the same god. He liked that. He liked the thank you note and told me he would post it in a prominent place as a memento from the time a foreigner came to stay in their village.

At that point the bakkal became very busy with the day's field workers stopping in to buy bread for their lunchtime, so I took my leave and headed out to the main highway.

On the road out of the village a man greeted me near the mosque where the woman had told me the night before that I could not camp. He apologized and said that they actually had a spare room, and that had he been home when I arrived it would have been no problem. I assured him that it was not a problem anyway, that I had found a great place to stay inside the village.

I reached the main road a few minutes later and began my day's walk south.

I felt happy and congratulated myself that I had pushed myself to keep going when I had wanted to hop a bus back Konya where the surroundings were familiar and there were people I'd already met.

HANGING WITH THE COPS

A few kilometers later, as I walked along the shoulder south of Çarıklar, two very friendly cops in an oncoming car slowed and pulled alongside me. The one in the passenger seat stuck his head out the window.

"How are you, is everything okay?" he asked.

"Yeah, thanks, everything is great."

"Do you need anything?"

"No, I'm fine, thanks."

I pointed at the sky, which was gray and overcast. A little light rain was falling that morning.

"It's kind of rainy today," I said.

"Yeah, but my iPhone says it'll clear up later today," the cop responded.

We continued making small talk for a few minutes, and then he suggested I stop by the police station in İçeriçumra, the next town. He and his partner wanted me to meet their colleagues, have some tea, and rest a bit.

When I got to İçeriçumra an hour later I was shaking from hunger, so I stopped at a gas station to ask where I could find a restaurant. The attendants, Fatih, Harun, and Deniz, greeted me eagerly and invited me to join them in the office for a couple of cups of tea. I took them up on their offer, hoping that there would be some snacks inside, too.

They were deep into a discussion about their hunting and fishing experiences in the local area, and as we waited for my tea they invited me into the conversation. I had neither hunted nor fished nearby in the recent weeks, so I just smiled and listened. And tried not to look too greedy as I munched on the large pastry they had set out on the office desk.

They chatted on, and my mind wandered as I reevaluated how long I would need to cover this stretch of road between Konya and the edge of the plateau. For a couple days I had been wondering if I could compress it into four days, so I would have an extra day when I went back to İstanbul the next week to pick up my residence permit. But as I sat there munching on cake and listening to stories about fish, I realized that that compression probably wasn't going to happen. It was barely noon, and I had already been stopped multiple times, including by cops on the highway, simply because people wanted to chat. And the day before, the same thing had happened. No, I probably wouldn't be able to blow through this stretch. The people were way too chatty for that.

A young boy briefly entered the room to deliver a cup of tea to me. As he hurried out the door I turned back to the ongoing fish and game conversation. One of the three men was describing how large the fish was that he had caught in a nearby stream last weekend.

I finished my tea, said goodbye to the three men, and hurried back out to the road to resume my walk. Maybe I could get further than İçeriçumra before it was time to bed down for the night.

As I reached the southern edge of town I saw the police station. I thought back to my promise to the policemen to stop and say hello to their colleagues, but I could see that the edge of town was only about a kilometer further. So, in order to make better time I decided to try to sneak past the police station and get out of İçeriçumra without stopping. As I passed the station I muttered to myself, "Free at last."

But then about 100 meters after passing the station, I heard someone call, "Hey, come back here!"

Damn! I thought, *spoke too soon!*

I turned around, walked back, introduced myself and shook hands with the cop who had run out after me.

He said it was important to check in at the police stations and to give them my information. I had heard that that was true, and I thought it sounded like a very good practice, but I'd been walking for two months and not once had I done that. *May as well start now,* I thought to myself, *a third of the way across the country.*

So I walked back to the station with the cop, and he introduced me to one of the other cops, and then more cops started flooding into the room. Pretty soon there were a dozen cops, all smiling broadly and talking amongst each other excitedly in Turkish. One of them turned to me and mentioned he had seen me on TV.

"Oh yeah," I said, "What did they say?"

I don't think he heard me above the excited din in the room because he quickly turned to his colleagues and jumped back into their lively banter about me.

The room calmed down and everyone went back to work, leaving just me and three of the cops to sit around and kill time in the main office. They asked me if I had eaten. I lied to be polite, and told them I had. No, that was breakfast, they said. They were talking about lunch. I told them that no, I had not eaten lunch. They ordered me a couple servings of *etli ekmek* (meaty bread, a local specialty) and an *ayran* (a yogurt drink).

After lunch we sat around watching the TV news, and the cops began to ask me questions about politics in the US. Someone commented that President Obama and Tayyip Erdoğan were awfully close. I didn't want to wade into a cesspool of alligators, otherwise known as "political conversation," so I just smiled and kept my mouth shut.

They warned me of the dangers ahead. I thought back to the early days of the walk, and how a couple months ago Turks were telling me the Turks in this area would be bad people. I noted that the bad people were always to the east, and I wondered if I would ever find them.

They offered me the use of the station's shower. I gladly accepted and disappeared down the hall for an extended soak in hot water.

By the time I got out of the shower the whole day was shot—it was about 3:30 p.m., so I wouldn't be doing any more walking that day. Conversation with the cops got around to what my plans were for the rest of the afternoon. I was tired. The day's prime walking hours had passed. I had walked a lot the day before, and I knew now that I was never going to cover the Konya-to-Karaman leg in four days. I just said I wanted to stay in a hotel for the night, and I asked them to recommend something. They said there was a hotel in Çumra, a town nearby.

"How can I get to Çumra?" I asked.

"Ride with us, a couple of us are going out on patrol in a few minutes. We'll take you to the hotel."

"Sounds good," I replied, noting to myself that I hadn't ridden in a patrol car yet and would now be able to cross that item off my bucket list.

We walked out of the station, piled into the patrol car, and pulled out onto the highway. On the 15-minute drive to Çumra the cop in the passenger seat called ahead to the hotel and made sure they had room for me. I sat back and smiled, noting to myself that in the past 24 hours I had slept in an unused Koran classroom and I had been escorted by cops through a village that almost never saw foreigners. I loved traveling like this.

When we got to the hotel, the cops helped me check in and then came up to my room to make sure everything was working.

"Yep, everything is fine," one of them said as he turned off the bathroom faucet. "Enjoy your stay."

I closed the door behind them, plopped down on the bed, and took out my computer to check my emails and upload some photos.

Within a few minutes the hotel manager knocked briefly. Before I could answer, he entered and sat down in a chair beside the desk.

"How is everything?" he asked.

"Excellent, thank you."

I looked at him waiting for him to tell me his reason for entering my room. But then I thought back to how social the people in this area had been, and realized he was here simply to kill some time with idle chat, and expected I wanted to do the same.

"The weather is nice," he said. "Sunny."

"Yes, it's great. Is that normal around here?"

"I guess so. Where are you from?"

"California. Have you been there?"

"No, just around here. So you're walking across Turkey, huh?"

"Yep, from Kuşadası to Van. Have you been to Van?" I suspected the answer would be no, not just because he had just said he didn't travel much, but because I was learning that most Turks had never been to Van, even though it was only a couple hours away from any point in the country, closer than Seattle is to San Francisco.

"No, haven't been to Van either." He changed the subject. "There are a couple markets and restaurants down on the street for dinner. Do you like köfte?"

"Of course," I said. Even the sound made my mouth water.

"Well, they have some great köfte at the place across the street."

He stood up and left as abruptly as he had come in. I went back to uploading my photos. I never made it to the köfte restaurant. I was so happy to have a soft bed that I hurried down to the market for a can of Pringles, scurried back up to my room, and fell asleep before the sun set.

WOULDN'T YOU LIKE TO BE A PEPPER TOO?

Thursday, 15 November

The next day I woke up, stuffed everything into my pack, and caught a bus back to the main road through İçeriçumra to begin my day's walk. As I stepped off the bus I bumped into four guys getting off another bus. They had worked the night shift at a nearby packaging factory. They apparently recognized me as they greeted me enthusiastically.

The four guys and I walked shoulder to shoulder down the road a ways, and then they bid me goodbye and headed down a side street. I continued along the main road and finally reached the outskirts of town. *Thank god,* I thought to myself, *now maybe I'll be able to make some distance.*

A few kilometers out of town I stopped at a gas station, Cevahir Petrol, to buy some water. I figured I had broken free of the orbit of İçeriçumra and could afford to be social again, so I introduced myself to the station owner, a friendly man named Ramazan.

Ramazan was in the middle of a business meeting with his District Manager, Mehmet, who had come down from Ankara. He invited me to take a seat with them in the office. We shared tea while Ramazan and Mehmet talked about things like who was going out of business and how to get more minibus accounts.

When the business meeting was over, I asked Ramazan a few questions about his family. He eagerly volunteered that he had seven children, one of whom was working at the gas station at that very moment. On the wall behind Ramazan was a photo of Atatürk and three family photos, two of which were headshots of Ramazan. I smiled and thought to myself, "At least no one has to worry about Ramazan forgetting what he looks like."

South of Cevahir Petrol was, well, nothing. Just vast expanses of desolate, flat, treeless rocky land with a few small rolling hills and no people. There were plenty of sugar beets, though, enough to give rise to an entire sugar processing company, Torku. I had seen the Torku name on sugar packets many times both on the walk and in İstanbul.

All that broke the desolate monotony of the land was the series of Torku billboards spaced about every 200 meters advertising the company and its products.

As I walked I began debating again whether or not I could blow through this area in four days instead of five. İçeriçumra had been very social, and I had not made very good time. I wanted to walk further now, but in the end, my tired body won out and I began looking for a place to camp. There wasn't a lot of tree cover though, so I was scraping the bottom of the barrel campsite-wise when I finally saw four or five poplars and a bush by the side of the road and figured that was probably the only place I would be able to camp.

I selected a one-meter space (about 3 ft.) that couldn't be seen from the road and pitched my six-foot tent in that three-foot space. It was the best I could do. I didn't really need to worry about being seen, though, as there was no traffic on the road to speak of. I'd spent my first night in Konya province sleeping by the side of the road, and I would be spending my last night in Konya province sleeping by the side of the road. Konya had been good practice for my hobo skills.

The night was clear. There were no lights, no traffic. I had just come from the clamor of İstanbul and Konya and the sociability of İçeriçumra and now, in this completely desolate and unpopulated area, I gazed up out of my tent at the panorama of stars gleaming across the sky and soaked up the quiet magic of the land as I fell asleep.

Friday, 16 November

I woke up the next morning to the surreal beauty of the sun rising above a 20-foot-deep layer of wispy fog hovering over the flat landscape. The only sound I heard was a dog barking about a quarter mile away. I couldn't see it at first through the fog, but after staring in its direction for a few minutes I could make out its shape enough to realize that it wasn't looking my way and was barking at nothing in particular. I relaxed, comforted that I was not bothering anyone in my half-hidden campsite.

The wispy layer of fog burned off quickly in the sun, and within 10 minutes my campsite was no longer hidden by the fog. I worried that a passing driver might wonder what this strange foreigner was doing camping next to a bush at the side of the road, so I hurriedly broke camp, stuffed everything into my pack, and began my walk for the day.

The fog came back, so thick this time that I was unable to see even 10 feet off the side of the road. The land around me was still board flat, but I knew from the day before that the tall, snow-capped peaks of the Taurus mountain range were looming just a few kilometers to my right, and that I would be passing through those mountains within a few days.

As I walked I looked for the road sign marking the provincial border between Konya and Karaman. Those provincial border signs had become important milestones to me, appearing every week or two and reassuring me that forward progress was being made, but this one I couldn't find in the fog. However, I knew from the map that I would be crossing into Karaman province within the first hour of the day's walk, so after about an hour I pumped my fist in the air and hollered to celebrate moving into yet another province. However, walking with a backpack in the fog that morning was starting to remind me of the 1981 British-American horror comedy film *An American Werewolf In London*, where David Naughton was attacked by a werewolf while backpacking on the British moors. Scared that I might attract a werewolf out of the fog, I put my fist back down and tried to walk quietly. A few minutes later my courage returned and I started singing, at the top of my lungs, a jingle from a David Naughton advertisement from about the same time, "Be a Pepper, drink Dr. Pepper."

The fog burned off later that morning, about 30 minutes before I reached a small town called Kazımkarabekir. As I entered the town I passed by a construction site. I heard shouts, and glanced around but couldn't see what the ruckus was about or who was shouting. I stopped walking to look more carefully, but I still couldn't see who was shouting at whom. Were they shouting at me? I shook my head and continued walking. Within moments a young man ran out from the site waving his arms to greet me. He introduced himself as Abdullah and invited me to come back with him to the site for tea. I went back with Abdullah, shared a couple cups of tea with him and his coworkers, took a photo, and then walked back to the road to continue.

Saturday, 17 November

Before passing through the next town of Karaman, I passed a hotel advertising their all-you-can-eat lunch buffet. Other than a can of Pringles and some crackers, I hadn't eaten since lunch with the cops in İçeriçumra, so, with my mouth watering, I happily strode into the hotel lobby and asked where the restaurant was.

After lunch, my stomach bursting from the onslaught of food, I waddled back out to the road and continued my walk. But 30 minutes later, I passed another hotel advertising another all-you-can-eat buffet, and I figured I could find room in my stomach for that one, too, and again strode into the lobby and asked where the restaurant was. *What a veritable orgy of food*, I thought. *When it rains it pours!* This restaurant featured a heaping bowl of Nutella on its buffet line, and I piled my plate high with the chocolaty goodness. I ate it straight, no bread or anything to cut it. I made sure that by the time I walked back out to the road to resume my walk, my head was buzzing from a sugar rush.

OFF THE PLATEAU

Within the first hour of the day's walk, I passed through the town of Karaman. This would be my last full day walking on the plateau. I would be glad to descend to the warmer climes, since the weather was becoming chilly on the plateau and I was now wearing my winter coat and wool scarf and hat, even when I walked. Today and tomorrow I would have a bit of a grade to climb before reaching Sertavul Pass, the point which would mark the beginning of the descent to the Mediterranean.

The walking after Karaman wasn't easy, since the road was surfaced with my least favorite material to walk on — tar with a layer of sharp rocks thrown down over the top. The rocks pressed through the soles of my shoes into my feet as I walked. Thank god I'd only run into this kind of pavement a few times so far on the walk, so it was no big deal. But man, it hurt to walk on it. I suspect it was the cheapest surfacing option, and that it was what they used for lightly-trafficked country roads.

I'd started out the day on flat plain with a slight uphill grade but the terrain began alternating between sections of flat plains and sections of rolling hills. Again it felt like the earth couldn't decide whether to be a flat plain with little foliage or a mountain with lots of evergreens. I was in a transition area again.

Off to my right to the southeast rose a lone snow-capped peak, my sole companion for the day. Though it seemed only a short distance from me, the peak was in the Taurus mountains, a range running along the southern edge of the Central Anatolian plateau where I was walking. Named for Taurus the zodiac bull, the Taurus range marks the southern edge of the plateau. That day's walk was uneventful, one of those *just bang out the miles* sort of days.

The icy air made me grateful for my wool scarf, gloves, and hat. The only life I saw along the way was a gas station, where the attendant told me snow was expected the next day. For dinner I bought potato chips, cracker-and-cheese sandwiches, and a carton of peach juice. I hesitated for a moment before turning to the attendant to pay. I realized I would need breakfast too, so I doubled the quantities before paying.

A few minutes before reaching the gasoline station, I had spotted a grove of trees next to the road on the other side of the gasoline station, and I intended to check it out for the night's camp spot. I reached the grove, looked both ways to make sure no one was watching, and walked off the road to inspect the grove. The ground under the evergreen trees looked well-traveled and there were leveled-out places where people had set up tents before. I saw footpaths headed out from the area. To the side was an area with enough waist-high brush to hide my tent. It wasn't great cover, if I stood up at all I could be seen clearly from the road if a person knew where to look. But there was no other option. I tamped down an area with my feet and pitched my tent. I ate my chips and sandwich cookies while hunkered down amongst the shrubs. I was cold and the cover wasn't good, but I was happy, feeling free, and excited to finally be walking off the plateau the next day.

I finished my dinner and dug into the warmth of my sleeping bag and gazed out at the full moon above me. The sky was clear and blanketed with stars.

In the morning I woke up feeling cozy, warm, and right at home. In fact, I didn't want to leave. But, leave I must. Clouds had rolled in during the night and I needed to get out of there before it started snowing.

Thursday, 29 November

The climb to the summit of Sertavul pass the next morning was short and steep. The few trucks climbing the pass with me were almost slower at climbing it than I was. They belched out huge clouds of exhaust as they labored up the hill. I remembered the gasoline station attendant's comment, and thought, *Yeah, it's probably going to snow today.*

After about five or ten kilometers I reached Sertavul pass, took off my pack, and stood for ten minutes to mentally "celebrate" in the icy wind that whipped around me. Reaching the summit was a major milestone, marking the end of my days on the Central Anatolia plateau. It was a little like standing on the moon. Nothing but gravel and sparse, low mounds of grass covered the hills for as far as I could see. At an altitude of 5400 feet (1650 meters), the summit was also the end of Karaman province and the beginning of Mersin province. I'd begun walking on the plateau at the end of September when I was 12% through the walk. Now at the end of November and at the end of the plateau I was almost 40% through.

But I was in no mood for an extended celebration with the cold wind blasting into my face, so I shouldered my pack and began the descent. The road was so steep in places that my main goal was just to keep from falling forward.

As I descended I started seeing eerie shelters carved into the hillsides that had openings sheltered by crumbling walls of piled-up rock. Their roofs were made of rusted tin and supported by upright, weathered branches. The shelters appeared to be abandoned. There was no sign of life, not one that I could see anyway. I did not want to go look in them to find out. Just days before, while in İstanbul, I had finished reading Cormac McCarthy's *The Road*, and I was still under its spell. The book speaks of a post-apocalyptic world where barbarians have killed off or enslaved most survivors, and here, alone in this deserted area with these shacks, and with the wind blowing around me like crazy, my fertile imagination began to run wild. I could almost see starved, crazed barbarians flooding out of the abandoned shelters to capture and enslave me.

I hurried nervously past the shelters, and as the wind subsided I began to enjoy the natural beauty of the area, with the Göksu River flowing through the valley off in the distance, eventually emptying into a Mediterranean I couldn't yet see. A blue haze hovered over the hills next to the valley. I planned to walk through that valley out to the Mediterranean. It would be a full week still before I reached the sea. I squinted to see if I could spot the road on which I'd be walking.

For shelter that night I found a little outcropping, sheltered by rocks and trees, where I could look off into the distance. Up on the pass the land had been barren and rocky, but now it was covered with mile after mile of evergreen forest. Not that there was much to hide from here — I had seen only one person all day, in the morning, and a car passed me on the road only once every five or ten minutes. There wasn't even a gas station, so there would be no lunch or dinner for me that day.

Fortunately, warm air was blowing up from the Mediterranean to replace the cold air up on the plateau. I sat on the rocky outcropping, my legs dangling over the side, and absorbed the view of the river valley disappearing into the distance, happy to know that I had reached a Mediterranean climate and wouldn't have to hide in my down sleeping bag as soon as I stopped walking each day.

I had no food for dinner, so I crawled into my tent and fell fast asleep, a warm breeze blowing gently past the tent. In the morning I awoke suddenly, surprised by the tinkling of sheep bells that sounded very close. Panicked and thinking that I was surrounded by sheep, and that my secret hideaway in the forest wasn't so secret, I jumped out of my tent to look, but there were no sheep in sight. I relaxed as I realized the sound had just been carrying very well, and that no one had spotted me.

SLEEPING WITH THE PEACHES

Wide awake now, I grabbed my camera and ventured out onto the rock outcropping near my tent to take photos of the valley and hills below. Then I broke camp and got an early start down the hill. There were still no signs of life. The road was mine alone, and I reveled in the solitude. But I hadn't eaten since breakfast the day before, and I was starving.

Out of the solitude came my second surprise of the morning. Ahead of me I saw a tiny green shack, on the right, just off the side of the road, perched precariously above the drop-off into the valley below. I walked up to it tentatively, wondering if my early morning presence in such a remote location would draw suspicion. By the door of the shack was an open ice chest filled, from what I could see at a glance, with an assortment of food items such as cheeses, olives, cucumbers, and tomatoes.

Inside the shack a young man stood next to a rickety stove preparing to cook on one of the gas burners. He looked up, smiled, and offered his hand. I shook it, smiled, and introduced myself. He said his name was Ramazan.

He didn't seem at all surprised to see me. It was as though hungry foreigners carrying backpacks and speaking pidgin Turkish hiked through there regularly.

I asked if he was open for breakfast yet. Of course, he said. I eagerly took a seat at the makeshift restaurant's one table.

By even loose standards of restaurant hygiene this setup would be completely unacceptable. But this was the biggest "restaurant" I'd seen in days, and I was starving. The simple breakfast of eggs, cheese, olives, and cucumbers was like manna from heaven to me. I greedily scraped every crumb off my plate like some starved homeless person.

While I ate I counted thirty goats in a pen next to Ramazan's "restaurant." Ramazan mentioned that there were a few people who lived down the hill in the nearby village of Mut who commuted to work back up the grade in Karaman, the small town I had walked through a few days before. He was getting ready to handle the early morning rush of commuters. I asked him how many that would be. He said, excitedly, five or six cars.

I finished my breakfast, paid Ramazan, shouldered my pack, and strolled outside to continue my descent down the pass. Who would have thought eating a breakfast of questionable hygiene while sitting in a small shack hanging off the side of a cliff could have seemed so luxurious. And yet I felt like a king. My stomach was full. The sun was bright. The air was fresh. I continued down the mountain, passing through more rugged rock outcroppings and lush evergreen forests.

About four hours later, after seeing very few people and only an occasional passing car, I came to a village called Geçimli, population 200. I spied a tea garden and figured it was about time for a couple glasses of tea and some human contact.

"Hello," I called out to the only two men I saw, "can I take a seat?"

"Of course," one of them replied as he jumped up from his short stool and disappeared into a nearby shack. He and his friend both looked like they were about 80 years old, and had seen better days.

The man emerged from the shack with my cup of tea. "I saw you on TV," he said as he brought it over.

"What channel?" I asked.

"TRT," he replied. It was a channel I recognized and had watched many times.

"What did they say?"

"That you are walking around the world, and that you walked 7,000 kilometers (4,200 miles) before arriving in Turkey. What countries have you walked through already?"

"Sorry to disappoint you," I said. "I am not walking around the world, just through Turkey. And I haven't walked 7,000 kilometers. And I have never walked across a country before. Turkey will be the first."

It wasn't the first time the media had gotten it wrong about me. *Why don't they contact me beforehand?* I thought. *It's not like I'm hard to find. I'm walking by the side of the road all the time, for god's sake.*

Conversation turned to small talk about the weather. I tried to stifle my feelings of peeve at the journalists, who had been getting my story wrong from the first day of the walk. *Why are you getting angry at people you've never met?* I asked myself. *There's a perfectly good 80-year-old man sitting right in front of you. Pay attention to him.* I tried to stay present, and wasn't sure why it was so hard.

I finished my tea, thanked both men for their conversation, shouldered my pack, and continued down the hill.

Within a few hours I reached the bottom of the hill, and the terrain became mixed again, with large flat treeless areas interspersed with orchards here and there, mainly olive groves. I couldn't see the river yet, and I was still a few days from the coastline. It seemed the land in this area couldn't make up its mind, whether to be flat and treeless like the plateau above, or rolling and lush, like the river bottom I'd seen from higher up the mountain. I walked a long way across one of the sparse areas thinking, *Man, if I can't find shelter I'm going to have to walk up on one of the hills over a kilometer off the road to try to find some.*

I forged ahead though, determined to get through this sparse area and find an orchard I could camp in. Within an hour, I got lucky. Up ahead in the distance was a peach orchard. There would be great cover amongst the trees, and soft grass growing from the dirt between them.

Shortly before sunset I reached the orchard. I looked up and down the road, and in a quiet moment between cars, when I felt safe that no one would see me disappear into the orchard, I scrambled up the embankment and hurried into the orchard. The soil was hard, dry and crumbly, but I had a sleeping pad, which would even that out. I walked to the back of the orchard, where I was sure to be hidden from the road. The sun had set, but it was still light out, so I hid behind some trees to kill some time. While hiding in the trees, though, I realized I was perched just meters from a bluff overlooking dozens of orchards below, and I wavered between the safety of hiding in the trees and the pull of the view I would see if standing on the bluff.

Of all the places I had camped so far, this location had the most natural beauty. It was much like a bluff above a town aptly called Vantage, in the arid central part of Washington State, where my family and I had camped out while helping my dad with some orchard work many years ago when I was a kid. Like I had then, I stood at the edge of the bluff taking in the bird's eye view of the rolling hills covered with orchards. It was exhilarating to gaze at such a great view, but I was also a bit nervous that someone leaving the fields at the end of the day would see me standing on the bluff, and my cover would be blown.

When it got dark, I set up camp and went to sleep.

OATMEAL DOUGH AND BIG STORMS

Monday, 3 December

The next morning, I finally reached the Göksu River. I knew from the satellite photos that just a few kilometers down the road it would start flowing through a dramatic canyon with steep rocky cliffs a thousand feet high, but here it looked more like an irrigation ditch, straight, calm, occupying only the space man had given it, its banks littered with trash and sunflower seed shells.

I stopped to look back at the hills I had just descended and squinted to see the road I had walked. The descent had been fun, if not a little eerie, but I knew I would reach the Mediterranean in a little over two days, and it was calling to me. I turned and resumed walking.

The road along the river took me through a village too small for a name. As I entered the village I spotted a family working together in front of a tidy market rolling dough. I walked up to introduce myself. The man introduced himself as Yunus. I asked him if the nearby apricot and olive trees and the grape vines were his. Yes, he said, and he held up his grandson, a toddler, also named Yunus. I briefly thought back to the turnip farmers weeks ago on the plateau, and how one of them had also held up a toddler grandson named after him.

He pointed to his wife on the ground rolling dough and mentioned proudly that they had been married 30 years. She looked up and smiled at me.

"Are you married?" she asked.

"No," I replied, "but I used to be married to a Turkish woman."

The entire group laughed knowingly.

"Would you marry another one?"

"Sure," I said, "of course."

They laughed even harder.

"What are you doing?" I asked.

"Rolling *yulaflı* dough for oatmeal bread."

My stomach rumbled.

At his wife's suggestion, Yunus went inside to grab some cheese, which they then rolled up into two of the yulaflı breads for me for breakfast.

I thanked them, and continued walking down the road, happily eating my bread and cheese roll.

About two hours later, I entered the village of Karadiken, population about 500. I was still basking in the social high of chatting with Yunus and his family, and was hoping for more of the same in Karadiken. But the sole group I met was a dour, unfriendly cluster of about 15 men, some sitting, some standing, in a large circle out in a dirt driveway, drinking cup after cup of tea and complaining about their lives and the government. It seemed they had been here for quite a while, commiserating, and that they had no plans to move on or do anything about the things they were complaining about. No one offered me a smile or a cup of tea, not even a place to sit. I stood with them for a short while, but after a few minutes felt like a clumsy interloper injecting unwanted optimism and friendliness into their litany of complaints, so I left.

By the end of the day I began to enter the narrow river valley, where the forest cover became much denser, and I easily spotted a tree to sleep under. I picked that tree just in time, too — moments before I climbed the embankment to get off the road, raindrops began to fall against my face. A storm was blowing in.

The storm quickly intensified, with a few stray drops becoming a torrential downpour in the 10 minutes it took me to set up my camp. Within seconds of getting the tent set up, I jumped into it to get out of the rain and lay on top of my sleeping bag listening to the rain beat against the tent's nylon fabric walls. Tree branches above the tent protected the tent from the full force of the storm, and I knew that if I was hearing raindrops pounding against the protected tent, that meant this was a really big storm. I love a good storm, but like most people, am happiest when I can witness it from a dry place, so I thanked god for the shelter of my tent and of the tree above, and I drifted off to sleep.

About 11 p.m., I awoke suddenly to a crack of thunder so intense I thought the tree above me had been hit by lightning and I was sure to be crushed any second by a fiery branch falling from above. But when that didn't happen, I exhaled and reveled in the fact that I was hearing one of the most dramatic storms of my life. My excitement at the storm drama competed with my tiredness from walking, and I drifted in and out of a shallow sleep as the storm raged above me.

About 2 a.m., I woke up to an eerie calmness. I stepped out of my tent to investigate. The big storm had passed, leaving just a few silvery wisps of cloud to blow in front of the full moon. The storm had come from the Mediterranean, just 25 kilometers to the south, and the air was warm. I stood in a nearby clearing for 15 minutes, marveling at the peace the storm had left in its wake, loving the fact that I was probably the only person for miles around. If I hadn't chosen to walk across the country, I would not be standing there, by myself, in a clearing, out in the middle of nowhere in a foreign land, looking up at those particular wisps of cloud passing in front of the moon.

The surrounding air was uncommonly warm, and I stood there drinking in the serenity for another 15 minutes, before I started to get cold and had to return to my sleeping bag.

CRASHING THE JANDARMA POST

The next morning, I woke up just before dawn to the howling and yipping of coyotes a few hundred meters away. They either didn't know I was nearby listening, or they didn't care.

I stepped out of my tent, put on my boots, and noticed that the soil under my feet, because it was sandy and porous, had dried quickly from the night's rain. In fact, because a steady, warm breeze had blown almost all night, my tent was dry and only some moist wood laying on the ground indicated that a heavy storm had blown through during the night.

I broke camp and began walking about 7:30 a.m. A few minutes after I began walking it began raining again, but this time it was only a light drizzle. With the mist, the rolling hills and road lined with evergreens reminded me of mountain roads I've walked in the Pacific Northwest.

About five kilometers down the road I came upon a *Jandarma Komutanlığı* (jandarma command post). In Turkey, the jandarma is a branch of the military. Their job is to keep the peace in rural areas and along rural highways, kind of a combination of a sheriff and a highway patrol in the US, except with a military flavor. The day before, a few people had told me about this jandarma post, so I was expecting it. And, I had heard that as I walk across the country I should keep in touch with the jandarma. So I figured now was as good a time as any to see what it was like to crash a jandarma post.

I walked up to the front gate. The guard was about 20 years old. He was wearing fatigues and a helmet and carrying a machine gun. I didn't realize machine guns were so large.

I told him I was walking across Turkey, and I asked him if I could come in and rest a bit. He radioed his commanding officer. His commanding officer said he would check with the post commander.

The guard and I made small talk while we waited to hear back from the post commander. I tried not to be intimidated by the gun. The guard tried to keep his cool too. I suspect it's not every day the monotony of guarding a rural military post is broken by the approach of a foreigner walking across the country alone with a backpack.

Word came back over the radio that the commander had approved my entrance. Another guard waved me through the gate and escorted me to the headquarters' front door. Once inside I was shown to the commander's sparse office.

The commander's first name was Nihat. Nihat was about 35 years old. He was a busy man, taking — and making — a number of phone calls and reading reports that were brought to him, but he and I made small talk when he was between tasks.

Nihat put the phone down and looked at me. "Have you eaten breakfast?"

I had not, and the day before I had eaten only one meal. I was ravenous. I tried to act with restraint when I shook my head and started to ask if there was food. Before I could get the words out though, Nihat called to one of his soldiers to make me some *menemen* (a dish of eggs scrambled with tomatoes and peppers) and bring me some tea, and make it snappy.

A few minutes later a soldier came in with the dish of menemen, a basket full of bread, and a cup of tea. I plowed into that menemen with almost no concern for decorum or restraint whatsoever. It was one of the biggest servings of menemen I had ever seen, and I had the entire thing eaten, and all the juice and grease sopped up with bread, in just a few minutes.

After the plates were cleared away, Nihat told me a bit about his personal history. He was single with no kids. He said the itinerant life of a military commander is not conducive to raising a family. He had been working at that particular post for about two months. Before that he was in the special forces in Mardin, Diyarbakır, Tunceli, and Urfa, all cities in east and southeast Turkey.

He asked me what countries I had been to, and I asked him what countries he had been to. He replied that he had been to Syria, Iraq, and Afghanistan, all on military assignments. Originally from the town of Osmaniye, Nihat had one sibling, a younger sister, who lived in Osmaniye and ran a grocery store there. I told Nihat I would be walking through Osmaniye in about a month, and he responded that he would tell his sister about me and ask her to show me around.

Nihat asked me about my route. He made some suggestions about tweaks to make to it. I asked him if gasoline stations and mosque gardens would continue to be good places to stay in the eastern half of the country. He recommended that I stay instead at facilities run by the city and town governments, and at the police stations. He said that in the east most of the towns would have one or two spare rooms they kept available for travelers. These were not hotels, they were free places they opened up for people traveling through. "Ask about these," Nihat told me.

Also, he said, "don't camp by the side of the road once you get east of Osmaniye."

Nihat asked me how far I was walking that day. I told him the name of the village I planned to stop in, and he recommended a particular restaurant in that village. "Stop there," Nihat said, "and ask for a man who goes by the name

Hoca. Tell him I sent you, and he will take good care of you."

It was time for me to go. I thanked Nihat for his hospitality and for welcoming me into his facility. He ordered me a couple cheese and tomato sandwiches for the road. The sandwiches were ready a few minutes later. I took my leave and walked back out the front gate, carrying the bag of sandwiches. I waved goodbye to the guard with the machine gun and felt less intimidated by it.

After I left the Jandarma Komutanlığı I spent the day walking a two-lane road hewn into the side of the mountains rising above the Göksu River. The road rolled up and down between 500 and 1000 feet above the river. Areas of yellow and red deciduous forest in fall splendor alternated with areas of evergreen forest that made me feel again like I was walking through the mountains of the Pacific Northwest near Seattle.

DINNER WITH HOCA

Nihat had told me to find and say hello to Hoca at the end of the day, so all day long I walked thinking, *I can't just camp anywhere tonight, I've got to find Hoca. Whatever I do, I've got to find Hoca.*

In the early afternoon I stopped off at a tea garden near Ortaören with an irresistible view of the river valley below. I ate *patatesli gözleme,* a pancake stuffed with boiled and lightly-seasoned potatoes, drank some tea, and had some conversation with Hilmi, the grown son of one of the tea garden's owners. Hilmi was a sailor with the merchant marine and at sea for six months out of the year. When he was home he worked the tea garden owned by his mother and uncle.

But as I was looking out at the view from the tea garden I saw the storm rolling back in and knew I had to get going, because I still needed to find Hoca.

Shortly after I left the tea garden the storm rolled in, except this time from the opposite direction. Instead of a warm rain coming from the Mediterranean, the storm was blown back in by a cold wind from the north. The rain was colder than it had been the night before.

After a few minutes a car pulled up beside me and stopped. It was one of the guys I'd seen at the tea garden.

"Get in the car!" he called out. "I'll take you wherever you want to go."

I said to him, as I'd said to countless people on the walk, "Thank you very much for the offer, but no, I've got to walk."

He insisted again a few more times, then finally gave up on me and turned around and disappeared back the way he had come.

Fortunately, the rain lasted only a short while. The clouds and the wind remained, however, and I was left cold and soaking wet but happy to be walking through such beautiful territory.

About 3 p.m. I reached Değirmendere, the village where I was supposed to find Hoca. Değirmendere is just a couple kilometers from where the steep v-shape of the river valley ends and turns into rolling hills through which the river meanders until it reaches the sea.

I came up on a section of the road crowded with parked trucks and thought that looked like a good sign. I started asking around about Hoca, and the third person I asked pointed to a nearby restaurant with a sign that said *Hoca'nin Yeri* (Hoca's Place). I'd find Hoca there, the man said.

I walked into Hoca's Place and started asking for Hoca. At the back of the restaurant I met Hoca and told him I'd had breakfast with Nihat the jandarma commander, and Nihat had told me to find Hoca and say hello from him.

Hoca smiled and shook my hand and invited me to sit down next to the fire they kept going for the barbecue. I began telling Hoca, and the people sitting nearby, who I was and what I was doing.

Within moments, and without my even asking, someone brought me a plate of barbecued *sucuk* (sausage), a huge pile of bread, and a salad. I bit into the sucuk. It was the most delicious sucuk I had ever tasted. I asked Hoca about it. He told me they made it there, themselves, with their own mixture of spices. I asked Hoca what they called the sucuk. He told me it was named after him.

After eating I sat around the restaurant with Hoca and a handful of the villagers making small talk. I could barely understand a single word they said. Their accent was very different from the Konya accent, and to me it was equally unintelligible. Sometimes I could barely identify their words as Turkish.

Hoca got up every few minutes to greet customers as they came into the restaurant. He acted like he was mayor of the town, greeting people like they were long-lost friends, even though he had probably last seen them less than 24 hours before.

As darkness fell I asked Hoca if I could camp somewhere in the area. I told him I had everything I needed in my backpack — tent, sleeping bag, everything. He said of course, you can camp anywhere you like. I asked if I could camp out on the restaurant's balcony, which was closed off for the winter. I thought the balcony would be a great place to camp, especially since it was right above the Değirmen creek (for which the village was named), and I could fall asleep to the sounds of running water. Hoca said sure, of course, no problem.

A few minutes later though, one of the earlier patrons in the restaurant, Ali, a man in his early 30s, came back, sat down next to me, and said come with me, you can sleep at my place tonight. I jumped at the offer, especially since I had camped outside in rainy weather the two nights before, and was in fact still a little wet from the afternoon's rain.

Ali and I left the restaurant and walked the short distance, maybe just 100 meters, to his apartment. Inside the apartment I changed into dry clothes while Ali built a fire in the TV room. The TV room was small, and by the time I finished changing clothes the fire had turned it toasty warm.

I took a seat amongst some pillows on the floor next to the fire. Ali spread out on the couch. He offered me some baklava, and we settled in to watch *Evlen Benimle* (Marry Me), a popular matchmaking show on television.

At one point one of Ali's neighbors brought over her two kids to meet (read: play with) the foreign visitor. They were Enes, a boy of about 5, and his sister Elif, a girl of about 2. Ali left to take care of some business elsewhere, and I played "horsey" with Enes and Elif. I was surprised that after a full day of walking I still had the energy to let a couple kids climb around on me simultaneously, but I dug deep and found it somewhere. I had no problem with Elif, who was about as light as a feather, but when Enes would decide that the back of my head made a great saddle, I had a hard time supporting his weight with my neck muscles. I didn't complain when Ali returned and told the kids to settle down.

After the kids' mom came to collect them, Ali and I watched the second half of *Evlen Benimle*. We drank some cinnamon and ginger tea that Ali had been brewing next to the fire. When *Evlen Benimle* was over Ali and I went back to Hoca's restaurant, and to the next door kahvehanesi, for some tea and village conversation before bed.

While at Hoca's restaurant I asked Hoca if he had any children. He said he had two, a daughter, aged 19, and a son, aged 16. Both lived in the nearby town of Silifke. I asked Hoca what his son's favorite subject was in school. Hoca laughed and said girls, and sports. I told him those were the favorite subjects of just about every 16-year-old boy. He laughed and said he just wanted to see his son go to college. Everything changes if you go to college, Hoca said. Life is different. Work is different. Everything is different.

That night I slept incredibly well, spread out on a comfortable couch, the fire still going, a drama show on TV. I couldn't believe how lucky I was, being that a mere 24 hours earlier I had been camping out on the side of the road, hiding from one of the most aggressive thunderstorms I had seen in a long time. I'd always found it so easy to take a warm bed and a roof over my head at night for granted, and at some point I probably would again, but for now at least I recognized how there was almost no price that could be put on small creature comforts like that.

REACHING THE MEDITERRANEAN

In the morning Ali and I both woke up around 6:30 a.m. We got up and walked down the street to Hoca's restaurant for breakfast but found it not open yet. We hung out at the kahvehanesi a while instead. When Hoca finally arrived we stepped into his restaurant for breakfast. It turned out breakfast was not a regular meal served publicly to restaurant patrons — it was just Hoca, Ali, me, and a young man named Şahin, the village's butcher.

While Hoca was away from the table I asked Şahin how Hoca had come to be called Hoca, since I had never met someone whose real name was Hoca (Hoca is just a nickname given to some people, and means "teacher"). Şahin told me that Hoca had once been an imam. With that piece of information, something about Hoca fell into place for me. He had a way of looking at me that made me squirm a bit — a calm, self-assured gaze that said, "I'm looking into you, but I don't need anything from you, and you don't need to do anything that you're not doing right now."

I remembered Enes, the imam I'd met a couple months before. He'd had a similar steady gaze that made me want to squirm. Maybe they teach you how to look at people that way in imam school or something.

Breakfast over, I said my goodbyes and thank you's, took a self-portrait of the four of us, and began my day's walk.

At no point had anyone asked for, nor would they have accepted, any money in return for the delicious dinner, or the dozens of cups of tea, or the breakfast, or the warm bed. I was simply the village's guest for the night. For eighteen hours it was their mission in life to see that I was taken care of. After almost a week camping by the side of the road, getting rained on, and eating food wherever and whenever it appeared, I drank that in like a man just in from crawling through the desert would drink in a tall glass of water.

As I left Değirmendere I noticed a man tending his sheep in a grassy area on the other side of the road. I crossed over to say hello and realized it was Ahmet. Ahmet and I had sat by the fire next to each other at the kahvehanesi earlier that morning.

We said hello again, and Ahmet gave me four tangerines from his orchard to tide me over until my next meal.

A few hours later as I began the final descent to sea level and into Silifke, I could finally see the Mediterranean. I was so happy that I dug my camera out of my backpack and filmed a video of myself congratulating myself for reaching this milestone. The sea looked to be five or ten kilometers off in the distance still, but I'd been looking forward to that moment for a long time.

I ended my day at the Oğretmen Evi in Silifke. I had reached the 40% mark.

Layover in Silifke

A teacher at a nearby international school, Tarsus American College, had heard about my walk and invited me to spend a few days at the school talking to the students. That was still 4 days away, so I had some time to kill in Silifke. After breakfast on my first day in Silifke, I took a seat on an overstuffed couch in the lobby of the Oğretmen Evi. I knew I had some problem solving to do, and welcomed having a few days in a comfortable place to do it.

I never seriously considered Nihat's admonishment not to camp by the side of the road. I'd heard it so many times on the trip. The problem was that this next section, the Çukurova plain, was densely populated. There would probably not be many areas where I could find a couple consecutive kilometers in which to camp. My daily operational model of sleeping under trees and behind rocks and in the gardens of remote village mosques was not going to work on the Çukurova. I would need places to stay for three weeks while crossing the Çukurova, so this was a more significant problem than if it would only last for a couple nights.

But I faced another problem too. As much as I enjoyed sleeping under the stars, even when it rained, what I craved at this point was sleeping in a warm bed with a roof over my head. I craved hot showers, washing machines, and more substantive human contact. I was emotionally exhausted from the daily need to say goodbye to people I had met the night before. I wanted a little more time to form friendships.

As I sat on that couch, wondering how to solve these problems, I thought of something: Couchsurfing!

Couchsurfing.org is a website that connects travelers looking for a place to stay with local hosts. I had never tried Couchsurfing, but a friend had used it to travel the world a few years back, and he raved about it. The more I thought about it the more Couchsurfing seemed a simple, practical way to solve my problems, both logistical and emotional.

But I wondered, was I being a sellout?

Would I be giving up an authentic life on the road for an inauthentic, sanitized walk across the country? Would using the internet to make friends and find places to stay turn this into Walk Across Turkey Lite?

What would it look like, logistically, day to day? How would I stay in the same house for a week, but still make regular progress across the country?

I got up from the couch to get myself a cup of coffee, pace around the room, and think this one through.

I know, I thought to myself as I paced the room, *I'll base out of one house for a week, and on the first day take a bus 90 kilometers to the west, and then walk 30 kilometers towards the city and go home for the night, and the next day I will take a bus to where I finished the day before, walk another 30 kilometers towards the city and then go home for the night, and the third day I will take a bus to where I finished the day before and walk the last 30 kilometers into the city. Then I will spend three days doing the same to the east of the city.*

I'll call this "throwing," my personal slang term for this model. Basically, I'll be commuting to work each day.

I decided to give it a try. I would throw my way across the Çukurova plain. If I didn't like it or it felt wrong, I could just stop doing it when I got across the Çukurova. I set up a Couchsurfing account, uploaded a profile photo, and sent out my first messages to members in the area.

BORROWED TIME IN THE GARDEN OF EDEN

On Sunday, I rolled out of bed and, before going down to breakfast, gathered up my stuff and prepared to check out of the Oğretmen Evi. Later that morning I would be hopping a bus to the nearby town of Tarsus to visit the students at Tarsus American College, a private middle and high school, for a few days.

Since I didn't have much stuff it took me only a few minutes to pack. I pulled on my freshly-laundered nylon track pants and black T-shirt with no dried sweat or dirt on them and headed down to breakfast. Having been at this hotel for four mornings now, I had gotten used to a new routine. Put on clean clothes every morning. Go down to breakfast. I felt like I was living in the lap of luxury.

After breakfast I hopped a bus for the two-hour ride to Tarsus American College.

As I neared the school I thought back to my first phone conversation with the American teacher who had invited me to the school. It had been back in November, over a month earlier. I had been walking along the side of the road when my phone rang. I pulled the phone out of my pocket and stared at it. It didn't ring often those days, and I barely recognized the ringing sound. From the foggy reaches of my distant memory I remembered that when someone calls you, you typically answer. So I'd clicked the button for "answer."

"Hello, this is Matt," I began.

"Hello Matt, my name is Stacey Brown. I am a teacher at Tarsus American College, a school in Tarsus, a city on your route."

Of course, Tarsus, I thought. I recognized the town's name instantly, having pored over the satellite maps of my route many times.

"Yes, I know of it. How can I help you, Stacey?"

Stacey told me that one of her friends had read an article about me in *Outside Magazine* and told her I would be walking through Tarsus. That friend had suggested Stacey call me.

Stacey asked me if I would in fact be passing through Tarsus, and if so could I come visit her students for a few days?

"Sure," I said, "I'd be happy to. How do I find your school?"

"Walk through the city's Cleopatra Gates, and then face east. You can't miss us."

The Cleopatra Gates, I thought to myself, *sounds great!*

"Could you check your calendar," she continued, "and let me know when you'll be in the area? I will need to talk to the school and get their approval for those specific dates."

Almost no one ever asked me for specific dates. Most people thought this walk was a footloose and fancy-free gallivant across the country. But actually, because I had planned it so carefully beforehand, I knew months ahead of time the specific day I would be passing through even the tiniest villages out in the middle of nowhere. It was refreshing to hear someone ask me for specific dates about something that would happen over a month later.

I smiled. *A kindred spirit,* I thought to myself.

"Sure," I answered, "give me two days, and I'll look at my calendar and let you know when I'll be in the area."

That was how I met Stacey Brown. Now, over a month later, here I was approaching the gate of her school.

As I walked up to the guard station, I imagined that I would be received like a rock star, that the guards at the gate would know immediately who I was, and would be as impressed with me as I was with myself.

I had let it conveniently slip from my memory that St. Paul was from Tarsus, and thousands of years earlier he had walked across Turkey proselytizing for Jesus. People had been walking across Turkey for thousands of years.

"Hello," I said to the guards as I walked up to the school gates. "My name is Matt, and I'm here to see Stacey."

I expected them to know exactly who I was, that my appearance would be the highlight of their day.

They looked up at me with blank expressions.

"Matt who?"

"Matt Krause. I'm here to see Stacey. Stacey Brown."

"Ah yes, Stacey Brown." They picked up the phone and dialed someone somewhere.

They couldn't find Stacey. After a few moments of confusion, they widened the search and began supplementing the landlines with their cell phones until they reached someone who knew where to find Stacey.

"Yeah," the guard on the phone said into the receiver, "there's some guy out front, with a big backpack. Says he's looking for Stacey."

So much for the rock star treatment. I was just "some guy." I thought back to the moment when I stepped off the bus in Kuşadası, watching the waiting cars whisk the other passengers away, leaving me alone on the blacktop, thinking to myself, *you are not of this world anymore.*

I waited about five more minutes and Stacey and Mr. Hanna, the school's headmaster, appeared to greet me at the gate.

They escorted me inside to my suite in the guest wing of the teachers' housing complex. The suite had a soft, inviting bed, a sparkling clean bathroom, and a sitting room with a computer.

"Is this acceptable?" Mr. Hanna asked.

I tried to act cool but blurted out, "Of course, it's more than acceptable!" I blurted out. I added, silently, *you have no idea where I've been sleeping, do you?*

As they prepared to leave, Mr. Hanna asked me if I wanted to use the WiFi. He said he was embarrassed, though, because it would take them a couple hours to find the password. *No problem,* I thought to myself. *I might not be used to beds anymore, but I have become amazingly resourceful when it comes to connecting to the internet.*

I simply said, "No, that's okay, I'm sure I'll be fine."

Stacey told me she and Mr. Hanna would pick me up a few hours later for dinner. Seconds after they pulled the door shut behind them I spread my arms and fell backwards into the soft white comforter splayed across the bed, rested there for a few minutes, and then got up for a long hot shower.

Later, when Stacey and Mr. Hanna returned to pick me up for dinner, they were accompanied by two more people: Filiz, Mr. Hanna's translator, and Pınar, one of Stacey's students. We walked to a nearby restaurant. Almost as soon as we sat down, the four of them began peppering me with questions in fluent English. I was so happy to be speaking my native language, and to be speaking with people who understood all my words, that between their eagerness to ask me questions, and my happiness to talk, I barely touched my food.

Filiz and Pınar wanted to know what I had been doing in the evenings along the walk. I mentioned that usually I spent time in the village socializing, but for the past few weeks I hadn't been in many villages and had been camping alone by the roadside.

"What do you do when you are all alone in the dark?" they wanted to know.

"Well, I tried reading with a book light in my tent after going to bed, but soon had to dispense with that."

"Why was that?"

"With the light on I couldn't see out of the tent, and I have to be able to see my surroundings, even in the dark," I said.

"How do you see your surroundings in the dark?"

"Well, of course, I can't see them like I do in the daylight," I explained as well as I could, "but in the dark, shapes take on a different personality, and I need to know that personality. Plus, I could have a light anywhere in the world. The point is, I'm sleeping in a tent in Turkey. I need to experience that and not turn on a light and start reading."

Filiz and Pınar stared at me without saying a word. I was afraid that next they'd tell me it was time for us to go home. I was afraid they were thinking, "Who is this crazy man, sleeping by himself in the dark at night?"

But Mr. Hanna smiled and began reciting a poem by Wendell Berry, "To Know the Dark":

"To go into the dark with a light is to know the light
"To know the dark, go dark, go without sight
"And find that the dark too blooms and sings

"And is traveled by dark feet and dark wings."

I relaxed. They weren't puzzled by me. They understood me quite well.

Filiz pointed at my plate and reminded me to eat. I finished my dinner and the five of us strolled back to the school slowly, taking in the warm Mediterranean evening air. I would need a good night of sleep, they told me, because the next few days would be very busy. I wasn't sure what they had in store for me, but I was happy to place my trust in these people I had just met.

Monday, 10 December - Wednesday, 12 December

What they had in store for me was three whirlwind days of running up and down stairs, from building to building, from classroom to classroom, and from auditorium stage to auditorium stage. Pınar and 5 of her classmates (Bade, Elif, Oya, Dilek, and Lara) had been appointed by Stacey to be my guardian angels for those three days. They picked me up from my apartment each morning and led me to a huge breakfast spread in the school cafeteria. They escorted me from classroom to classroom each day, where the other students would pepper me with an endless array of questions: What do you eat? Where do you sleep? How do you wash your clothes? What kind of social life do you have? Do you ever worry? Are you ever afraid? The students wanted to see what I carried in my pack, so often I would empty it onto the classroom floors. Shortly before the end of a class, one of my guardian angels would show up and wait by the classroom door. When the bell would ring, I would hurriedly stuff everything into my backpack, and the two of us would run to the next classroom, pushing our way through a sea of admiring students. The guardian angels were the cool people, trusted by the school to escort this VIP from class to class. Not only was I a rock star now, they were too.

I had grown accustomed to walking alone for hours each day, talking mostly to 65-year-old men outside mosques or 25-year-old attendants outside gasoline stations, and now I was surrounded by a bunch of secular English-speaking Turkish kids from wealthy families in urban areas. I had grown used to being cared for by strangers, but within hours the students did not feel like strangers anymore, they had become family. They even got worried that I might be homesick and one day organized a "Taste of Home" luncheon where they presented me with a platter of peanut butter and jelly sandwiches. They took care of me, and I wanted to take care of them.

The teachers made sure my after-school social needs were taken care of, too. One evening they invited me to play in their indoor soccer game. I told them I had no soccer skills, but they insisted skills were not necessary for this game. "Then I'm perfect," I said. "I'd love to join."

The game was like no soccer game I had ever seen. It was played on a basketball court, and it was perfectly acceptable to bounce the ball off the walls and ceiling. It was basically a three-dimensional game played on a hardwood floor with a ball ricocheting off the walls and ceiling. I loved it. The teachers had even done away with the rule "no blood no foul" — when one of the teachers got hit in the face with the ball, she just wiped away a rivulet of blood, laughed it off, and went back to playing.

From sunup to bedtime the school kept me busy. I was happy, cared for, and comfortable.

Thursday, 13 December

On Thursday morning I said goodbye to my bed, took one more hot shower, pulled on my pack (now stuffed with clean clothes), pulled the apartment door shut behind me, and walked toward the school gates. For three days I had swum in a sea of warm, friendly people. For three days I hadn't had to think of anything. All I had had to do was put my hand out, and one of my six guardian angels would appear to take me to where I needed to go next, or to feed me, or to show me back to my apartment at the end of the day. Outside of the school gates I would need to do those things for myself again. The transition back into the real world was going to be tough.

As I neared the gate, one of the students ran up to me. He asked if he could take a photo with me, and if he could get my autograph. While I was signing one of his books, another student ran up to us. Then another. Then another. Within seconds I was surrounded by a hundred students, all clamoring for a photo and an autograph. The warm human sea was back, and I was happy to swim in it for a few more minutes. I signed one autograph, and then another, and then another, for about two hours. Then the crowd began to dwindle, and I knew my borrowed time in the Garden of Eden was about to end. The world was calling.

When the last autograph was signed, I sighed, pulled my pack back on, and walked out onto the street. The school gate shut behind me.

I sighed again, hitched up my pants, and began walking towards the city center.

OUT OF EDEN

Thursday, 13 December

My short stay at TAC had been an emotional high, and as I walked away from the school I wondered what would come next. I remembered that now I was shifting into Couchsurfing. *That should shake things up a bit*, I thought. I wondered what it would be like.

I arrived at the bus that would take me the 30 kilometers to the nearby town of Mersin where my first Couchsurfing host, Melih, lived. I was feeling emotionally low. It would be hard to match the high I had experienced at TAC. But by that time I was beginning to learn: *When you leave something great, just get to the next thing. You'll find something great there, too.*

I ate lunch at the bus station after arriving in Mersin, then sat drinking tea while uploading photos, updating my journal, and answering emails.

Then it was time to go meet Melih. I had looked up his neighborhood on Google maps and knew I had three or four kilometers to walk to reach his neighborhood. Most of the walk was along the Mediterranean shore, so I didn't mind. On one side of me were palm trees and grassy parks, and on the other was the marina with its fancy boats and old men fishing. For weeks and hundreds of kilometers I had been looking forward to walking next to the Mediterranean, and here it was, finally.

Via messaging on Couchsurfing, I had arranged to meet Melih at 2:30 on the steps in front of the municipal arts theater next to the seaside. Melih had said his apartment was a five-minute walk from the theater. At 2 p.m. I arrived at the theater, pulled off my pack, and sat on the concrete steps. It was December but I was wearing short pants and a t-shirt, sitting in the shade of palm trees. The plateau, where I had been two weeks ago, was now covered with snow.

I thought back to the times I had sat outside a mosque, hoping they would let me camp outside, and marveled that for the first time on my walk sleeping arrangements for the night had already been made.

I had never met Melih face to face and had only an idea of what he looked like from a photo on Couchsurfing, which had been our only contact. Since I wasn't sure who to look for, any male passing by was a Melih suspect, and it occurred to me that I might look a little weird, sitting alone on the stairs, smiling at every approaching man.

Melih didn't have a problem finding me and spotted me very quickly, perhaps because I was the only foreigner stretched out on the front steps with a humongous backpack. He was wearing old khakis, his hands thrust into the pockets of a red jacket he'd probably been wearing for several days in a row. His shoulders were a little slumped.

"Hi!" he said in a flat monotone, "Let's go back to my place." He turned abruptly and began walking back to his apartment.

I hopped up to follow. But since I had to pause to pull my pack on, I had to hurry to catch him.

He didn't seem very excited to see me, but as I followed him back to his place I was excited to see how easy Couchsurfing made it to find a place to sleep. *So much for chatting up gas station attendants,* I thought, *hoping they'll like me enough to offer me a place to sleep.*

We went back to Melih's small apartment.

It wasn't a fancy apartment. In fact, it was kind of dingy. The shower was just a nozzle on the wall next to the washing machine. Under the nozzle was a plastic bucket for pouring water over yourself. The kitchen sink was full of dishes that had been dirty for weeks. Scattered crumbs and stray dust bunnies littered the floor, so I kept my shoes on as I walked across it. Melih's desk was covered with stale cigarette ashes and overflowing ashtrays.

However, I reminded myself that for the last few months I had been sleeping in abandoned pear orchards. Plus I knew this was Melih's first Couchsurfing experience, so maybe that explained his mood.

I set my pack down in one of the four rooms of the apartment, a room Melih had designated for Couchsurfers — in this case me, and we went to have a meal and get acquainted.

Friday, 14 December

The next day I resumed my walk, this time Couchsurfing style. I woke up at 6:30 a.m. and walked a couple kilometers to the main road. I caught a bus for the 90-kilometer ride to Silifke, found a seat, and propped my red knapsack on my lap. At Melih's the night before I had filled that red knapsack with supplies I would need for the day: my iPhone, my camera, a bottle of water, a pair of gloves, and an extra shirt in case it got cold. I reached into the bag, pulled out my camera, and filmed a couple minutes of footage just sitting on the bus. I was almost as excited to be on a bus commuting to work like a normal person as I had been on the first morning of the walk back in Kuşadası. The woman across the aisle from me watched me as I filmed, looking puzzled, probably trying to figure out what was so interesting about sitting on a bus that it warranted filming.

I stepped off the bus in Silifke, pivoted, and began the day's walk, 30 kilometers back towards Mersin. I figured that without a pack, I would be able to cover 30 kilometers, not my usual pack-carrying 20 kilometers.

Two weeks before, I had been walking through forests and river valleys. Now I was walking through a string of sandy beach towns along a road lined with hotels, shops, and restaurants for vacationers. The sparkling waters of the sea were 100 meters to my right, and the hills of the Taurus mountain range to my left.

At the end of that day's 30 kilometers I hopped the mini-bus back to Mersin and walked the final one or two kilometers from the main road to Melih's apartment.

So that's how it's going to be for a while, I said to myself as I climbed the stairs to Melih's apartment. *Take the bus to work. Walk. Take the bus home. Repeat that process the next day.*

That evening Melih and I sat in his apartment drinking a couple beers. Melih was silent for a moment, then looked me directly in the eyes and said, "Matt, I'd like to come with you on your walk tomorrow."

I was surprised and happy to hear he wanted to join me, figuring that having company might be fun. But I was also a little nervous. I was aware most people do not walk 6 hours a day.

Melih smoked and was a little on the heavy side and got no exercise that I was aware of. I said, "Well, I walk 30 kilometers. Are you sure you are up for that?"

He replied, "Whatever you do, I'm determined to do it too."

A fire in his eyes told me that yes, he was determined to do it. But could he do it? I did it, but I was used to it. He wasn't.

"Do you want to walk the whole thing?" I asked. "Or just the beginning or the end?"

"I want to do the whole thing," he said.

"You'll probably be pretty sore the next day. Are you okay with that?" I asked.

He said, "Yeah, I'm okay with it. What you are doing is a test for me. I want to do it."

"Well," I said, "I'll be glad to have you. I leave about 6:30 in the morning. Are you okay with that?"

"Yes, no problem," he said.

WALKING WITH MELIH

Saturday, 15 December

The next morning I got up at 6:30. Melih was still sleeping. I knocked on his door to wake him up.

"Hey, I'm leaving in a few minutes," I called through the door. "Do you still want to join me?"

"Yes," he called through the door, "I still want to join you. I'll be out in a couple of minutes."

Melih got up and got dressed, and we walked two kilometers out to the main road and caught the bus I had been on the day before. We rode back to the point where I had stopped walking the day before, a landmark called Kız Kalesi (Maiden's Tower), a small fortress/lighthouse rising out of the sea about a hundred meters off the shoreline.

When we stepped off the bus I ran over to a dumpster and touched it with my hand and ran back to Melih, who was now standing in the cloud of dust left behind by the departing bus.

Melih looked at me, a puzzled expression on his face. "Why did you run over and touch that dumpster?"

"Well, that's where I finished yesterday," I said, "And I'm walking across the country, which means wherever I stop one day, I have to start the next."

"If you don't, who's going to know?" Melih asked.

"I'll know."

Melih and I took a few selfies with the Kız Kalesi in the background, and then we began the day's walk.

The first ten kilometers went pretty smoothly. Melih walked with pep in his step, and for the first time I could hear lightheartedness in his voice.

The road took us through an area that, in the days of the Roman Empire, had basically been a Roman suburb. We stopped to climb around on the ruins of an amphitheater, and later to take a photo of me standing in front of an old Roman aqueduct nestled between lemon trees. I marveled throughout the day that in most other places sites like these would be hidden behind closed gates and entry fees, but here they were just scattered rocks and pillars farmers drove their tractors around.

We passed a new building complex. Melih pointed out the complex and said that he had designed the electrical systems for these buildings.

Between kilometer 10 and 20 Melih started to tire. I could see on his face, and in his gait, that he was starting to hurt.

"Are you okay?" I asked him.

"Yeah, but my feet are hurting a bit, and my legs are getting stiff. My back hurts, too."

As we neared kilometer 20 I looked at my watch and noticed that it was 4 p.m. *Man,* I thought to myself, *if I were by myself I'd be finished for the day by now but we still have ten kilometers to go!* It would be dark when we finished. I was starting to get nervous.

At kilometer 22 we stopped for börek and çay. Melih took his shoes off. I could see he was starting to blister. I thought, *Man there is no way he is equipped to finish this next ten kilometers.*

I asked him, "Melih, are you sure you don't want to pack it in? We could get a bus right now back to Mersin, we'd get home early. Why don't we just do that?"

"No! I want to finish," Melih said.

I pointed to the road behind me. "Are you sure? The buses are right there, we could flag one down."

"No!" Melih insisted, "I want to do this!"

"It'll be dark when we finish," I said, hoping he would give in.

He smiled back at me. "No, Matt, I want to do this."

"Okay then, let's finish up our çay and then get back to it. Daylight's burning."

We gulped down the rest of our tea and crossed the road to finish the last ten kilometers of the day's walk.

For seven kilometers, Melih did okay, but for the final three kilometers, I was sure that every step was going to be his last. For about 30 seconds I would walk at what I thought was an incredibly slow pace, and then I would turn around and wait while Melih caught up with me. He was not talking at all, and his face was frozen in a grimace of exhaustion. I was afraid he was going to collapse.

"We're almost there," I reminded him. "Just a couple kilometers."

It was nearing dusk when we entered the small town of Arpaçbahşiş, with Melih still hobbling through every painful step and me turning around to wait for him every 30 seconds or so. We finally reached the flagpole at the municipal building which we had agreed on the bus ride would mark the end of the day's walk. It was well past the time I would normally want to pull off the road and stop working for the day.

At the flagpole, I turned one last time and watched Melih trudge toward me. Even though he could barely walk, when he spied the flagpole he found it within himself to skip like a kid through the final few steps. As he reached the flagpole he raised his hand and we did a high-five. I said, "Let's go home,

Melih!" A look of relief crossed his face and he broke into a huge smile and said, "Yes, let's do that."

On the minibus ride back into Mersin, Melih fell into a desperately-tired sleep while I looked out the window at the passing trees. I sensed that the day's walk had addressed a deep need for Melih. I didn't know what that need was, but a few days earlier at TAC the universe had made me a rockstar. Maybe my job this week was to repay the favor, and help Melih find the rockstar within himself.

The bus let us off at our corner in Mersin at 9 p.m. I shook Melih awake and we stumbled the last two kilometers back to Melih's apartment.

DESSERT WITH REFUGEES

Sunday, 16 December

The next day, Sunday, I woke up at my normal time, 6:30 a.m., and knocked on Melih's door to ask him if he wanted to join me again. He called out good morning through the door, but he sounded like he was in pain. *Probably sore from yesterday,* I thought. I let him go back to sleep as I laced up my shoes and headed out the door.

I hopped the bus and rode back to the flagpole in Arpaçbahşiş where we'd finished walking the day before and began my walk back into Mersin. It wasn't a pretty walk-by-the-seaside day. Most of the time that day I walked past tall buildings and through heavy traffic. It was a day to knock out the smelly, exhaust-filled kilometers. Nothing more, nothing less.

Mid-morning, as I was standing on the side of the road struggling to open a particularly reluctant roll of sandwich cream cookies, up rode five Turkish cyclists decked out in lycra and helmets. They pulled up next to me and stopped. I had not met them before, but they greeted me by name in English.

"Where are you headed?" the lead cyclist asked.

"Back into Mersin," I responded. The roll of cookies popped open, and a few of them dropped onto the ground.

"Looks like you lost part of your lunch," the lead cyclist smiled. She continued, "We're going to Kız Kalesi to greet some Germans who are cycling to China. Have you been to Kız Kalesi before?"

"Yeah, I was there yesterday."

"Of course you were. Well, good luck with your cookies. We've got to go, it was nice to meet you," she said, as she clipped back into her pedal and started away.

As the line of cyclists pulled away, I thought, *Wow, they knew my name. For thousands of years people have been crossing this country, and now I'm one of them. It's quite a club, and now I'm in it.*

When I got back home Melih was out of bed, but said he had been too sore and stiff to walk across the apartment, much less leave the house that day. I showered and rested, and then attended a potluck dinner hosted by one of the faculty members I had met at Tarsus American College. I was loving my new Couchsurfing travel method. People had been feeding me all the way across the country, but now they were friends I had met a week before, and here I was getting to see them again. What a treat!

Monday, 17 December

Since I had now finished walking towards Mersin, it was time for a day or two off before I started the walk away from it. As I rolled out of bed Monday morning, I decided that my first act of my first day off under my new Couchsurfing regime would be to walk across the street to a bakery I had seen, and buy a bunch of stuff.

The bakery attendant asked me how many people I was buying for.

"Two," I said.

He took out a small bag and shook it open.

"I'm going to buy a lot," I told him, "You might need a bigger box for this."

He got a box and followed me around the shop while I pointed at things I wanted to buy. When the box was full, I told him, "There's more. We're going to need another box."

I carried my haul back to Melih's apartment, brushed away the cigarette ashes on the desk of Melih's home office, and dropped the boxes down.

"Breakfast is served," I said to Melih with a flourish.

I ate my half of the pastries in about three minutes, eyed Melih's half and decided not to eat it. Instead, I went back to bed and slipped into a happy carbohydrate coma. *This place is starting to feel like home,* I thought as I drifted off to sleep.

Though I was close to halfway through the walk, I had yet to meet any of the "dangerous" people I had been warned about. I did meet a young man, a 17-year-old kid from Croatia who was staying with Melih for a few days while I was there. He was hitchhiking to Iran. He told me that during school breaks while the rest of his friends were hanging out at the mall, he would walk to the edge of town, stick out his thumb, and hitchhike. A couple of months before this trip he had hitchhiked through Ukraine, Siberia, Mongolia, and into China. He had gotten to Shanghai and he looked at the calendar and thought, *Oh, I better get back home — school's starting again.* So he hitchhiked back to Croatia from Shanghai.

This guy is young enough to be my son, I thought. *If my son were doing this I would be much more relaxed if I knew somebody was taking care of him.* So that evening, after my carbo-high wore off, I said to him, "You haven't eaten yet so let's go out to dinner." And with as few resources I had myself, the three of us — the Croatian kid, Melih, and I — went out to dinner and had some *tantuni* (a local specialty, basically a burrito containing beef or lamb).

Melih and I had arranged a small party that evening so we could get better-acquainted with the local Couchsurfing community. After dinner with the

Croatian kid, Melih and I went to a nearby restaurant famous for the local dessert specialty, *künefe*, to meet some of the community members. There were ten of us: Stew, from Ireland, Ziad, a refugee from Syria, Milad, a refugee from Iran, Milad's Turkish girlfriend, three other Turks, Anisa, a refugee from Afghanistan, and Melih and me.

Thirty percent of the people at that table were refugees, and none of them fit what I imagined a refugee to be: someone running across the border carrying blankets and then sleeping on the streets begging for money. Ziad, Milad, and Anisa weren't carrying blankets, and they slept in their beds at home. They were more educated than I, and their English was quite fluent.

As the group broke up for the evening, a voice at the back of my head told me I needed to learn more about Anisa's story. While the rest of the group had been chatty that evening, she had been fairly reticent, and the few words that she did say suggested she had a very unusual background.

So I asked her if we could meet again so she could tell me her story. She nodded yes, and we agreed to meet a few days later, on one of my next days off.

NOT AS YOU THINK IT IS

We met on a rainy evening in the park next to the seaside. It was a warm rain, but it was enough to drive all the evening strollers out of the park, so we had the park to ourselves. A strong wind blew the drops sideways, but we found a pagoda sheltered by a tree where we could sit out of the rain. Neither of us had an umbrella, and I noticed that water was pouring off Anisa's windbreaker.

"You look wet, are you cold?" I asked after we took a seat.

"No, I'm fine. This jacket is actually waterproof."

I sat down across from her, and as we huddled in the rain I learned that she was from western Afghanistan, near the border of Afghanistan and Iran. Because the educational opportunities were better in Iran, her parents sent her to school at a regional city in eastern Iran. She was 16 at the time. By the time she was 18 or 19 she'd completed the normal high school curriculum, as well as mastering technical courses in computer programming and networking and earning various Microsoft certifications. When it was time for her to find her first job, it was easy. She was in high demand and went to work setting up and running the computer systems for a company in Iran.

I figured I had misheard about her age because it would normally take about ten years to get the kind of education and experience she was describing. I asked her how old she was when this happened.

"I was nineteen at that time," she told me.

I realized that I was sitting across from one of the smartest people I knew.

She returned to Afghanistan in 2001 or 2002, shortly after the US invasion, to take a job with the UN setting up computer systems for the refugee office in western Afghanistan. She soon moved up into an administrative position in the refugee office.

Shortly before leaving for my walk across Turkey, I read a book by Rory Stewart, *The Places in Between*. He had walked across Afghanistan shortly after the US invasion, about the same time Anisa was working at the UN.

I thought of Ismail Khan, whom Stewart had mentioned in his book, a local warlord who was fighting against the UN control of the region. At the time of the US invasion, Khan controlled the borders of western Afghanistan, had his own import taxes, and was running his own small regional government when the UN arrived to take over the administration of the whole country. Not surprisingly, Khan and the UN butted heads.

I asked Anisa if she had run into Khan.

"Of course, Ismail Khan," she nodded quickly. A look of fear and disgust crossed her face.

"He attacked the office regularly," she continued. "A couple of times while I was at work, he shot rockets at us. I'd be sitting at my desk, and rockets would explode outside or crash into the building walls."

"Once some of his soldiers made it past the security gate. They stormed into the building, running around with their machine guns. I ducked under my desk and hoped not to get shot."

I watched the woman sitting before me as she talked. Not only was she smart, she was brave. She hadn't stayed away from her country even though it was a war zone. She had returned to it and taken a job there. I started to connect her story with my own images. I had imagined refugees were unwashed masses with blankets and no shoes, escaping the chaos in war-torn countries. But this refugee had been a woman in her early 20s with a desk job, typing at a computer.

"One day some of the soldiers followed me as I walked home from work. They started harassing me, but some neighbors broke it up. However, then the soldiers followed me at a greater distance and saw where my family and I lived.

"I could deal with rocket attacks at work, but when they knew where my mother, brothers, and sisters were, that was enough. For months my family had been saying, 'No, no this is our home. We want to stay here.' But finally that became, 'Okay, let's leave the country. The time has come.'"

"We found our way to the eastern Turkish city of Van, where we lived for about two years.

"I got a job helping other refugees with their own resettlement. And then, after the big earthquake in 2012, my family once again did not feel safe, so we moved further west to Mersin. And that's how I came to be here."

By that time it was getting late, and the blown rain was starting to soak our table. We stood up, said goodbye, and I leaned into the wind and walked back to Melih's apartment, all the while thinking, "See the world as it is, not as you think it is. Don't ever forget that."

CHRISTMAS AT BURGER KING

Monday-Wednesday, 17-19 December

Oh, the food in Mersin!

After subsisting for a couple of months on gas station junk food, whenever real food was presented to me I gulped it down unquestioningly. And Mersin was full of good food. In fact, during the time I took off for the holiday season, I developed some food-related rituals. In the mornings I would cross the street to the bakery and buy a box full of enough pastries to feed two people for three days. This was my breakfast.

After my carb-heavy breakfast, and the nap that inevitably followed, I would schlep myself down the street to the *künefe* restaurant for dessert, even though it was barely 10:30 a.m. (Künefe is a disk of cheese surrounded by shredded wheat, soaked in honey water)). Then I would schlep myself back to Melih's for another nap.

After my nap I would lug myself downstairs to lunch at the hummus restaurant below Melih's apartment. In İstanbul there is very little hummus. But in Mersin, which is nearer Syria and the Middle East, there's a lot of hummus.

The hummus restaurant staff got to know that when I came in, made eye contact, and held up one finger, it meant one order of hummus, and mere moments after I took a seat, they would set before me a huge bowl of hummus drizzled with olive oil and sprinkled with spices and garlic sauce. Moments after that they'd bring a basket of bread. I broke off pieces of bread to sop the hummus bowl clean. And because I was in the habit of eating all the bread that was presented to me, I ate all the rest of the bread too when the hummus was gone. If there was anything else like parsley or fruit garnishes on the table I ate those, too.

After lunch at the hummus restaurant I would walk back to the künefe restaurant for the second time in about six hours and chow down on yet another dish of künefe for dessert. Then I would go back to the apartment for an afternoon nap.

When I finished my nap, Melih was usually finishing up his work for the day and was hungry for dinner, so we would walk to a nearby restaurant for tantuni.

Yes, Mersin was a veritable orgy of food!

When the food parade was not enough, Melih and I would go to a nearby *hamam* (a Turkish bathhouse where you can get scrubbed down with a sponge until all the dead skin is gone and you walk out pretty raw). I opted to skip the scrubdown because I didn't want the intimidating guy dressed in a bath towel scrubbing my skin raw. So while Melih volunteered for this service I just lay on the marble in the steam room. That felt really good. For months I had been walking by the side of the road camping in weird places like abandoned pear orchards, and now here I was in a hamam with abundant water, a steam room, swimming pools, and hot showers. It was great!

But I had a job to do, so the food orgies and the hours whiled away under luxurious streams of hot water could not last forever. I still had a country to walk across. I lived the life of the hedonist only on weekends and during the few days off I'd planned for this time of the year. I would never have completed a day in my walk being weighted down with carbs like I was during my days off.

Thursday and Friday, 20 and 21 December

On Thursday it was back to work, and I took the bus to Adana where my Couchsurfing host Utku had arranged to have me speak at the mountaineering club, ÇUDOSK (Çukurova Mountaineering and Nature Sports Club). I stayed in his home that night.

Then on Friday I walked east from Adana to Yakapınar on the Çukurova plain, where I would be walking for four or five more days. I dedicated the day to Pinar Seydim, the lead guardian angel at Tarsus American College who kept everything organized so I didn't ever have to think about where to go or how to get there. I wanted to make sure each member of the guardian angels team at Tarsus was acknowledged, as I owed them big time for their help.

For a few days I stayed at Utku's house in Adana, temporarily skipping the Mersin-to-Adana segment of the walk. Melih and I had become good friends by then, and I planned to return to Mersin later and walk that segment when Melih could do it with me. Also, I wanted to be in Mersin for Christmas.

Saturday, 22 December

I woke up at 6:30 a.m., my normal wake-up time for a work day, and lay in my sleeping bag for 15 minutes flirting with the siren who sang to me each morning. She whispered softly into my ear, "Oh, this sleeping bag is so warm and fluffy and comfortable, you could just stay here all day, yes, couldn't you?"

I had heard this song many times in the past few months, and was starting to realize it was not going to go away. It was not a sign that something was wrong, it was just a sign of a conflict that was never going to go away. So I told myself what I told myself every morning when the siren sang to me like this: *This kind of comfort will not last and when it is gone, I will need to be, too. Get out of bed! Must get to work.*

The day's walk was a 20-kilometer walk east from Yakapınar (aka Misis) to Ceyhan, a city of about 100,000 people between Adana and Osmaniye. I dedicated it to Bade Turgut, the guardian angel at Tarsus American College who brought me brownies that I'll never forget and guided me tirelessly from classroom to classroom.

As I walked I could see the mountains east of Osmaniye. It would be another week or so before I climbed into those mountains and left the Çukurova plain behind. I had a string of holidays (Christmas, New Year, my birthday) and a few social calls to make in Mersin before then.

It wasn't a straight shot to those mountains. But they were there, looming behind the clouds. I had seen them. I loved the mountains. I missed the mountains. I was looking forward to climbing into those.

One of the features on the day's walk, midway between Yakapinar and Ceyhan, was Yılankale, or Snake Castle.

The castle was built on top of a high hill in the 11th or 12th century by the Armenians, and was probably used by the Crusaders too.

There's another hill right next to the one where the castle was built. Much of that second hill has now been carved away to supply a cement factory, but I could see that the hill had in the past partially blocked the castle's sight line across part of the plain. So as I approached I was wondering what the castle's occupants did about that blind spot.

Then at the end of the day I went back to Utku's to meet with people, as was becoming my habit now that I was Couchsurfing.

Sunday, 23 December

I stayed three nights in Adana with Utku, and on Sunday I walked to the train station in the rain and took the train back to Mersin to Melih's for Christmas and the holidays.

Monday, 24 December

On Christmas Eve, Monday evening, I attended a rehearsal for a Christmas program done by Mersin's Nevit Kodalli Chorus. Nevit Kodalli was a Turkish opera and ballet composer born in Mersin. I went mainly because I had friends connected with this chorus, but I especially wanted to hear my friend Ayşe from Tarsus sing a solo of Silent Night.

Tuesday, 25 December

My Christmas celebration was meager. But having been in Turkey for several years, I was rather used to that and appreciated the kind-hearted Merry Christmas wishes I received from my Turkish friends on that day as they went to work as usual. In a few places I would see decorated Christmas trees, mostly because generally people in Turkey like the idea of Christmas and the decorations and the lights. They just don't celebrate the holiday.

Christmas morning I got up and worked on emails, photos, and the usual stuff. Toward noon, as I read my emails and the posts on the website I saw a greeting from an eight-year-old boy, Pryor Gibson. Pryor is the son of some very good friends of mine in Seattle, George and Napua. They had posted a picture of Pryor holding up a drawing he had made for me of Santa and two reindeer. Pryor had written a note at the top of the drawing wishing me the "merriest Christmas ever."

In turn I walked to a Burger King not far from Melih's and took a selfie standing in front of the Burger King and posted that along with a Merry Christmas note, telling Pryor that I missed playing with him this Christmas and wished I could be there doing that now, but I guessed I'd have to settle for something else. Then, to complete my Christmas nostalgia for things American, I walked into the Burger King and ordered a Whopper.

UNIFRUTTI

Wednesday, 26 December

I had spent a few days leapfrogging ahead and walking east, into and out of the nearby city of Adana. But Melih wanted to walk another leg with me, and I with him, so the day after Christmas the two of us hopped a bus to Tarsus. We rode to the main intersection in Tarsus and got off at the *Nüsret* minelayer display. The Nüsret is a ship which mined the Dardanelle Straits in World War I and helped the Turks stop an Allied invasion. From there we began our walk back to Mersin. But first we dedicated the day to the pink-booted Oya Zaimoğlu, another one of my guardian angels in Tarsus.

This time we planned to walk a shorter 20 kilometers, rather than the 30 kilometers Melih had to walk the last time he walked with me.

Neither pretty nor idyllic, the area we walked from Tarsus to Mersin was a semi-populated, heavily industrialized area with lots of smog and narrow shoulders and busy roads filled with trucks rumbling by belching exhaust fumes.

Later, after Melih and I had stopped for lunch and begun to enter Mersin, I felt a bit of *deja vu* when we approached some acres of neatly trained, manicured orchards behind a steel fence, and I thought, *Oh wow, they train those trees like they train peach trees in California.* As I've said before, "You can take the boy off the farm, but you can't take the farm out of the boy." Then I saw the huge sign on the fence — *Unifrutti of Turkey.*

I quickly snapped a picture of the sign and the orchards on the other side of the fence and posted it for my dad. I knew this name, Unifrutti, since I had heard my dad speak of it often. Luis, a good friend of my dad's from Santiago, Chile, worked with Unifrutti in establishing the nursery and these orchards for the Turkish Government, and with the help of the Turks in the area, Luis was responsible for planting these trees. My dad knew Luis from working with him on cooperative projects over the years between their respective agricultural companies in Chile and California. Strange the connections we can find with what we know, even in the remotest of places.

As Melih and I threaded our way through through the various

neighborhoods on our route through suburban Mersin, Melih said, "Matt, come this way just a bit. I want to show you something."

I didn't know what to expect. Melih's face was expressionless. I followed him down a side street about two kilometers off our route until we came to a walled-off neighborhood. To enter this area we had to go through turnstiles where guards stood waiting to check our IDs.

We passed groups of men coming toward us to exit the turnstiles through which we had entered. The buildings were dark, hollowed out storefronts that had seen better times. None of them seemed to have electricity. Prostitutes stood outside the doors laughing and making loud, crude comments to each other from across the street. I realized Melih was showing me a darker side of Mersin.

My skin crawled. We had only been inside the gates for 1 or 2 minutes, but I turned to Melih and said, "Melih, I'm not going to last even ten more seconds. I've got to get out of here." Melih saw how uncomfortable I was. "Sure," he said, and we left.

That was my first and last foray into the underbelly of the sex trade in Turkey.

It had taken a huge amount of open-mindedness for me to sleep at the side of the road. It had taken a lot of acceptance to be kind to people trying to convert me in the villages when I just wanted to make friends.

This walk was also forcing me to dig deep and take my own advice to see the world as it is, not as I think it is.

You are not of this world, I reminded myself.

Melih and I walked back to the main road and finished the day's walk into Mersin. That day, plus the sections I had already walked, into and out of Adana, put me at 51% of the total distance walked. I'd walked more than halfway across Turkey! It was an honor to clear the halfway mark with someone who had become such a good friend. And to do it one day after Christmas, and a couple of days before my birthday. A great way to mark the holiday week.

BIRTHDAY

My birthday!

What better way to celebrate a birthday than walking for six hours? I was joined that day by a young man, Barış, who had contacted me via the Couchsurfing website and asked if he could join me for a day. He was originally from Denizli, but now lived in Adana with his wife and daughter. He worked for a cruise line and had a few days off before he would fly to Miami to get on the ship again.

I was still commuting to work from Melih's place in Mersin, so Barış met me at the start of our day's walk in Tarsus. Our destination that day was Arıklı, a village about 25 kilometers east of Tarsus on the way to Adana.

Barış was no stranger to traveling long distances solo. He had ridden his motorcycle across the United States twice, the first time from Florida to California, the second time from California to Florida. The experience of a long solo journey, no matter what mode of transport is used, is similar, so we shared a mutual understanding of what each had gone through.

I started the day's walk by dedicating the day to Elif Başak Kürkçü, another TAC guardian angel who had tirelessly herded me through hallways and up and down stairs.

Along the way that day Barış and I stopped at a gas station for a snack. When I told the attendants what I was doing, they said, "Wow! If we had the money, we would walk across the country, too!" I got comments like these often — people's eyes would grow dreamy, as though they thought I was doing something exotic, when most of what I did was actually boring scut-work. Besides, they spent more money not doing what I was doing than I spent doing it.

As we left the gas station, Barış also commented on that irony. I smiled. It was good to spend time with someone who understood.

That evening, after Barış and I finished the day's walk and said our goodbyes, and I had taken a short nap, Merve, a friend I'd met on Couchsurfing, came to get me. She arrived carrying a shopping bag full of goodies. She had been concerned that I might pass my birthday alone, and considered it her mission to make sure that didn't happen. We walked to the beach, and as we sat on the rocks visiting she pulled two bottles of beer and some chocolate bars out of her shopping bag.

I admired Merve. She represented what I loved most about Mersin. Mersin reminds me of what Ellis Island was for the United States — a welcoming haven for refugees from war-torn countries.

Merve, like many people in Mersin, comes from a refugee family. She is Kurdish and is originally from a small town near Diyarbakır in southeastern Turkey. In that area the Kurds are the majority — between 65% and 70% of the population. During the establishment of the Turkish nation, there was no provision made for a separate country for the indigenous Kurds who then populated southeastern Turkey, spilling over into the surrounding border countries of Syria, Iraq, and Iran.

In the 1990's, the Turkish army conducted military operations in the area as part of a violent civil war with Kurds who were demanding a separate country and government. One of the military's tactics in these operations was that if there was a village suspected of harboring rebels or having rebel sympathies, the military would burn it down.

When Merve was about 10, the village where she and her family lived was burned to the ground during one of these operations, and with it, the family home where she was born. The family witnessed not only the destruction of their home, but the death of Merve's brother at the hands of the soldiers. Having lost everything, including their son, the parents picked up the rest of the family and fled to Mersin to begin again.

As in many immigrant stories, including those of the immigrants who came through Ellis Island in the US, the first hurdle facing the family is often for the father or mother to earn some money to put a roof over the heads of the family and some food on the table.

Merve's father found odd jobs at construction sites. This led to his starting a construction business. Over the next twenty years he grew that into a thriving real estate development business, where he bought plots of land and built apartment buildings on the land. Today the company still buys plots of land and builds apartment buildings. Merve and her siblings sit at desks in the ground floor of the new buildings and sell the apartments. By the time the apartments are sold in one building, Dad has usually finished another building, so the siblings move on and sell the apartments in the new building.

There are a lot of stories like Merve's in Mersin. If you are from a small village that has just been destroyed and you want to move your family to a place that's not so big that you are going to get lost, but big enough to find work quickly so you can put some food on the table, Mersin is a good place to go. The people used to come from Turkish cities like Diyarbakır. Now they come, increasingly, from places like Syria.

The people who passed through Ellis Island, people we admire and consider our heroes, were often refugees too. We've forgotten that the same process still goes on. Humans leave one place and go to another. That's just what humans do. Few of us have to go back very far in our family lineage to find someone who did just that. Merve didn't even have to go back one generation. So it was an honor to spend my birthday with her, sitting on the beach drinking beer and eating chocolate.

EDGE OF THE PLAIN

Saturday, 29 December

After my day of walking with Barış, I still had one leg I needed to walk in order to complete the stretch between Mersin and Adana. I decided to wait on that, because the social life was so active in Mersin, and I had social calls I needed to make before I moved on. So I took few days to make those social calls.

Ayşe and Rüstü from TAC had invited me to spend some time at their home in the country. On Saturday they had a dinner party for some of their friends and me. I also got to meet their dog Buğday, who became a close buddy of mine for the next couple of days.

While I was with Ayşe and Rüstü, I visited a children's chorus that Ayşe was involved with. The group, *Umut Işığı* (Light of Hope), was made of kids about 8-10 years old. I enjoyed being their audience of one while they serenaded me with Turkish songs in clear, enthusiastic voices.

I stayed the night with Rüstü and Ayşe, and the next morning I got up and spent a little time out on the porch swing basking in the sun and enjoying the expansive view of the green countryside, before going inside so Rüstü and I could dig into a huge breakfast Ayşe had prepared for us.

After breakfast I spent more time kicking back on the porch swing, this time joined by the dog Buğday. He shared his sloppy tennis ball with me. I didn't eat too much of that.

Tuesday, 1 January

I passed New Year's Day back at Melih's house catching up on emails, doing an update on the walk so far for my sponsors, and taking care of various other administrative tasks.

I'd been on the road for four months and had walked across 53% of the country. I'd walked a total of 1109 kilometers (689 miles). That was an average of 277 kilometers (172 miles) per month. Months before the trip I planned on 300 kilometers per month, so I was pretty close to my target.

These were the numbers broken down by month:

Sep: 399 kilometers (247 miles)

Oct: 238 kilometers (148 miles)

Nov: 165 kilometers (102 miles)

Dec: 302 kilometers (187 miles)

As is obvious in the numbers, I'd hit it pretty hard in September. November, the month with two trips to İstanbul, was very light. December was actually right on plan, even with large changes in my traveling style and more social activity than in the three preceding months combined.

Money spent over the four months was over budget. My total was US$3979, an average of US$995 per month.)

Monthly numbers:

Sep: US$737

Oct: US$1303

Nov: US$1143

Dec: US$684

Those numbers included everything I'd spent including buying warmer clothing, an internet data plan, a new cell phone, two trips to İstanbul, food, lodging, health insurance, and residence permit. Everything.

All the months were over budget. December was pretty close to budget, but even it was too high.

I was liking the Couchsurfing method I'd started in early December. Physically, it was more comfortable, since I slept in a bed or on a couch. I could take showers and do laundry on a regular basis.

I commuted to work in the mornings, and returned to the same home in the evenings. Since I was based out of a given place instead of moving to a new location each day, I made closer friendships. Emotionally it was much richer.

The conversations were more substantive, too. Traveling old-style (pre-December), I had the same conversation over and over. What is your name? Where are you from? What are you doing? Where are you going? Why? With Couchsurfing, since we had more time to get to know each other, we talked about other things too. Politics, history, professions, money, life, philosophy, girls.

I've always kept close track of my weight. I wondered how walking 20 kilometers per day and not being able to always control my diet would affect my weight. For 10 years my weight had never gone far from 84 kilos (185 pounds). I regularly went 5 kilos (10 pounds) over or under that, depending on what I'd been eating and how much exercise I was getting. But my weight wasn't changing much on this trip. It was staying at 84 kilos, +/- 5 kilos.

Language-wise, the Couchsurfing community was heavily oriented towards English. In December I spoke way more English than I did Turkish. But I wasn't here to learn Turkish, I reminded myself. I was here to walk across the country and show it to people.

Still, the question stuck in my mind, unresolved: Would this be better if I were speaking more Turkish? So I asked my online followers. Some people said I should dive deeper into Turkish, some people said don't worry about it. Other people said, "Whatever feels right." It was inconclusive, so I decided only time would tell.

Another question that gnawed at me during the Couchsurfing experience was "Am I experiencing the country or not? Is my Couchsurfing experience an authentic experience?" It wasn't what I had set out to do. It wasn't what I had pictured as an authentic experience.

I decided that in traveling, no matter in what mode, you only get to experience a very small slice of the population in front of you. That slice might be peasant farmers, or it might be economically-upscale students at an expensive private school, or it might be the Couchsurfing community. If you want to have an authentic Turkish experience, any experience you have inside the national borders of Turkey will be a completely authentic Turkish experience. Even if you are sitting eating a waffle with American tourists while sipping a coffee from Starbucks, it's completely authentic because it's happening in Turkey. If a foreigner decides what is authentic and what isn't, he is asking Turkey to be something it is not. I stopped my thinking and analysis there, and walked the couple blocks to Burger King for dinner.

Friday, 4 January

The next day I traveled by bus from Mersin to Osmaniye, my next Couchsurfing stop. On the way into Osmaniye, I spied a highway sign for Halep (the Turkish spelling for Aleppo) through the bus window. This was exciting for me because it reminded me that the trip was shifting into another gear. Osmaniye, with a population of about 200,000 people, is about 28 miles from the Syrian border, closer to the border than it is to any major Turkish city. For a few days I would be staying at a college student bachelor pad. I was not expecting an elegant place, but it did have a lot of rooms, so I would have one to myself.

As the bus pulled into Osmaniye, I had a thought I wanted to commit to paper before I forgot Mersin. So I pulled out my notebook and quickly penned:

Occasionally someone asks why I don't mention his or her name on my website. People may wonder why I don't mention them in the book.

Well…

There's a scene in the movie Saving Private Ryan where Matt Damon and Tom Hanks are swapping stories about loved ones.

Tom Hanks tells Matt Damon about his wife back home. Matt Damon asks Tom Hanks to tell him his most special memory.

Tom Hanks declines, saying, "No, that one's just for me."

If I don't mention your name, or the times we shared, in my website or in my book, it might be because some memories are just for me.

Saturday/Sunday, 5/6 January

I began the walk into Osmaniye by taking the bus about 60 kilometers west of Osmaniye and then walking east toward Osmaniye to a town called Mustafabeyli. Then Sunday morning, which was gray and drizzly, I took the bus back to Mustafabeyli to complete the walk into Osmaniye.

When I got off the bus in Mustafabeyli, I stopped in at a market to pick up some bread and cheese for the road and began a conversation with the store owner, Cevdet Aksu. I downed three cups of tea and chatted with Cevdet while he took care of the Sunday morning rush of people buying bread and newspapers. I took comfort in the fact that Sunday mornings are pretty much the same whether you're in Manhattan or a small village in southern Turkey — carbohydrates and newspapers.

Cevdet had three children: a 23-year old daughter, a 20-year old son, and a 12-year old daughter. The son was a student at Korkut Ata University in Osmaniye, the same university my Couchsurfing hosts went to.

Between customers Cevdet pulled up Facebook on the computer near the cash register and asked me for my profile. I typed my username into the search box, and Cevdet sent me a friend request on the spot.

I was starting to find something quite comical during the last few days while entering the eastern half of Turkey. The people here were almost maniacal Facebook users. Even before Cevdet, when I would walk into a market to buy water and a bag of chips, attendants at the counter would have Facebook open while they worked.

The view on the walk that day was spectacular, even though it was a bit cloudy. Osmaniye is on the extreme edge of the Çukurova plain, and the mountains visible since Ceyhan were closer now and in clearer view. I was happy to be entering the rolling, mountainous territory that I loved.

OOPS

After a month of Couchsurfing, I started to settle into a routine: Walk three days into a city, take a day off, walk three days out of the city, move on to the next city, and then repeat the pattern. "Turn off your brain and just keep repeating the pattern until it's done," I told myself.

One of the friends I made in Osmaniye, İlgi Çelik, taught at a middle school in Tüysüz (translates to "hairless"), a small village just outside Osmaniye. She knew I had a day off coming up, and invited me to come visit her students.

I got up early, walked to the main road, and hopped on the service bus İlgi and the other teachers rode to the school. The kids all seemed to arrive at school at once, and while the teachers held their morning meeting in the schoolmaster's office, the kids waited and played unattended outside in the hallway. I didn't know humans were capable of creating as much noise as those kids did! I looked around at the other teachers in the room, expecting one of the teachers to open the door and shush the kids, but none of them seemed in the least bit bothered. I was already feeling out of place. There I was, a middle-aged man who walked alone on country roads with only the whooshing of cars, the roaring of semis, and the chirping of birds for my white noise. *I would never last a day in this school,* I thought. *Those kids would eat me alive.*

The teachers' meeting over, İlgi took me to her classroom. Mid-sentence in her introduction of me the students began cheering wildly. They exploded with energy, pulling one of the kids down on the floor and piling on top him in a wriggling, screaming mosh pit. I laughed to myself and realized I wasn't going to need to entertain them, they were perfectly able to do that for themselves. All they needed was a thin excuse, and I was that day's thin excuse.

When they finally settled down I told them some stories about my walk and invited questions. İlgi told them to ask their questions in English for language practice, but they were too shy, so they asked their questions in Turkish and I answered in Turkish. When I needed to speak English, İlgi translated my words into Turkish.

There were three boys named Yusuf in the class, and during a break from the Q&A they came to me and asked me to take a photo of them standing together. The largest Yusuf was a gentle giant who almost never spoke, and the smallest Yusuf, probably half the largest Yusuf's weight, had the biggest personality in class, never shy about anything including asking countless questions in English and coming out from behind his desk to stand at the front of the room when he did it.

After a couple of times having to walk from his desk to the front, he planted himself right in front of me asking his barrage of questions, one after another. Some of these questions I knew were asked only to control the platform from which he worked the room. Any platform would do. I knew the type. We were kindred spirits in that regard! As much as I wanted to think these kids would remember me because I had a story to tell, I knew they would probably remember Yusuf's performance more. I was just Yusuf's prop.

At lunchtime İlgi steered me into the teachers' lounge where I met and chatted with the other teachers and staff members. Then when I'd finished my Turkish coffee a staff member from the kitchen, Meryem Abla, read the grounds for me.

Back in class after lunch, I didn't realize how tired I was until I took a turn at the blackboard to solve a simple fraction addition problem. I could barely do it. I had no brain power left. At Tarsus American School I was thinking it would be fun to be a teacher and it was too bad I hadn't become one. Now, even though I'd really enjoyed interacting with the kids, I thought, "Thank god I'm not a teacher!" I was more tired than I was after most days walking.

On Tuesday, my next day off, I visited a local radio station in the evening with Alperşan, one of the university students I was Couchsurfing with in Osmaniye. Alperşan was a DJ with a night show on that radio station. He had asked me if I would come along and record some jingles for his show. Ever the performer and happy to get in front of a microphone, I had eagerly replied, "Of course!"

So I sat with a microphone near Alperşan while he did his show, which was called "On the Air With Alperşan." All I had to do was drawl in the deepest of voices several times on cue, "On the Air with Alperşan."

While we were getting the studio equipment ready for the recordings, one of the other DJs launched into a graphic story about a woman he had been "with."

Midway through the conversation, we realized one of the microphones had been left on. We had been broadcasting the conversation.

Oops.

ŞALGAM AND PEPPER SPRAY

The next day was a work day. I was getting used to my new routine: get up early, take the bus to work, walk for 6 hours, take the bus home.

In the evening, after I had rested up from my walk during the day, I met with İlgi again. With her was her colleague Dilara and Dilara's husband Mutlu. The three of them decided they needed to test my şalgam-drinking skills. They laughed sinisterly amongst themselves, knowing what I was in for. Me, of course, I had no idea. I didn't even know, until that evening, what şalgam was.

Popular in southern Turkey, şalgam is a non-alcoholic drink made of salted and spiced red carrot pickles flavored with fermented turnip.

İlgi, Dilara, and Mutlu quickly found a small deli that served şalgam. They ordered two glasses, one for me and one for Mutlu. I smelled mine. It smelled awful. I scrunched up my nose and took a sip. It tasted even worse. Mutlu gulped his down and wiped his lips. He looked at me with a big smile and asked what I thought.

"I guess it's an acquired taste," I said.

While I was nursing my şalgam, my new friends asked me if I carried a gun to protect myself while I was walking.

"Absolutely not!" I said. "There's no way I would carry a gun. Finding food and a place to sleep depends on my getting people to trust me very quickly. If I carry a gun that isn't going to happen."

The three were shocked. Dilara said, "Okay, but at least we've got to get you some pepper spray."

İlgi motioned at me to finish my şalgam quickly so we could go find pepper spray. I gulped down my şalgam, being careful to keep it off my tongue as much as possible, so it would be gone before I had a chance to taste it. I slammed the empty glass down on the table.

"You like şalgam, huh?" İlgi asked.

I smiled and said, "It's an acquired taste."

As for the pepper spray, I didn't want to carry pepper spray either. I figured that if I were attacked, I would probably accidentally spray it backward into my own face. But at least they weren't making me buy a gun, and if I had it in me to accept the "drink şalgam" challenge, I could certainly get out of buying pepper spray. Plus they seemed to be having such a great time teasing the foreigner. I didn't want to spoil the fun. So I followed them down the road on the search for pepper spray.

İlgi, Dilara, and Mutlu excitedly agreed that I looked exactly like Süleyman, a friend of Mutlu's who ran a gold jewelry shop nearby, so during the search for pepper spray we stopped by the shop so they could compare the two of us side by side. The three of them laughed and agreed again that Süleyman and I looked exactly alike. Süleyman and I looked at each other. I saw no resemblance whatsoever. Süleyman obviously didn't either.

"Do you know where we could get some pepper spray?" Dilara asked Süleyman.

"Try the army surplus store around the corner."

The army surplus store did indeed sell pepper spray, but I declined to buy it, telling the three that I needed to walk without carrying guns or pepper spray.

İlgi, Dilara, and Mutlu seemed to realize by then that I was a lost cause and that there was no way to weaponize me.

PEOPLE ARE STRANGE WHEN YOU'RE A STRANGER

Thursday, 10 January

The next morning, after staying out with my new friends relatively late the night before, I got up early, shouldered my backpack, and said goodbye to Osmaniye. It was time to move on. I was to meet Joy Anna on the road for that day's walk. She had joined me for my very first day four months before. Now, here I was, more than halfway across the country, and she was joining me again. I was happy to be seeing her. It was a reminder that I was making progress across the country, and I suspected that if we knew each other better, she would recognize that I was a different person from the one who started the walk.

That day we would begin our walk by climbing out of the Çukurova plain into the Nurdağları mountain range (Mountains of Heavenly Radiance). We would end the day halfway between Osmaniye and Gaziantep. Like we had done on that first day, Joy Anna would flag a bus back to the city after the day's walk, while I stayed behind and set up my tent for the night.

The air was cold, but the sky was clear and sunny. It had snowed a bit the night before, just enough to leave a light dusting in the shaded areas. I put my sweater on under my coat and donned my wool hat and gloves. I had foolishly left my scarf in Osmaniye in an attempt to lighten my pack, not thinking about needing it as I headed into higher elevations. I dug some clean long underwear out of my pack and tied it around my neck instead.

Joy Anna and I began the day's walk with a climb. I labored under the weight of my pack, cursing myself for not having lightened it more before I left Osmaniye. I tried to breathe normally enough to not interrupt the conversation with Joy Anna. Joy Anna pulled out her camera mid-conversation, crossed the road, and took a photo of me climbing the hill. She ran back across the road smiling and holding up her camera to show the photo to me. In the photo a tall, fit, angular man was confidently carrying a large pack up a steep hill. The man in the photo did not look like he was breathing hard and trying not to collapse.

Gradually the terrain smoothed into a plain where we walked for most of the rest of the day.

After we had been on the road for a couple of hours, Joy Anna and I stopped for breakfast at the Öz-Al Petrol Station and Restaurant. The station had been recommended to me by Mustafa, an online follower from Gaziantep whom I would be staying with, but hadn't yet met. Mustafa had commented on Facebook that we should stop by and say hello to his uncle and cousin at that particular station. His uncle owned the station, Mustafa told me. I marveled at how many people's uncles owned gas stations.

Mustafa's uncle treated us to a delicious breakfast. The *sucuklu yumurta* (sausage cooked with eggs) was some of the best I'd ever tasted. I noticed Joy Anna seemed mildly uncomfortable at the station, for reasons I didn't understand, so I ate quickly and politely declined Mustafa's uncle's offer of tea. I grunted as I struggled to pull my pack back on and muttered to myself that this Couchsurfing was fun, I was meeting some great people, but it was making me soft and weak.

A couple kilometers down the road, Joy Anna and I came upon a brand new bridge to and from nowhere. It was simply sitting on the dirt at the side of the road, parallel to the main bridge. Joy Anna and I looked at each other, puzzled. Why was this extra bridge here?

"Oh well," I shrugged, "it never hurts to have an extra bridge."

"That's right, you never know when you'll need it," Joy Anna responded.

We walked on. We began climbing a hill further into the Nurdağları mountains.

I had enjoyed having a friend to walk with during the day. For a couple of weeks I'd been very comfortable — sleeping in people's houses, having dinner with friends, shopping for pepper spray. But tonight when Joy Anna got on the bus I would be alone again. My mood began to sink.

I thought of a Doors lyric:

People are strange, when you're a stranger.

Faces look ugly, when you're alone.

Snow crunched under my feet, as if I needed reminding that the weather was freezing and the terrain inhospitable.

The hills began to pinch themselves into a narrow canyon. The climb steepened. Two highways squeezed through the narrow pass: the intercity freeway, and the local road I was on. Usually the two were at least a few kilometers apart.

I knew we would not clear the pass before the day ended, and that I would need to bed down for the night soon. I turned to Joy Anna and told her I needed to look for a place to stay that night. I scanned the surroundings, and noted that the presence of two highways was going to limit my options, since I wanted to find a spot away from the prying eyes of passing drivers. I looked at the few gullies nestled into the rocky slopes. They were covered with thorny raspberry bushes. There would be no soft beds of pine needles that night.

I spotted a small area that was out of the direct line of sight of passing drivers on both highways, and was almost large enough to accommodate my tent.

I pointed to the area and said to Joy Anna, "There you go, I'm going to camp there tonight."

Joy Anna looked at the site and then back at me. "Are you sure?"

"Yeah, I think I'll be able to make it work just fine."

"Okay," she said. We said our goodbyes and waited by the side of the road a few minutes to flag down a bus. One slowed down for Joy Anna, she hopped on board, and I scrambled down the slope and began gingerly tamping down prickly berry vines to make a place large enough for my tent.

NO TEA FOR YOU

The next morning I crept out of my frost-covered sleeping bag and with stiff, blue hands slowly began to break camp. I shook an icy crust off my tent, and the tent's fabric crunched as I stuffed it into my pack. I was having a hard time finding a source of inner strength to get started that morning, to shoulder my backpack, to place one foot in front of the other and get to work. In the past few months, finding that inner strength had usually only taken a few minutes, and by the time I had broken camp I'd usually felt it.

But this morning, camp was broken, and I still wasn't in touch with that strength. I stood there in the brambles, my hands on my knees. I dug around for an image or a thought, anything, that would get me up onto that road walking.

I thought about my friend Aly in İstanbul. She had been a staunch supporter of the walk since before Day One, and in fact had written an article about it for *Outsider* magazine. She had talked me through many a low moment on the walk. I could hear her voice now telling me, "Matt, man, you've got to do this!" Then the strength came. When I climbed up onto the road and realized I had the strength to continue, I took the whiteboard out of my pack and dedicated the day to her.

Then I brushed the dirt and brambles off my pants, and started walking.

The spectacular views as I descended the mountains into Gaziantep province soon distracted me from my doldrums. I was awed as I looked down on the sweep of the lush green plain below me, with its thick carpet of farms and villages. The busier toll road had disappeared somewhere into the hills, so the air was quiet now and I could hear nothing but my footsteps.

Around mid-morning I approached the day's main town, Nurdağı. As I neared the town, I spotted the cold, square government buildings of the Jandarma post at the edge of the city. As I walked past the post's front gate I waved hello and nodded to the guard. I was just being polite and friendly — I wasn't planning on stopping.

The guard followed a quick "good morning" with more small talk. "Where are you headed?" "It's awfully cold out!" "How heavy is that pack?" With each comment I would pause, turn around halfway, and answer before continuing. His curiosity, and his questions, continued and warranted more attention than a quick "good morning." So I stopped, turned, and started walking back towards him. He got nervous. A look of panicked uncertainty crossed his face, and he waved his gun and called out to me, "No, no, continue, continue!"

Other soldiers, hearing the commotion, started to appear at the gate. They were curious, calling out questions over the driveway that separated me from them. "Hello, good morning, where are you from? Where do you sleep at night? Do you like Turkey?" I wasn't sure whether to approach and talk to them, or heed the advice of the first guard to keep moving. I thought of news footage showing Iraqi civilian drivers with their brains splattered over the back seat after getting shot in the head by nervous US soldiers at security checkpoints. I decided to keep moving. Better to seem rude than to get my brains splattered all over the road.

A few minutes later I came upon the local police station. I decided to stop by and see what kind of reception I'd get there.

I walked up to the guard booth at the front gate and said hello to the two policemen inside.

"Good morning," the first policeman said to me, a huge grin crossing his face as he looked up from his paperwork. "It's a little cold out, huh?"

"Yeah, it's a little cold, but it's warming up. The sun's out." I looked at the second policeman and said, "Hello."

He responded with a curt "Hello." As cold as ice.

"What's your name?" I asked.

"My name is hello."

The first policeman said, "His name is actually Ali. Ha! Ha!"

The first policeman invited me in for tea. The second policeman quickly put a stop to it:

"No," he said, waving his hand dismissively, "keep moving!"

I think it was the first time ever in Turkey that someone had said to me that no, I couldn't drink their tea. I sensed this was an interpersonal conflict between the two cops, and I didn't want to get involved. I had avoided getting my head blown off a few minutes before, and I didn't want to get arrested. So I said goodbye and kept walking further into the village.

I figured I would just keep walking and blow right through Nurdağı. *Zero for two in this town*, I thought. *Just keep going. You don't need them anyway.* But then I saw yet another set of government-looking buildings and the naughty part of my personality came out, the part that loves being a bull in a china shop. I stopped walking. *No, I'm not done with this town yet.*

I walked up to the buildings and picked the nearest one, which turned out to be the local Agriculture and Animal Husbandry Government Administration office. I walked through the front door. There was no reception area, so I stuck my head into the doorway of one of the offices and called out, "Hello! How's it going? What's up?"

Before I could even focus my eyes on the room, someone grabbed my hand

and pulled me in. He told me to put my bag down, sit, rest.

While I sat resting on one of the chairs saying hello to the four or five men in the room, someone thrust a cup of tea into my hand. Within minutes the office was full of curious workers wanting to find out who this foreigner was who had just walked in wearing an enormous backpack. I was the center of attention, and word was quickly spreading through the building that a visitor had arrived.

The conversation quickly turned to a debate about where they should put me up for the night.

"How about the office?" one man asked no one in particular.

"No, it's unsatisfactory," said a second man.

"How about the town hall?" volunteered one man who had just stuck his head in the door.

The chatter continued. How about this? How about that?

I stopped them. It was barely 9:30 in the morning. It was too early for me to quit for the day.

"Thanks, but no," I said to the group, interrupting the debate. "I need to keep moving."

"Have you eaten?" someone asked.

"Take him to the cafeteria!" someone else suggested.

"It's closed!" said another.

"Order him some take-out!"

Three men lunged for the phone. *It's nice to be so warmly welcomed,* I thought, *but you don't get many visitors here, do you?*

Within minutes I was eating a chicken wrap and drinking ayran.

Then we stepped outside for some photos, came back in, and friended each other on Facebook. At that point I felt it was time to go, so I said my goodbyes. I could see they were disappointed to see me leave, as it meant going back to crunching numbers about, probably, things like soybean production.

The town was small, so within a few minutes I was clear of it and back out on the open road. I smiled to myself and thought,

This was what I love about this walk. Sometimes I walk up to a Jandarma base and I'm told to move on. Sometimes I walk up to a Jandarma base and I'm ushered in and fed more food than I've ever seen. Sometimes I check in at a police station and I'm told to keep moving without being offered a sip of water or tea. Sometimes I check in at a police station and spend the next two hours watching TV and eating dinner with the cops. Sometimes I walk into offices where I am stared at like a space alien, and sometimes I walk into offices where I am met with an overwhelming explosion of hospitality as if I were a gift from God. What happens in one situation never provides any indication of what will happen in the next.

At the end of the day, I stopped to wait for the bus back to Osmaniye out in the middle of what I thought was nowhere. Up pulled a car. The driver was none other than the son of the man who fed breakfast to Joy Anna and me at the gasoline station the day before. He gave me a huge bag of peanuts, waited with me by the side of the road until my bus came, and then insisted on paying my fare. I hopped in the bus and headed back to Osmaniye and the Oğretmen Evi for my days off and planned to visit with my new friends, İlgi, Dilara, and

Mutlu.

HANGING WITH THE TAX INSPECTOR

Saturday/Sunday, 12/13 January

I spent most of my three days at the Osmaniye Öğretmen Evi catching up on administrative stuff, doing laundry, taking care of personal needs, and visiting with friends.

One of the first things I did during my long weekend off was to get some new shoes. It wasn't easy to find my size in Turkey, but I walked into a store in Osmaniye and lo and behold, they had not just a few shoes in my size, 12 ½, but a bunch of them, and at great prices! I usually had to buy my shoes from a website called iriadam.com (giantman.com).

One evening I went to dinner with İlgi, Dilara, and Mutlu. What I love about the typical Turkish dinner table is that before the main course even arrives, the table is filled with food, and that evening the array included two salads of lettuce, carrots, and tomatoes; bread; a mound of yogurt made from buffalo milk with walnuts and honey on top; a plate of greens; a plate of four toppings — hummus, yogurt, a carrot salad, and an "American salad" (something I'm not a big fan of because of its high mayonnaise content, and which I've never seen in America); a plate of chopped onions with parsley and balsamic vinegar; and some plates of things I could not identify.

For the main course we had two different kinds of kebap: Adana kebap and beyti kebap. It was another food orgy.

After dinner we watched a football (soccer) game on TV. Mutlu and I bonding over the fact we were both Fenerbahçe fans. Well, anyway, Mutlu was a Fenerbahçe fan. I couldn't care less about football, but I had fun bonding anyway.

Monday, 14 January

The next day I packed up my stuff, checked out of the Öğretmen Evi, and grabbed a bus to Gaziantep to meet my new Couchsurfing host, Mustafa, a tax inspector for Gaziantep province.

I found his office and waited next to his desk for about an hour while he finished up some work. When it was time to go we walked out to the parking lot. Mustafa picked up my backpack and grimaced at its weight, commenting on how much I was carrying. He tried to shove it into the trunk of his car but it was a tight fit. Eventually, together we got it crammed into the trunk. Then we loaded into the car and took off toward his home.

Mustafa and his wife lived on the outskirts of town. My room was not in his apartment but was in a nearby apartment occasionally occupied by his in-laws who were out of town. He told me he didn't want to have any sign that anyone had stayed there. So I was a surreptitious guest in this very spacious apartment with a big kitchen and a couple of big bathrooms with a couple of big showers but I could leave no trace that I had been in the apartment — no water rings in the kitchen or anything.

Still, Mustafa was a very gracious host. After he made sure I got settled in okay, he went across the street to his home to greet his two young sons. Then we went out for döner and rice at a nearby restaurant.

Before bed I looked at the map to see where in Gaziantep I was, and how I would get out to the highway the next morning to continue my walk. I discovered that the road I needed to walk the next day was at the northern edge of the city and Mustafa's place was on the southern edge, so I would have to commute about an hour on public transportation to get to the beginning of my walk.

Tuesday, 15 January

I got up about 5:30 a.m. so I could commute and begin my walk by 8. Mustafa came by to say hello before I hopped a minibus for my commute back to work.

Shortly after boarding a bus to the northern edge of the city, a truck driver from Syria tried to board. He was heading back to the border and had only Syrian currency with him. The driver would not accept it, and he told the Syrian guy to get off the bus and find a currency exchange. I called out to the Syrian guy to get back on the bus, I would cover his fare. People did me favors on the road all the time. I was happy for the opportunity to help out a fellow traveler. It was the least I could do.

After transferring buses a couple times, I got off where I had finished walking before the weekend's break, and started walking back towards Gaziantep. Within a few minutes my cell phone rang. A journalist from *Sabah*, one of the national papers, was on the line. He was doing some fact checking for an article he was writing about me. I was happy to help him check his facts, so I stood by the side of the road and answered his questions, speaking loudly into the phone so he could hear me over the din of truck traffic.

But my main job for the day was not to pay Syrians' bus fares or talk to journalists. It was to get a particular climb out of the way, from the valley floor to a village called Atalar a couple thousand feet above.

Midway through the climb, I stopped for a late-morning breather. I perched on a highway turnout bench and took in the scenery. This was a beautiful climb, offering a panoramic view of the fertile green valley below, sprinkled with tiny villages and farmhouses. I squinted to make out the ribbon of road leading back to where I had begun the walk that day.

At my elevation there were traces of snow along the sides of the road, and rocks, so many rocks. Rocks everywhere. This was the rockiest place I'd ever seen. The mountains were covered with baseball-sized rocks. Rocks had been piled along the sides of the road to get them out of the way, and rocks lined the green fields where it looked like attempts were being made to farm inside walls made of the rocks. I wondered how the farmers got any farming done with so many rocks around.

After resting for about 15 minutes, I stood up from the bench and walked back out to the road to continue my day's work. I thanked god, and knocked on wood, that I could walk for hours and not stop. I realized (and knew from my own experience) that many people are not able to walk that much.

By mid-afternoon I reached Atalar. The hill had been climbed, my kilometers for the day had been walked, and I was ready to go home. I flagged down a passing bus and rode it back to Gaziantep. Mustafa had a delicious dinner of köfte and pilav waiting for me. After dinner we had tea while I uploaded photos onto the web and he studied for a tax law exam. I smiled at the "odd couple" image: a tax accountant cooking dinner for a cross-country walker, in an apartment the walker wasn't supposed to be in, the two of them quietly drinking tea while one played with his computer and the other read a thick book on tax law.

THAT'S NOT APPLE JUICE

Before leaving Gaziantep to begin my final day of walking back into Gaziantep, I met Mustafa and a few of his colleagues at a bakery for a breakfast of *katmer*. Katmer is a favorite breakfast food in Gaziantep. I had never eaten it so I entered the bakery with curiosity running high.

Mustafa called out to the man behind the counter that he wanted a couple servings of katmer and tea for everyone at the table. The katmer arrived in moments. Starved, I gulped down my first serving in a few bites, astonished at the sugary sweetness. Katmer is a pastry piled high with thin layers of phyllo dough. Each layer is sprinkled with powdered pistachios and white sugar, slathered in sweet cream, and then the process is repeated on the layers after that.

In other words, if you want to start the day with a sugar buzz, eating a couple servings of katmer for breakfast is the way to do it.

Since I was the guest and it was my first time eating katmer, Mustafa and his colleagues insisted that I eat a lot of it. Two servings were not enough, so Mustafa turned to the waiter and waved at him to bring us more. I wondered, *do they really want me to eat a lot of katmer, or are they just using me as an excuse to eat katmer themselves, or both?*

Four servings of katmer later, our little group broke up as abruptly as it had formed. Mustafa and his friends scrambled off to work, and I, hands shaking and head buzzing from all the sugar, stumbled out to the main highway to begin my final stretch back east into Gaziantep. I boarded a bus and headed back to the place I had stopped the day before.

The day's walk was pleasant, most of it a very gradual downhill slope on a curvy road for 30 kilometers. Hills all around me. The bright sun reflecting off patches of snow still on the ground. And lots of rocks. Rocks, rocks, everywhere.

I came upon a small plastic water bottle filled with a yellow liquid. I had seen hundreds of these on my walk. For months I had been wondering why people across the country on long inter-city drives were filling water bottles with apple juice and then throwing them out onto the shoulder.

This time I paid more attention, peering at the bottle and finally realizing, "Oh, hey, I'll bet that's not apple juice!"

I don't know why it took me 4-1/2 months to that figure out.

Later in the day as I walked into Gaziantep, 61% of the way across Turkey, I met up with statues of a Silk Road camel caravan carrying loads of spices west out of Gaziantep. I snapped a photo of the caravan. I remembered that my mom was having knee replacement surgery the next day, and I thought it might inspire her to get up and walk on that new knee if she saw the photo. If people could walk to Gaziantep from China, my mom could walk on her new knee, and I could walk across Turkey.

STUMBLING INTO A REFUGEE CAMP

Arriving home at Mustafa's each day had meant I ended the day with a warm, home-cooked meal and a hot shower in a spacious bathroom, but all good things must come to an end. Mustafa's in-laws needed their apartment back. They lived in Kilis, a city adjacent to the Syrian border about 50 kilometers away, and were coming for a visit, so I would need to find another place to stay.

During that day's walk, a few miles east of Gaziantep, I pulled out my cell phone and called Tomas, an Italian Couchsurfing hitchhiker I had met a couple days before in a cafe.

Tomas answered: "Hello?"

"Hi Tomas, it's Matt Krause from Couchsurfing, remember me?"

"Sure, what's up?"

"I'm looking for a place to stay tonight. I know it's kind of short notice. Do you know of anything?"

"Probably. Tonight I'm staying in the attic of a friend of a friend's place. You might be able to crash there."

"Have you stayed there before?" I asked Tomas.

"No."

"Have you met the host before?"

"No."

The connection sounds kind of tentative, I thought. *But I sleep in ditches by the side of the road. Beggars can't be choosers.*

"Can I join you?"

"I think so," Tomas responded. "Meet me in the square downtown at 5 p.m."

I breathed a sigh of relief and stuffed my phone back into my pocket. "Good, that's taken care of."

I continued walking.

A few kilometers later, a village appeared on the horizon and I spotted, at its edge, a collection of tents with people milling about. *Cool, a market,* I thought, *I'll drop in and take a look.*

I came to the outskirts of the village and began walking towards the market.

I noticed that the women wore bright colors — purples, reds. I generally didn't see Turkish women wearing robes that colorful.

I noticed lots of children running around unattended. *Huh, that's different,* I thought. *At most of the Turkish markets I see, there aren't a lot of children, and the mothers generally hold the ones present close.*

I noticed lots of men sitting on the ground in small groups. *Huh, that's unusual. I almost never see groups of Turkish men sitting around at a market, especially not on the ground.*

I noticed the tents were empty, save for a few bunks and some scattered bags of clothes. *Huh, that's unusual too. Most of the markets I see have tents overflowing with goods for sale.*

I stopped dead in my tracks. I looked around closer at the women in robes, at the children running around, at the men sitting on the ground outside empty tents.

I wasn't standing in a market. I was standing in a refugee camp.

I looked around some more, wondering if it was always this easy to walk into refugee camps.

A truck pulled up on the road a hundred meters away. Some men got out of the cab and began pulling temporary fencing from the back of the truck. *I guess this is a new camp,* I thought. *They haven't even put up fencing yet.*

I resumed walking. Another quarter-mile and I had left the village and its new refugee camp behind. Back out onto the open road. Only mile after mile of gently rolling hills and row after row of pistachio trees. And the occasional Syrian family making its way to the camp I had left behind me.

After the day's walk I hopped a bus back to Gaziantep. I met Tomas on the square. We picked up my backpack from Mustafa's office nearby. We went back out onto the square and met Sara, an Italian exchange student who had helped Tomas find the attic where he and I would sleep that night.

"Where is this place," I asked Sara. "Is it far from here?"

"I don't think so," Sara responded, "but I've never been there."

We wandered up and down streets, in and out of blind alleys, and finally found the place. It was behind a locked gate. Sara tried a bunch of keys on a ring full of them, and finally found the key that unlocked the gate. It popped open into a small courtyard. We entered the building and climbed the stairs to the attic. Tomas and I dropped our packs onto the attic floor.

I looked at Tomas. "You hungry?"

"Yeah, I'm starved."

"Let's go eat, then," I said.

We descended the stairs and found a nearby restaurant for dinner.

That night as I fell asleep, I worried about Tomas. It was cold in Gaziantep, and especially cold in that attic. My sleeping bag was toasty warm, having been designed for sleeping on snow and ice. But Tomas had only a summer bag. It was going to be a cold night for him.

The next morning, I woke to see Tomas sitting next to a glowing space heater, cupping his hands and breathing into them.

"Are you okay?" I asked. Mist came out of my mouth as I spoke. "It was kind of cold last night."

"Yeah, I'm fine," Tomas answered, shivering, "just trying to warm up."

"Come on," I said to Tomas, "Let's get out of here and go get some breakfast."

It was my day off, and I was looking forward to a leisurely breakfast in a warm restaurant followed by some sightseeing. Besides, back in Osmaniye I had promised İlgi that I would introduce foreigners to şalgam whenever possible.

"Have you tried şalgam?" I asked Tomas as we descended the stairs.

"No, what's that?"

"It's a local drink, it's delicious. You'll love it."

After breakfast we wandered around the city sightseeing, knowing that we had only a few hours to give to a city that had taken thousands of years to create. Later that day, Tomas' phone rang. It was Sara. We would need to clear out of the attic later that day. The owner was coming back and would need the space.

"I guess we'll need to find another place to stay tonight," I said to Tomas. "Any ideas?"

"No. You?"

"No, none. I guess we'll have to look for a place. But first, let me introduce you to şalgam. Come on, there's a shop across the street. They'll have some." We crossed the road and entered the shop. I ordered two şalgams.

Tomas grimaced as he took a sip of his. "Is there something wrong with this?"

"No," I said, "it's supposed to taste like that. Drink it fast, it'll be easier that way. Besides, we should start looking for a place to stay."

After drinking and grimacing his way through şalgam, Tomas and I walked around Gaziantep looking for a cheap motel to stay in. The shadows grew longer and longer, and then the sky dimmer and dimmer, and we had inquired at almost a dozen places, but they were all too expensive, or full, or, if they fit into our budget, didn't have hot water, which was kind of a deal breaker since it was so cold outside.

Finally, we found one which fit our budget AND had hot water. And, to make it even better, the manager took pity on the two homeless strangers wandering around the city looking for a place to stay, and he gave us an especially deep discount. We went up to the room. The water was hot and the sheets were clean.

CRYING INTO MY TAHINI

The next day, before resuming my walk, I went downstairs to the hotel's breakfast buffet and took a seat next to the window. A cold rain was beating against the glass. I was happy to see on the buffet a bowl of tahini, an oily spread made from pressed sesame seeds. At most places in the US that little bowl of tahini would cost about $20.00. In this part of Turkey there was so much tahini that it was a complimentary breakfast buffet item.

The TV was playing in the dining room while I ate, and as is usually the case on TV news someone was crying about something. I watched closer. A Turkish mother was crying about her dead son.

Fat drops of water were splattering against the window now, beckoning me to the long, tedious day of walking through deserted areas in the rain.

I hunched over my tahini feeling sorry for myself like a poor old man hunched over crying into his bowl of soup.

Then there was that mother crying some more on television. "God, life sucks so much!" I said to myself.

"Hold yourself together!" I said back to myself. "Do not start crying into your tahini! That's going to look really bad. Do not go there!"

Once I finished breakfast, though, and got out on the road and started my work for the day, I got caught up with executing the daily routine: Get to where you're going to walk. Walk. Get back. Eat. Sleep. Wake up the next day and do it again.

On the way out of Gaziantep I passed another stone camel caravan. This one, like me, was walking east out of town.

As I walked through the edge of town, breathing exhaust fumes and trying not to get hit by cars, I thought, *sometimes walking across a country is boring scut work, not that much different from sitting in a cubicle answering emails*. The difference was I didn't mind this particular variety of scut work.

East of Gaziantep were rolling hills, green grass, rich but rocky soil, olive trees, and some other kind of trees I could not identify. I remembered that a few weeks ago I had learned that southeastern Turkey and Iran supplied more than half of the world's pistachios and wondered at the time where they grew all those pistachios. Duh! I looked around and realized that those trees I couldn't identify were pistachio trees.

At the end of the day I took a minibus back to Gaziantep to meet up with Tomas and stay at the hotel another night.

Glad they didn't blow me up

Friday, on the climb into Urfa, I ran into what seemed to be road construction. I didn't see any machinery moving though, so I figured the entire crew was on break, and I kept walking. A cop car came down the hill toward me from Urfa. It pulled over in front of me and stopped. Three policemen got out to greet me.

"Is everything okay?" they asked.

"Yes, thanks," I replied, "everything is fine."

They looked at me uncertainly, as if they had something to say, but didn't want to say it.

"Are you going to Urfa?"

"Yes," I replied.

"You should get into the car. We will take you there."

"Thanks," I replied, "but no, I need to walk."

One of the officers repeated, "You should get into the car. We will take you to Urfa."

"No," I repeated, "thanks, but I will walk."

The three of them gave up and climbed back into the squad car. They turned around and drove back toward Urfa on the wrong side of the highway.

I thought to myself, *That's dangerous. What if someone hits them?* Then I noticed there were no cars in either direction. It was normally a busy road, so I thought that a little strange. I hitched up my pack and continued walking up the hill.

I climbed another two or three kilometers, wondering why this uncanny lack of traffic? Then as I entered the city limit I saw a roadblock about 200 meters ahead and the cops who had greeted me earlier were parked there with a long line of traffic behind them. It slowly dawned on me that they must be waiting for me, and I thought, "This is not going to go well for me. The cops have lost patience with me. They are not going to allow me to continue walking. I'm going to have to walk this last part later. As soon as I reach that roadblock they are going to make me get in the car."

I stopped to take a picture of the city limit sign before the cops could stop me.

When I arrived at the roadblock, all the cops said to me was, "Hello! Welcome to Urfa." One of them got on the radio and I heard him say, "Okay you can blow it up now." Then came the deafening blast of dynamite behind me where I'd been walking.

Why, I wondered, hadn't they told me they were dynamiting? I would have gotten in the car immediately and come back later to complete those kilometers. As it was, the cops and that string of cars had had to wait all that time for me to walk to the city limits.

The cop on the radio turned to me and said, "Okay! Now you've got to get in the car! We need to take you to the station."

This time I got into the police car and we rode to the precinct station. I sat in the precinct station for a little while, drinking tea and watching television while the cops took photocopies of my passport and residence permit and faxed them to another office to make sure I wasn't a terrorist.

I didn't know whether I was free to go or not, so after about ninety minutes I finally asked them. They said, "Yes, of course, you are free to go."

They gave my passport and paperwork back to me. I shoved them in my back pocket, pulled my backpack on, and walked out to the main road. I asked the cops, "Which way do I go toward the city center now?"

They said, "We'll drive you to the bus station."

I told them, "No. I need to walk to the bus station."

They said, "No, no, no! We absolutely insist. You must get in the car and we will drive you to the bus station."

I had turned down enough rides from the cops that day, and I figured I would just come back and walk this leg later. So I got into the back of the police car and they drove me to the main bus station.

When I realized we were going to the main bus station, I said, "No, I need a local bus because I am just going back to Gaziantep."

They said, "No, we're taking you to the main bus station. The local buses are not trustworthy."

I repeated, "I need a local bus back to Gaziantep."

They insisted, "No!! You need to take one of the main buses here at the main bus station and go on one of the main roads back to Gaziantep."

At the main bus station, I opened the car door and entered a sea of men and women in colorful baggy pants and dresses dancing and banging on drums. However, I had told the cops I would buy a bus ticket right away, so I paid no attention to the festivities and just walked up to the ticket counter and bought a ticket for the next bus to Gaziantep.

Ticket bought, I finally looked around to see what the commotion was about. The dancing men and women had come to the station to see off their young men who were going into the military to do their mandatory service. Urfa was one of the intake points.

The part of southeastern Turkey that I was in now — Gaziantep and Urfa — was the area people in the west had been referring to when they pantomimed machine guns and warned me that all the people "over there" were terrorists. But all I was seeing here so far were people who wore more colorful clothes than they wore in the west and, yes, their language was different. But they were here at the bus station seeing off their sons into mandatory service for the same country that the people of the west served. I'd seen no machine guns yet. And the police with the string of cars at the roadblock into town had sat and patiently waited and stopped a dynamiting project for me, a foreigner, even as I refused to cooperate with them.

I was entering another world, and I knew that in order to survive I had to remember that I was never going to understand what was going on in any given situation. I was just going to walk and hope they let me do it.

Once back in Gaziantep I took a couple of days off in the nearby city of Kahramanmaraş to work on the book.

BAT OUT OF HELL

After taking a few days off for vacation and writing, I slide into my pack again and walk out of Urfa like a bat out of hell. My first thought: *Oh shit! I want to finish this up by the middle of April and I still have one-third of the country to cross without injuring myself!*

On the outskirts of Urfa, I pull a calculator out of my pocket. How many kilometers will I need to walk each day to meet my goal? I punch a few numbers into the calculator, and breathe a sigh of relief. It's doable, but I'm going to have to walk twice a much as I've walked in previous months. There will be a lot of wear and tear on my body and I will be very tired at the end of the month.

Urfa, with a population about 600,000 and one of the oldest cities in human history, is considered to be the hometown of Abraham but there is no more room in my schedule for visiting historical sites — not even Urfa's iconic Balıklı Göl (Fish Lake). The story with Balıklı Göl is that King Nimrod had Abraham burned on a funeral pyre, but God turned the fire into water and the burning coals into fish. This pool of sacred fish remains today. No one eats these fish. Legend has it that if you eat one of the fish you will die.

Tourists flock to Urfa for this and other "cradle of civilization" sites. But I have a job to do.

I think of a friend, Yonca from İstanbul, and dedicate the day's walk to her. On Twitter Yonca goes by @epithetankgirl. March is going to be my busiest walking month yet, so all month I'll be needing the inspiration of, for example, indestructible tank girls.

I stuff the calculator back into my pocket and resume walking. My goal for the day is the airport about 35 kilometers outside the city.

Around 10 a.m., I stop at a gasoline station for a mid-morning snack of a bag of potato chips and a candy bar. A group of farmers squatting on the pavement, also taking their mid-morning break, invites me to join them for tea. I squat down next to them.

"What are you doing?" they ask me.

"I'm walking across Turkey. I've been on the road for six months," I say.

"Where do you sleep at night?" they ask.

"Sometimes I stay with friends," I say. "Sometimes I camp on the side of the road."

"Like a spy," says one of the farmers.

"Yes," I reply, "like a spy."

Further down the road, I come across a young man, a shepherd named Şahin. He walks with me for about a kilometer, which is unusual, because shepherds are usually busy managing their flocks.

"What are you doing out here?" Şahin asks.

"I'm walking across Turkey. I've been on the road 6 months. I'm walking towards Diyarbakır."

Şahin's face lights up. "That's great," he says, "what a grand adventure! I will probably live my entire life right here, just a few kilometers from my village, watching these sheep every day. I wish I could do something like that."

A few kilometers later, I run into another young man on the side of the road. He asks me, "What are you doing out here?"

"I'm walking across Turkey. I've been on the road 6 months. I'm walking towards Diyarbakır."

"That's impossible," he says, "you can't do that."

"I have been walking for six months," I repeat.

"That's impossible, you can't do that," he repeats.

"Okay, thank you," I say, as I wave goodbye and continue walking.

Life is so much simpler now that I am not trying to respond to everything people say or to defend myself. All I'm thinking is — 17 kilometers, 18 kilometers, 19 kilometers, 20 kilometers. Put one foot in front of the other. Put it down. Pick up the other foot. Put it down in front of the first one. Repeat until you've crossed the country.

I reach the airport and wait by the side of the road twenty minutes for a minibus to ride back to Urfa.

Saturday, 2 March

I wake up in Urfa. I take the bus to the airport, where I ended my walk the day before.

Green blankets the rolling hills for as far as the eye can see. There is not a tree in sight. The villages are far apart. From what I understand it is like this all the way from Urfa to Diyarbakır.

I walk 30 kilometers further. Then I take the bus back to Urfa.

Sunday, 3 March

I wake up in Urfa, board a bus, and ride 60 kilometers to where I left off yesterday. There is nothing in sight but rolling hills covered with green grass, and a blue sky above. At the spot I stopped yesterday I tell the bus driver to let me off the bus. He looks at me, puzzled. His face says, *Why in the world would you want to get out here?* When he sees my increasing urgency he pulls to a stop and opens the door and I climb off.

Today, if I walk 32 kilometers I'll get to Siverek, a small town of fewer than 10,000 people between Urfa and Diyarbakır.

Before I walk I dedicate the day to Mary Baba. Tomorrow is her birthday. Mary is my aunt (my mother's sister). Her birthday actually isn't until tomorrow, but I won't be walking tomorrow — I'll be moving on to Diyarbakır.

"Mary," I write. "I have a photo of me at the Euphrates river the other day. I'll drop that in the mail to you."

I begin walking. I am again in the middle of nowhere, but in Turkey, people appear even in the middle of nowhere.

I meet two men on the side of the road. I greet them and ask them if everything is okay. They tell me they are looking for their horse. I wish them the best of luck and continue walking.

A few hours later I come across a truck stop with a cafe. It's probably the only food place I'll see today so I stop for lunch.

I order the ground beef with eggs. It looks like it has been around for about 37 years, but I'm hungry, and I am craving protein, so I cross my fingers and hope for the best.

While I am eating it occurs to me I ought to start a travel cuisine blog called QuestionableTruckStopGrub.com. I chuckle at myself. After all, there aren't many people around today to laugh at my jokes. If I don't laugh at my own jokes, who will?

After lunch I begin walking again, facing traffic as always. Once or twice a day drivers suggest to me that hitchhiking would be so much easier if I would cross the road and walk with traffic, not against it. I thank them for their concern. If I were hitchhiking I would probably have picked up on that idea on my own by now.

I walk for a few more hours and reach Siverek, midway between Urfa and Diyarbakır. I hop a bus back to Urfa, glad that tomorrow I will be moving on to Diyarbakır.

DO YOU HAVE ANY INFORMATION?

Tuesday, 5 March

The day after moving to Diyarbakır, I hop a mini-bus back to Siverek to begin the three day-long legs of my walk toward Diyarbakır. The plains now are windswept, the winds high.

I dedicate the day to Merve, the friend of mine from Mersin. Diyarbakır is her hometown.

Merve was the first one to teach me the Kurdish greeting "roj baş," and I notice that in these parts "roj baş" brings on some pretty big smiles. People love to hear foreigners speaking their language.

As I start my walk out of Siverek, a group of about eight 10-year-old boys runs up to me.

One of the boys jumps up and down, gesturing wildly and pointing at me, his face contorted in anger. He yells, "Syrians are not welcome here. Move on!"

I turn my back to him and face the other boys. I take off my sunglasses.

While the angry boy jumps and screams, I chat with his friends and introduce myself.

"Where are you from?" one of the boys asks.

"I am an American," I say.

Upon hearing this, the angry boy calms down a bit and pushes to the front of the group. He introduces himself as "Ronaldo." Ronaldo is a famous Portuguese footballer.

"Nice to meet you, Ronaldo," I say. I hold out my hand. He shakes it. Then I shake a few more hands before turning around and continuing to walk.

By now the angry boy has calmed down enough such that the expression on his face says, "I should still be angry about something, but I'm not sure what now." Before I get too far away he catches up to me and reintroduces himself using his real name.

The boys fall away as we pass a soccer field. A group of men are sitting on the sidewalk drinking tea. I say hello to them. They nod at me, and one of them strikes up a conversation:

Man: Where are you going?

Me: Today I am walking towards Diyarbakır.

Man: Are you hitchhiking?

Me: No, I am walking. On foot.

Man: Are you riding a bicycle?

Me: No, I am walking. On foot.

Man: (after a pause) Are you taking a car?

Me: No, I am walking. On foot.

The man looks at me with a surprised look that says, "You're crazy!"

I smile and wave and resume walking.

At the beginning of the walk, I wanted people to understand what I was doing. But it's been six months, and even I barely understand what I am doing. All I know is that I have to do it. I've stopped caring what other people think. I just want to bang out the kilometers and be done with it.

A couple hours outside Siverek, two men pull over on the other side of the road. They are driving a rusty old Datsun. The front bumper looks like it's about to fall off onto the pavement.

"Do you need a ride?" they call out to me.

"Thank you," I say, "but I am walking."

The driver jumps out of his car and crosses over to the median strip to say hello.

I too cross over to the median strip. The man and I shake hands.

"Where are you from?" he asks.

"I am an American," I reply.

"Excellent." He leans in and looks both ways. "Do you have any information?"

"Information about what?" I ask.

He leans in further, raises his eyebrows, and says cryptically, "You know, information. I am a Turkish agent."

I look closer into his eyes and notice that they are not connecting with mine. My instinct tells me this man is crazy. I feel my protective shields going up. I tell him in English that I cannot speak any Turkish. The conversation grinds to a halt. I don't want to talk to crazy paranoiacs, especially not in this area. I just want to walk.

He hands me his business card and reminds me that he is a government agent and I should call him if I have any problems. As I cross back to my side of the road, and he to his, I call out thanks in Turkish and assure him that I will do so. As he and his friend pull away in their rusty old car, I turn his card over and take a look. His cover: dried nuts salesman. *So that's what spies are doing these days.* I smile as I crumple up his card and stuff it into my pocket.

THOSE AREN'T SHEPHERDS

Wednesday, 6 March

Today's walk is 32 km (20 miles), starting at the provincial border between Urfa and Diyarbakır, and ending at the village of Tokaçlı.

The temperature is 0 degrees Celsius (32 degrees Fahrenheit), and the crosswind so strong the bus is shuddering and the bus door won't open until the attendant rams his shoulder into it.

When I step out of the bus into the freezing wind, all I can hear is my brain yelling at me to "go! go! go!", not "stop and take a photo." I usually take photos of the road signs at provincial borders, but I glance at the sign and decide not to today. To keep from getting blown over while I walk, I lean hard to the side. I gaze out at the windswept plain. It is barren, just like I feel inside.

I'm not bored, though. I only feel bored when I am looking for distraction. If I were looking for distraction I would be tremendously bored, since for the next six hours I will do nothing but walk on this windswept plain. But I'm not looking for distraction. I know from experience that there is nothing over the next hill. There's only another hill. So I empty my head and bang out the kilometers.

A man who I think is a shepherd waves me over to a small stone shelter next to the road. I eagerly head in his direction.

"Roj baş," I say as I duck into the door and hide from the wind. Greetings.

"Roj baş," he smiles and says back.

He motions me further into the shelter and invites me to sit down for tea. I sit down next to the stove and warm my hands.

When my eyes adjust to the darkness I notice there is another man standing near the door. The shepherd introduces him. They are friends. The friend and I greet each other. Roj baş.

The friend is brewing tea. He points to the kettle. "It's not ready yet," he says. "Give it a few more minutes."

A random thought flashes through my mind: *Where are the sheep? I didn't see any sheep outside. Aren't these guys shepherds?*

I take a closer look around the room and see a half-dozen automatic rifles leaning against the wall.

I didn't know shepherds carried automatic rifles.

I look at the shepherds a little closer. They are wearing camouflage fatigues and headscarves.

Wait a minute, a voice in my head tells me. *These aren't shepherds.*

I stand up. I don't know where their loyalties lie. I don't want to. I tell them I'd like a rain check on the tea and that I really must be going.

We shake hands, say our goodbyes, and I head back out into the wind.

Thursday, 7 March

Today is the last leg of my walk into Diyarbakır. I hop a bus to where I left off yesterday so I can walk the 30 kilometers back into Diyarbakır.

I climb down off the bus and take out my writing stuff. The clean whiteboard I used to use for my daily dedications is gone now, crushed by the other things in my backpack. I discarded it hundreds of miles ago. Now I write my daily dedications on scraps of paper.

A memory has popped into my head and I dedicate the day to Bill Munn, a friend of mine from my teenage days. I stand by the side of the road and write the memory on paper so I can type it into my computer later:

When I was 15 I lived in Visalia, California. On Saturday mornings a bunch of us would ride our bicycles to Rocky Hill, one of the foothills of the Sierras.

One day Bill Munn came with us. He was a patriarch of the Visalia cycling scene at that time, but he wasn't always a regular at the Saturday morning rides, even though they started in front of his shop.

At that time Bill was about 35, I guess. He was, shall we say, a little bit heavier than the rest of us.

We young bucks got to the top of Rocky Hill way ahead of Bill. While waiting for Bill, some of us rode around idly in circles, while some of us just sat on our bikes, leaned against the bars, and watched him sweat his way up the hill.

At the top he pulled to a stop and gasped out some words I'll probably laugh at for the rest of my life: "I can't breathe, I need a cigarette."

By the time he came to a full stop he had pulled a cigarette out of his pocket, lit it, and started puffing away.

I notice that while I've been writing in my notebook I've been standing in front of a police station. I figure I have mere seconds before the cops show up to find out what I'm doing. Sure enough, three of them appear as I close my notebook. They greet me and pat me down. They check my documents and rifle through my notebook.

"Who is Bill Munn?" they ask, pointing to his name on the page, perhaps suspecting that he is a spy higher up in the organization.

"An old friend of mine."

They eye me suspiciously and hand the notebook back to me. I say thanks, turn around, and begin my walk for the day.

Six hours later I walk into Diyarbakır. I stop briefly to take a photo of the city limit sign: Diyarbakır, population 875,000.

Over the past 7 days I have walked from Şanlıurfa to Diyarbakır. 185 kilometers, or 115 miles. I suspect I am tired, but I also suspect that if I were tired I would not know it. So now that 77% of the walk is done, I will be taking 3 days off. I will be visiting a school, and I'll also have two days of napping and eating. I might try to catch a movie too. I don't watch too many movies these days.

Friday, 8 March

I spend the day at Rekabet Kurumu Cumhuriyet Fen Lisesi, a science-focused high school in Diyarbakır. I am a guest of Nazile Çelik, one of the school's English teachers. She is a friend of my hosts in Diyarbakır.

This particular school is pretty competitive. The students have to pass a special exam to enter, and then once they're in, they not only go to school during the week, they also take 4 hours of additional classes at private study schools on Saturdays AND on Sundays. Chess, table tennis, and volleyball seem to be the most popular extra-curricular activities. Almost half of the students want to be doctors.

Visiting schools is exhausting for me, but it is, hands down, my favorite activity on the trip. If I had the invitations, and the endurance, I would spend every single spare moment of this trip visiting schools. I don't care if they are primary schools, middle schools, high schools, or universities. I LOVE visiting schools.

The students get excited, and I get confused and overwhelmed, and in the hallways a million people talk to me at once and I don't know who to focus on. But once I get in front of a class and start talking with the students the rest of the world falls away. It's just me and the students in front of me.

Saturday, 9 March, and Sunday, 10 March

I spend one of the days touring Diyarbakır with four students of Nazile Çelik: a young man named Diyar, and three young women named Ezgi, Esra, and Aysel. We climb around on the city walls, visit the city's four-footed minaret, and relax with a hot cup of *menengiç*, a hot drink made with terebinth berries.

I spend part of the other rest day helping my host with the ironing. Some people, like my host, hate ironing. I love it. It brings me peace.

I spend the rest of the time sleeping and eating. My host asks me if I want to go out and explore. I say no, I do enough of that these days. I just want to rest, thank you.

Monday, 11 March

On the walk today a man asks me, "What's this region called?"

There are a couple possible answers to that question, and for those answers wars have been fought, and are still being fought, and people give, and take, lives.

I don't want to get involved. It's not my fight. I just want to finish walking across the country. I answer the best I can: I smile and say, "I don't know, you tell me."

He smiles back and declines to answer, too.

The day is sunny and warm with big blue skies. There is no wind. Rolling hills as far as the eye can see, with a change in the ground cover now. West of Diyarbakır the land was covered with rocks and was used only for grazing. East of Diyarbakır it's the opposite: no rocks, and all farming. Mostly wheat, barley, and lentils. Fresh green sprouting grasses cover the rolling hills. Last time I saw a wheat field was in December and it was brown.

I stop for lunch at Ortaçlar Petrol in the village of Köprübaşı ("Bridge Head"). Lunch is two ice creams, a bag of nacho cheese Doritos, and some water. Doritos enjoy a large distribution network in eastern Turkey; you can find them almost anywhere.

İsmail and İshak, the owners of Ortaçlar, ask me to make sure I mention their gasoline station in particular. So the next time you find yourself in need of fuel in Köprübaşı, 20 kilometers east of Diyarbakır, be sure to stop by Ortaçlar Petrol. Ask for the fill-up special, and tell them Matt sent you.

My walk's 1,000th mile matches exactly with the middle of the Tigris river. I stop briefly to note that to someone in a less utilitarian, more poetic mood, the combination of rolling the odometer to 1,000 miles while crossing a river considered by many to be the cradle of human civilization would probably be more significant. I resume walking across the bridge. Two more days of this and I'll be ready to move on to the next town, Silvan.

Tuesday, 12 March, and Wednesday, 13 March

I can see a few mountains have started to appear in the distance. In about a week I'll start the climb up onto a higher plateau, and I'll finish the walk on that plateau.

On one of my breaks I stop at a gasoline station for some tea. They ask me about federalism in the US. In my Tarzan Turkish I try to answer questions like, "In America, are the state governors appointed by the President, or are they elected by the people?"

As I walk back out to the road, I reflect that in western Turkey, when I would tell people I was heading east, they would almost invariably pantomime machine gun fire. Now that I'm in the east, I am answering questions about federalism.

When I reach Silvan, my destination for the day, I snack on peynirli kol böreği and çay. While I eat someone explains to me that the Bible is broken. I thank them for the information and hop a bus back to Diyarbakır.

Thursday, 14 March

As the bus leaves Diyarbakır I pull out my notebook and pen this:

There was a squirrel. He was out hunting for nuts. He saw a big one down in the well of a tree. He grabbed the nut. He tried to pull it out, but the nut was too big. It, plus his hand, wouldn't come out together. So he had to make a choice — let go of the nut and live, or hold onto it and starve.

Today I am leaving Diyarbakır. I have been here for over a week — three days to walk toward the city, one day to visit a school, two days to rest, and then three days to walk away from it.

I am moving on to Silvan, and then Tatvan. People are waiting for me in those places. I know from experience now that some of them will become great friends, but in order to meet them, I have to say goodbye, at least for now, to my old friends.

It is like breaking up with people every day, day after day, and I don't like it a whole lot. In fact, it is the single most emotionally exhausting aspect of this trip.

But the soon-to-be-new-friends are waiting for me, and so I've got to say goodbye, at least for now, to the old ones. Thank you Diyarbakır, it's been real.

IN THE HOUSE OF İSLAM

Thursday, 14 March

When the bus nears the center of Silvan, it gets stuck behind a stopped delivery truck. I decide to get off and walk the rest of the way. All I know is I am looking for the Oğretmen Evi. I don't know where it is, but Silvan is a town of only 40,000 people, so how far can it be? I poke my head into an unlit shop and call into the darkness, "Which way to the Oğretmen Evi?"

My eyes, slowly beginning to adjust to the darkness, make out the forms of two men. One of them, the shopkeeper, points down the street and begins an explanation. Then he turns to the other, a younger college-age man, and says, "Why don't you show this guy the Oğretmen Evi?"

I follow the young man down the crowded street, trying not to get hit by a passing caravan of delivery trucks. The young man stops, turns towards me, and introduces himself as Yunus. I introduce myself too. Yunus turns back abruptly and resumes walking.

After a few minutes he turns to look at me, puzzled.

"Why are you staying at the Oğretmen Evi?" he asks. "Why don't you stay with us?"

I don't know who he is referring to by "us" but this is Turkey, and it certainly isn't the first time a stranger has offered me the hospitality of staying in his home.

"Sure," I say. "Let's do it!"

Yunus takes out an ancient cell phone. The keypad is pretty much destroyed and he has to type in the number with a stub of a matchstick.

I hear a man answer on the other end. Yunus says to him, "I ran into this guy on the street and he's looking for a place to stay. Can we put him up at our place?"

The answer is apparently *yes* because the conversation is short, and immediately after Yunus hangs up the phone he turns to walk in the opposite direction, waving at me to follow him.

A few blocks away we meet some of his friends standing on the sidewalk, and we all take seats at a sidewalk tea garden a few doors down. More friends arrive, and pretty soon there are a dozen of us crowded around the small table, drinking çay and chatting.

I ask each one his name and find out they are all students at a university preparation school a couple of blocks away. They have taken the national university exam but haven't done particularly well, so they are spending the year getting the backup schooling they need to take the test again.

While we chat boisterously and enjoy our çay, a man, appearing to be in his 30s, walks up to us and says hello. He is selling socks. He leans over the table, looks at me, and says, "Hey. Who are you and what are you doing?" His words are disjointed and he looks a little crazy.

I tell him I am from California and that I'm walking across Turkey.

"Welcome to Silvan," he says.

He reaches over to his mortarboard of socks, takes off a pair, and hands them to me.

"Here," he says. "Here's a pair of socks. My gift to you."

I take the socks and thank him. We exchange Facebook account names. He tells me he mostly uses Facebook to play poker with people from the Philippines and Ukraine, but assures me that I will see him there.

Yunus and his friends nod at each other in agreement that it's time to go. They stand up in unison. I reach for my backpack. They refuse to let me carry it, and I know that insisting on carrying it myself will only insult them. One of Yunus' friends tries to pick it up but is unable to lift it by himself, so two of them grab one shoulder strap each and heft it together.

I look from person to person and realize I don't even know who I'm staying with, and I have no idea where these people are taking my pack. The pack contains every earthly possession I have, but by now I've gotten used to taking actions while not completely understanding the situation. I have learned to trust my ability to see in someone's eyes whether they are good or not, and I know I will be fine even if I am wrong.

We come to an intersection and the two guys with the backpack head off in a direction towards what they call home. I see that Yunus is planning to go in another direction. I don't know who to follow, the guys with my pack, or Yunus. I look at Yunus for some indication. I see from his body language that he wants me to follow him. He says he wants to show me around town first. I ask if we'll meet up with the others later. He says of course.

Thousands of years ago, Silvan went by another name and was the capital of the Kingdom of Armenia. Yunus and I visit the old castle, and climb around on some other ruins, which, if Yunus was not there to point out and identify for me, I would mistake for a pile of rocks. I like Yunus and am thankful for the tour and the hospitality, but half of my brain is preoccupied with the thought that my backpack is out of my sight.

The tour finished, Yunus sees the anxiety in my face. Don't worry, he says, let's go to the house now. When Yunus and I get back to the house, I am immediately relieved to see my backpack sitting in a corner. While Yunus and I were touring Silvan, his friends had cleared out a room for me to stay in. They tell me a couple of them rent the place, and the rest of them come and go during the day, mostly for naps between classes. I look around the apartment. *This is a student crash pad,* I note.

The main renter, İslam, introduces himself to me. A thought flashes through my head: *I will be staying in the House of İslam.* There's a pun in there somewhere, I suspect, but I am too tired to think about it. Can I wash up? I ask. Of course, İslam says as he points me to the sink in the kitchen.

Several of the students leave for classes. İslam and two others stay behind. After I wash up we sit on cushions on the floor and chat. They speak to me mostly in Kurdish. Turkish is as much a foreign language to them as it is to me. If they were speaking to me in Turkish I would understand a small amount of what they are saying, but since they are mixing Turkish and Kurdish, I understand even less.

I grab my cell phone and call a Kurdish friend I had made in Mersin. She is from this area. I tell her my situation: that I am staying with students, and they are being very nice to me, but since I don't speak Kurdish it's hard to break the ice with them. I want them to know that I have friends who are looking out for me.

I hand the phone to the students and my friend in Mersin says hello to them. They chat for a few minutes.

I see the students relax. I have been vouched for, in their native language by someone from their area. I'm not just a stray dog anymore.

I think to myself, *They take me in first, and then they find out who I am. Thank god the instinctive behaviors come in that order in Turkey. I have been able to walk across an entire country because of that.*

After the phone call the students and I chat a while longer, and then they decide they want to go out on the town.

They invite me. "We are going to go out in a few minutes; do you want to clean up again before we go?"

I've forgotten how dirty I am from traveling. It would probably take me days to wash off all the grime. "Yeah! I'd like to clean up," I say.

İslam tells me to grab my toiletries, my towel, and some clean clothes, and to follow him. He leads me out to the packed-dirt yard, where a shed I had thought contained only an outhouse also contains a shower. A goat is standing next to the shed munching on one of the few remaining patches of grass. I enter the shower and let my eyes adjust to the dim light, the shower lit only by a few rays of sunlight poking through holes in the wall. I shower while the goat chews patiently.

After my shower, İslam pulls the steel gate shut behind us and the four of us walk down the lane to meet some of their friends. We find the friends at a café, where we sit to drink tea and watch a football game.

As the game nears its end two of their female friends walk up to the table. They introduce themselves as Gülden and Dilan. They are sisters. "Come over to our house after the game," they say, "we'll cook dinner for you."

After the game we walk over to Gülden and Dilan's house. They are gardening in the front yard with their father, who shakes my hand and introduces himself as Mehmet. It is a lush garden, full of grasses and trees and flowers and bushes. Before dinner we take a seat at a table underneath one of the trees. Dilan, the older sister, brings tea.

Mehmet invites me to dinner. İslam and the other students leave, saying they have classes that evening. Mehmet, Dilan, Gülden, and I go inside the house, where Dilan has prepared a simple but delicious dinner out of grated carrots and beans and rice, plus a tomato-based stew. I eat one serving, then another, then another. I can't stop. I smile contentedly at Mehmet and tell him I feel like I've gone to heaven. Dilan apologizes for her meager cooking skills. I say, "Don't be ridiculous, this is delicious. You have no idea how happy I am just to sit here with the family and enjoy this meal."

After dinner Gülden brings tea and Dilan turns on the television. We watch a Kurdish-language news program broadcasting from Iran.

I can't understand what they're saying on the news, and I don't care. I'm just happy to be sitting in this living room soaking up the warmth of this family. Back in western Turkey, every time I told people I'd be walking through this area, they told me it was dangerous, that everyone carried machine guns and I would fear for my life. But that is irrelevant to me here, now, relaxing in this family room with this family who uses Kurdish words to speak kindly to each other, garden together, and cook for each other.

WHAT A MORON

Friday, 15 March

The Malabadi Bridge, an ancient bridge built in 1147, spans the Batman River just outside Silvan. Yes, that's right — Batman, though the name has nothing to do with the comic book hero Batman. It's a Turkish name, and the Batman river is a major tributary of the Tigris River.

That ancient Malabadi Bridge is where I'm supposed to be right now. In fact, I've planned for hours to be there so I could dedicate the day to Özgür Çelik, a friend of mine from İstanbul, and take a picture of the ancient Malabadi bridge for him.

However, I'm not at the ancient Malabadi Bridge. I am at the new Malabadi Bridge. It is so new, in fact, that orange construction cones still line the sides of the bridge, and there is no road signage yet. I look to my left. Two kilometers upstream I see the ancient Malabadi Bridge.

I wonder briefly if I should go see the ancient bridge. I've almost walked across an entire country, surely I can go a few kilometers out of my way.

No, I decide, *Özgür's going to have to make do with a picture of the new Malabadi Bridge. Sorry Özgür, it's the thought that counts.*

I finish my six hours of walking for the day, and then ride back to Silvan to spend my last night there.

Saturday, 16 March

I board the bus to move from Silvan to Tatvan. Tatvan is a town on the western edge of Lake Van in eastern Turkey. It lies about 2,500 feet above the Malabadi Bridge. It marks my last plateau. Only about three weeks of walking remain.

On the bus a young ethnic Turkish man sits down next to me. I ask him what he's doing in the area. He tells me he's a soldier stationed in Mardin.

"What is Mardin like?" I ask.

"Scenery's nice," he says loudly, "but the people are bad. You can't trust them."

I think, *Uh oh, you've got to be a major moron to make a statement like that when you're the only Turk on a bus full of Kurds.* I shut up and look straight ahead, knowing full well what is about to happen…

Within moments the other passengers begin criticizing him viciously and vocally. One man in particular, an older man I had chatted with at a rest stop 15 minutes earlier, goes on at the top of his voice for a full ten minutes. Erdoğan this, Erdoğan that. Turkish soldiers this, Turkish soldiers that.

The young Turkish man slouches down into his seat and tucks his chin into his jacket, his expression saying, "Oh why did I have to open my big fat mouth?"

The older man, growing angrier by the minute, repeats one phrase over and over: "We are not a question, we are a people!" referring to the way the Turkish government refers to Kurds.

The passengers around us start chanting like a choir in a church, probably saying the Kurdish equivalent of, "Amen, brother, you tell him!"

I marvel how vehemently the locals are laying into this young man. I briefly feel sorry for him, but mainly I think, "Sorry, kid, but someone's gotta teach you some manners. And learn some situational awareness, for chrissake."

I keep facing straight ahead. I don't want the other people on the bus to think I'm this young man's friend.

The bus slowly winds up the hill. I look out the window, knowing I'll be walking this section in a few days. I mentally rehearse my steps, especially through the washed-out sections where the road has been damaged by the raging river below, swollen with runoff from the snow at a higher elevation.

Soon we reach the higher plateau and the bus driver stops to let me off. I step out of the bus. It's snowing heavily at this higher elevation. The driver gets out and walks to the back of the bus, pulls my pack out of the trunk, drops it on the ground next to me, and then hops back in the bus and pulls away. I'm left standing by the side of the road in the middle of the snow storm, my pack at my feet. The snow is probably about three feet deep and is blowing horizontally. I have no idea where I am. I'd figured the driver would drop me off at a bus station in the middle of Tatvan. Instead I'm knee deep in snow by the side of the road out in the middle of nowhere with zero visibility in all directions.

About 10 minutes later a local bus comes by and pulls to a stop in front of me. I hop in and learn that Tatvan is within walking distance just a little way off the main road — four or five kilometers at the most. So I'm not in the middle of nowhere after all. I just can't see anything with the snow blowing. As I ride into Tatvan I call Veli, who will be my Couchsurfing host.

Veli tells me to get off at the big mosque, which is the main mosque in the middle of town. "I live right across the street. I'll come and get you," he says.

I tell the bus driver to let me off at the big mosque. He knows exactly where that is. At the big mosque he pulls to the side of the road and lets me off.

I walk into a store next to the mosque and buy myself a snack. As I make small talk with the store clerk, Veli crosses the street to pick me up and leads me to his apartment across the street.

Veli has a flatmate named Asım (pronounced awe-some), a common Turkish man's name. Veli and I joke about Asım's name: "Asım is awesome!" Veli explains the joke to Asım. Asım smiles.

Veli and Asım are both teachers — Veli an English teacher at a high school nearby, and Asım a primary school teacher in a small village outside Tatvan.

Real estate in Tatvan is pretty cheap, so between the two of them they can afford a large apartment with a panoramic view of Lake Van and the snowy mountains to the southeast. I am happy to be inside where it is warm. The scenery is breathtaking, but I like looking at it from a warm living room.

Veli is a member of an international postcard club. As we are getting acquainted he takes out his postcard collection and shows it to me. He has about fifty postcards from countries all over the world: Brazil, Germany, France, China, Japan. Some people he has talked to on Skype, and some others he has never met.

In the evening Veli and Asım invite me to join them and some friends for a night of traditional Turkish music.

Sunday, 17 March

Before I begin my walk for the day I pull out my notebook and dedicate the day to İslam in Silvan.

As I hold the notebook up in front of my camera, I notice the highway sign above me and break into a smile. It indicates the destinations ahead — Ahlat, Ercis, Iran. I snap a photo of the sign too. A road sign to Iran means I'm getting close to the end of the walk.

Today's leg is the 26 kilometers (16 miles) between the towns of Bitlis and Tatvan. I will spend the next few days walking the climb into Tatvan, leaving a few weeks for the snow to melt at the higher elevations between Tatvan and Iran. I don't want to walk through snow.

It's raining. Big drops. Trucks spew torrents of water at me as they pass. I have to hide the camera under my coat to keep it dry. But rain melts snow really fast, so when there's snow, rain is fine with me. I get wet, but the roads clear fast.

I'm not really fond of hail however, and for the first couple hours of the day's walk a stiff headwind blows hail into my face. Hail stings.

In a couple hours the sun comes out, and I spend the second half of the day's walk drying off and enjoying the scenery along the Bitlis River as it flows into Bitlis, swollen with the recent snowmelt and the morning's rain. When the day's walk is over I head back to my room at Veli's in Tatvan.

Monday, 18 March

I have the day off. Veli has invited me to visit a handful of classes he teaches at Tatvan's Hüseyin Çelik Anadolu Lisesi. One of these is an intensive English language class that meets for three hours in the same room. The students in the classes are 15 and 16 years old. The exercise Veli has prepared ahead of time for the students: 1) the students ask questions of me in English, 2) I answer, and 3) the students repeat my answers in their own words.

The students finish the language exercise halfway into the 3-hour class period, so for the rest of the period they raise their hands and ask me unscripted questions, using English when they can, and Turkish when their English skills are insufficient for the question. I can see a particularly urgent look on the face of one of the students, Zeynep. I point to her.

She asks, "What were you looking for on this walk, and did you find it?"

I lean back onto the teacher's desk and think about that one for a moment. Zeynep's question requires me to dig especially deep. I think to myself, *I can barely answer that question in English.* I answer, "I don't know, and I'm not sure yet."

After a brief period of laughter from the class, I can see on Zeynep's face that she doesn't consider her question answered. She wants me to press further and explain what I mean by that.

I scratch my chin and dig deeper. I really want to find an answer for Zeynep, but I get nothing. I shrug my shoulders and say, "Sorry, I really don't know."

I can't always find an answer to all their questions, but I love that the students are patient with me while I try. Like it has when I've visited other schools on this trip, everything else in the world has fallen away, and the only things that exist, as far as I can tell, are me and the students in front of me.

Thursday, 21 March

I dedicate the day to Veli and smile when I see the road sign "Welcome to Siirt province." *Getting closer,* I mutter to myself, because there's no one else there.

Siirt is one of the provinces in southeastern Turkey known for its separatist rebel activity. I see the province mentioned in the news a lot, and I expect armies of rebel soldiers to come running out of the forest. But I see no unusual activity. Just trees and a few cars passing on the road.

Tatvan, at a higher elevation, is covered in snow. But here, 2,000 feet lower, the road passes through green, grassy plains. Spring has come to this lower elevation.

Friday, 22 March

On my final day of walking into Tatvan, I take a bus to the nearby town of Bitlis. Because Bitlis is along the road I am walking, I have been using it for the past four days as a morning staging area for my walk towards Tatvan. Bitlis, population 100,000, is the home of the American author William Saroyan's parents. William Saroyan made his home in Fresno, California, a few miles from Reedley, California, where I spent time growing up.

Since I have been using Bitlis as a staging area, I have become well known at a tea house across from the bus stop. When I walk into the tea house on the third day I recognize some of the patrons and wave.

Two of the older men walk up to my table, greet me, and ask if they can join me. I say of course, and point to two of the empty chairs. The men sit, order tea refills, and ask me if I know the meaning of a particular phrase.

In Islam, one of the traditions is that if you utter this particular phrase then you are automatically converted to Islam. It's kind of like saying abracadabra and all of a sudden you magically become a Muslim. It is a long phrase, and I could never remember it well. In Turkey, and especially in southeast Turkey, many people have tried to teach this phrase to me, and I always pretend it is the first time I've heard it, and I fake an inability to say it, which frustrates them terribly, and entertains me to no end.

They say the phrase to me again, slower this time, and I repeat the first two syllables with no problem, but then I pretend to stumble over the third and fourth.

They repeat the phrase. This time I say the first three syllables correctly, but pretend to stumble over the fourth and fifth.

"Could you say that again?" I ask.

One of the men repeats the whole phrase.

I try the phrase again, but this time stumble over the third and fourth syllables again. I put on my best innocent face mask.

They get frustrated at my inability to learn this phrase, and grab a piece of paper so they can write it down for me. Still, I find it nearly impossible to get past the fifth syllable without a problem.

My would-be teachers become increasingly frustrated. Converting me, and thus entering Heaven, is going to be harder than they imagine. After half an hour of my saying things like, "What's that?" and "Huh?" they give up and we go back to drinking tea while I wait for my bus.

At the end of the day, after walking my 30 kilometers, I stick out my thumb to hitch a ride back into Tatvan. There aren't many buses, or traffic of any sort, along this stretch of road, but fortunately hitching is easy and people expect it.

About half an hour later a truck comes by and rumbles to a stop. I run up to the cab, say hello to the driver, who introduces himself as Hur, and ask where he is going. Ercis, he says, a town near Tatvan. I hop in.

As the truck lumbers up the hill, Hur asks me where I am from.

"California," I tell him.

"Is that near America?"

"Yes, it is," I answer.

Hur says, "Oh I've never been to America, but maybe someday I'll go."

Jokingly, I say, "Ah! We should go together."

"Will I need a passport?"

"Probably," I reply.

"I don't have a passport."

"That might be a problem."

We ride up the hill in friendly silence after that. At Tatvan I thank Hur for the ride and hop down from the cab.

I have finished the walk into Tatvan. I have walked 1,848 kilometers (1,148 miles) so far. I am 88% of the way across the country. Time for a hot shower and a nap.

THE LAST BIT

I wake up, walk to the kitchen, and look out the window. It snowed in Tatvan last night. I gaze further out the window at the road leaving town. It's covered in snow.

I go downstairs, push through the door onto the sidewalk, and crunch my way to the inter-city bus stop. This morning I will be riding the 150 kilometers (93 miles) from Tatvan to Van, and then back to Tatvan, to inspect the next segment of the road I'll be walking. I want to see if the shoulder is mostly clear of extensive snowy patches, so that I can walk safely without snow banks forcing me into the middle of the road.

On the bus ride I see that the road is not clear yet. I will need to rest a few days in Tatvan while the snow melts.

A few days later, when the snow has cleared enough to walk along the shoulder of the road, I resume walking. The road weaves along the south side of Lake Van, so sometimes I walk next to the water and sometimes I walk further inland, with a hill between me and the lake. There is almost no vehicle traffic on this road, so at the end of each day I hitchhike back to Tatvan with the first car that appears, rather than wait hours for a minibus. *Thank god hitchhiking is so normal in this part of the country,* I think. *Otherwise I probably wouldn't be able to make it through this section.*

At the end of the walk one day I stand waiting at the side of the road, ready to hitchhike back to Tatvan. I hear a distinctive sound. I've been hearing the same sound since Gaziantep. It is a flatbed truck carrying a temporary housing unit, and the distinctive sound is coming from mesh straps flapping in the wind. I can't see the truck yet, it is still a kilometer or so away, by the sounds of it.

I suspect what the trucks are doing with the housing units, but I'm not sure, so I welcome the opportunity I'll have in a few minutes to talk to the truck driver and find out for sure.

As the truck comes into view, I stick out my hand and wave it down. Sure enough, the driver pulls to a stop on the side of the road. I run up to the truck and climb into the cab.

"Thanks, much appreciated," I say to the driver.

"Of course, my pleasure," he replies. "Where are you headed?"

"Just down the road to Tatvan."

I marvel at how comfortable the truck is, and how bouncy the seat is. I guess that when you are traveling thousands of miles, having a seat that absorbs the road shocks is important.

I notice a plastic shopping bag full of road snacks on the floor. Doritos. Pringles. Cakes. Cookies. Cans of iced tea. This guy is ready for a long haul.

"Where are you headed?" I ask.

"Gaziantep. And then İzmir." İzmir is on the west coast, near Kuşadası, where I started this walk.

"How long will it take you to get to İzmir?"

"I'll be there tomorrow," he says.

Tomorrow, I think. *It took me more than half a year to cross this country. He'll do it in a day.*

"That housing unit on the back of your truck, who is it for?" I ask.

"Syrian refugees in Kilis, near Gaziantep. The government is paying us to move unused units from the earthquake relief here in Van down to Gaziantep for the Syrians."

We fall silent. I gaze out the window at the distance I walked today and yesterday. It will take only an hour to drive it in a truck.

A question from the driver pulls me out of my reverie. "Where are you from?"

"California. You?"

"Erzurum," he answers. A city in northeastern Turkey. "I don't get home much. I'm mostly on the road."

"Do you have family?" I ask.

"Yeah, a wife and two daughters. But I don't see them much."

We fall silent again. I turn and gaze out the window some more. In my peripheral vision I see the cans of Pringles on the floor. I crave salty junk food. I look forward to returning to Tatvan, and to buying my own can of Pringles before going back home to Veli and Asım's apartment.

The driver pulls into Tatvan. I thank him for the ride and wish him a safe journey. He wishes me the same, and I hop out of the cab and shut the door behind me. I walk across the street to buy a can of Pringles. *And some iced tea. I want some iced tea,* I think to myself. It's snowy on the ground but sunny and warm this afternoon, and I'm thirsty.

I take my snacks across the street, walk up the stairs to Veli's, and crash in the living room to check my emails. One is from my host in the next city of Van. He will be leaving town and can't host me after all. I will need to find another place to stay.

I'm too tired to deal with this now, I think. *I'll deal with it later.*

Another email is from my mom. She asks me if I have a girlfriend. I don't have a girlfriend, but my mom is the third person to ask that question this week. For almost two years no one has bothered to ask me if I have a girlfriend, and now three people in one week do. I email her back, asking her why she asked. Did I say something? Am I giving off some "I have a girlfriend" vibes?

Veli calls me to dinner. He and Asım have made a dinner of seasoned potatoes, pasta, and yogurt. I close my laptop and walk into the dining room. Two of their friends from the building join us for dinner. The five of us spread some newspaper on the floor, set the dishes on it, sit cross-legged around the food, and eat from common plates.

I wolf down the potatoes and finish off one of the bowls of yogurt. Veli offers me some of his potatoes. I politely turn them down. It is 9:30 p.m. I am exhausted. It occurs to me that I am walking six hours one day, and then getting up the next day to walk six hours again, and then getting up the next day to walk six hours again. I thank god that my knees and hips have held up this well.

I sit quietly, staring blankly at the empty plates in front of me, while the others chat excitedly about something. Veli notices I am tired. He excuses me from dinner. I take my leave, brush my teeth, and am asleep by 10 p.m.

The next day I tell Veli I won't be back for a couple nights and I leave Tatvan. I have two or three days of walking into Van, and I am determined to get that done. Van is 95% of the distance, and I have an emotional need to hit that milestone. I can't let the project linger in front of me, nearly done but not quite. I have to get the walk done, before the Resistance sets in.

On Sunday, 31 March, about 15 kilometers south of the city of Van, I stumble across a little place for lunch on the shores of Lake Van called Kadenbas Köftecisi. It's between the lake and a cement factory in a suburb called Edrimit. I have some of the most delicious *ızgara köfte* (grilled meatballs) and homemade ayran ever at that out-of-the-way restaurant. The outside of the kofte is crunchy, and when I break the köfte open with my fork the meat is so tender it flakes apart.

There are many things I will miss about this region. Kadenbas Koftecisi is one of them.

I enter the city of Van, population 353,000. I stop to take a photo of the city limit sign. I remember that one month ago, on 1 March, I walked out of Urfa, and promised myself I'd arrive in Van by the end of the month.

In under the wire, I think to myself. *But in nonetheless. Good job Matt.*

God, I'm so exhausted I want to cry. Almost done. Van is 95% of the distance.

I continue walking into the city, towards the inter-city bus station. I need to ride back to Tatvan tonight, since I still haven't found a place to stay in Van. I walk past a huge installation of hundreds of those temporary housing units. I pull out my camera and take a photo.

A man walks past. I say hello and ask him what those housing units are. He tells me they are temporary housing units for earthquake victims. Which earthquake? I ask. He answers the one last year, or maybe the year before. He's not sure. They have a lot of earthquakes around here.

Monday, 1 April

Now I'm walking between Van and the Turkey/Iran border. I couldn't find a place to Couchsurf in Van, so I will stay for a few days at the Oğretmen Evi while I bang out the last 5% of the walk.

All I want to do is crawl into a corner and roll up into a fetal position. My spirit and my legs are heavy. I want to quit. I want to quit more than I've ever wanted to quit anything.

I think back to a few of the moments I had back in California, when I spent 6 months practicing for this walk.

Back then, I noticed that whenever I approached a major milestone, such as 500 miles, or 1,000 miles, I would find myself feeling that the miles leading up to the milestone seemed more difficult than the miles that preceded them. My spirit would drag. I'd have a hard time getting out of bed in the morning, and I'd have to dig unusually deep to walk.

I asked myself, "Why is that?" Why is mile 999 harder than mile 257, or mile 676, or mile 819?

I answered, "Well, actually, it's not. Mile 999 is a mile, just like any of those other miles. So I will walk mile 999 just like I did the miles that preceded it."

I draw on that lesson right here in the final week of the walk.

Tomorrow's 30 kilometers (19 miles) will be just like all the other 30-kilometer walks I've done. Wednesday's 30 kilometers will be just like tomorrow's. Thursday's 18 kilometers will be just like every other 18-kilometer walk I've done, and Friday's 16 kilometers will be just like every other 16-kilometer walk. And then boom, I'll be done.

The last mile isn't the hardest unless I think it is, I remind myself. *Get it done.*

Tuesday, April 2

Today I will walk 30 kilometers, from Van to the town of Erçek. I start out at an elevation of about 5550 feet (1700 meters), but will later be climbing and spending most of the time between 6100 and 6200 feet (1900 meters).

On the way out of Van I pass a garbage dump. A bunch of mangy dogs turn, bare their teeth at me, and bark.

I walk a little further. A puppy, probably only about 10 weeks old, raises its head and starts screeching at me. "What the...?" I don't recall ever hearing a noise like that from a dog before.

I look closer. He is resting against his dead mother. By the looks of her, she was hit by a car maybe a couple days ago. The flies are settling in.

The puppy continues screeching. He runs over to me and begins following me, running about one step behind me on his little puppy legs. He is clean and fluffy and cute. He doesn't yet have any of that unkempt manginess that besets dogs living the stray life.

"No, sorry, I can't help you," I mutter. I speed up. I don't want to encourage him. "Go find some other dogs," I tell him. "I'm sorry, I can't help you." I pick up a stick and try to push him away. I know if I touch him we will start bonding. But he won't go away.

A few steps later we pass another puppy, this one slightly older. He is munching on the remains of another dog who has been hit by a car and whose body has been torn open by the impact.

Packs of mangy dogs. Orphaned puppies. Cannibalism. It's like I'm walking through a dog version of Cormac McCarthy's *The Road*.

The little puppy continues following me. He follows me for three kilometers, a full half hour of walking. Every once in awhile I look down and there he is, trying to keep up, running along on his little legs.

I try to explain to him, "No, I'm sorry, I can't take care of you. I'm going to have to leave you at the end of the day. Go! You have to go." I feel like Clint Eastwood in *Gran Torino*, the movie where he is torn between not getting attached to someone new, and playing father figure to a young Asian kid who needs some help.

I'm starting to get annoyed at the little puppy. He won't give up and leave me alone.

I think, *for 7 months I have been having to say goodbye to people, and now I'm going to have to say goodbye to you too?! I thought I was done with that. I thought I was going to get out of here without getting attached to more people I was going to have to say goodbye to! What the hell, puppy, don't ask me to do this!*

As I walk through a small village a larger dog comes running across the street at us. This other dog is not happy to have a stranger entering his territory. But the puppy starts screeching that desperate, lonely, orphaned screech of his, and the other dog slows down. He approaches the puppy carefully. The puppy continues screeching, like he's saying, "Don't hurt me, don't hurt me, I just need a home." My eyes water. There have been times in my life when I have felt like that, too.

The dogs touch noses as dogs tend to do when they say hello to each other. Three village kids come running out to the road to see what the commotion is about. They see the puppy, pick it up, and start playing with it. When it looks like the puppy might have found a new home, I walk on.

The high plains on the road to Erçek are flat as a board. The road cuts across the plain to the horizon in an unyielding straight line. Perched on the flat horizon sits a row of snow-capped mountain peaks that seem to move further east with every step I take.

Is this walk ever going to end?

Then I am walking along Lake Erçek, so flat it looks like a sheet of glass shimmering next to me atop the plain.

I stop to take pictures of the lake to post to the website, but my camera battery dies in the middle of the first photo. I guess that's it for photography today. *I don't care*, I think, *I'm too fatigued to think about it.* I stuff the camera back in the bag and keep walking. Three more days to go.

Wednesday, 3 April

I dedicate the day to "The Last Day of the 30's."

For more than 3 months I have been walking mostly 30's (30 kilometers, or 19 miles in a day). Today is the last such day. I have two days left, and they are both under 20 kilometers each.

It takes me 6 hours to walk 30 kilometers, today or any other day. I walk those 6 hours without stopping, not even for a few minutes' break, not even once. Once again, I am amazed and thankful that my hips, knees, and feet can keep moving like that for 6 straight hours, day after day. Thank god, the universe has smiled on me.

The territory is so barren here, and there is no one around to talk to. People have even stopped appearing in front of me by the side of the road. I am just banging out kilometers and thinking that if my body will hold up for six hours then I'm going to walk for six hours.

Thursday, 4 April

Today is my second to last day.

I'm walking to Saray, the last little town I'll see on the way to the border.

My heavily-accented Turkish doesn't work really well around here anymore. "Is this the road to Saray?" comes across as "Is this the road to Syria?" and is more likely to garner the response, "No, this is the road to Iran" than anything else. Good to know. At least I am headed toward the right country.

I finish the day's walk and hitch a ride back to Van with the driver of a pharmaceutical wholesale delivery truck. Tomorrow's walk will be 19 kilometers to a turnoff that marks the "5 kilometers to go" point. Then I'll go back to Tatvan for a week and leave the last five kilometers for Saturday, 13 April, when a handful of friends from around Turkey will arrive to finish the walk with me.

Friday, 5 April

I hop on the minibus out of Van and ride to somewhere in the-middle-of-nowhere. When I get there I dedicate my last day of walking to my mom and dad. Without them I would be unable to do pretty much anything in life because, well, I probably wouldn't be here to start with.

I begin the day walking silently through a brown landscape spattered with patches of quickly-melting snow and a chill wind that whips across the plain. The sky is gray and hung with heavy clouds. I'm about ten kilometers from the Iranian border.

I reach the walk's highest point — 7500 feet (2300 meters) above sea level.

I almost expect a marching band, a big parade, and a ribbon-cutting ceremony of some sort ("Matt has reached the highest point of his walk!"), but all I encounter is a stiff headwind. No traffic, no people, just wind.

Around lunchtime, I come upon a cement making facility. In a few weeks, when the land begins to thaw, the facility will mine rocks from the side of the hill to make cement. There are a few workers around, just a skeleton crew readying the facility. I study the facility as I walk by. I try to imagine what it looks like when it's buzzing with 100 workers.

One of the employees sees me and calls to me and waves at me to come over to join them for a lunch of beans and rice. I go over, sit with them, and savor the food as I tell them I can't stay long; I've got another five kilometers to walk yet today. Which, by the way, ends in the middle of nowhere.

"Where are you staying the night?" they want to know. I tell them I am staying the night in Tatvan.

They have the restraint not to laugh or tell me I'm crazy. They say instead, "Thank you for having lunch with us. If you need anything stop back by and say hello!"

As I leave I smile to myself, a smile of pleasant surprise. Here I am, a stranger, a foreigner nonetheless, by himself, miles from anywhere, talking some bizarre gibberish about walking all the way across the country. And the locals' first instinct is to share their lunch with me, as if something unusual happens here every day. Because, as I've learned, it kind of does.

A few hours later I finish my walk for the day and hitch a ride back to Tatvan to rest up for a week, write, work on my website, and wait for my people to come walk the last three miles with me.

Saturday, 13 April

My friends and I descend upon Van to walk the final three miles together. The early birds — Tolga, Yonca, Alper, Salih, and Donna — and I meet for a group breakfast.

It's yet another orgy of food! We order enough for two people, and the six of us barely eat half of it, try as we might.

Fortunately, Yonca suggests we pack the rest of it up and take it on the road with us so we can eat breakfast all day.

After breakfast the six of us walk to a nearby corner, where we meet up with Joy Anna and a few people she has brought with her from Ankara. Then we meet the rest of the group and wait for the minibus.

I remember that I forgot to get the champagne. We are still in Van and I know we are not going to find champagne in these parts. Sparkling apple juice will have to do.

I find a nearby market. Inside the market a Dutch woman is ordering some cashews. She is having a hard time explaining something to the shopkeeper. I play the translator. She pays for the cashews and leaves the store.

I buy my three bottles of sparkling apple juice. Back at the corner where I left the group the Dutch woman is talking to some of my friends. I figure they must know each other, so I just stand nearby waiting for them to finish their conversation. I find out they have just met.

It turns out the Dutch woman's name is Gerdi and she is riding her bicycle across Turkey and into Iran.

I turn to her and say, "We are taking a minivan to the border. Would you like to ride to the border with us?"

She says yes she would like that. When the van arrives we load Gerdi's bike into it, too.

I tell the driver we want him to drop us off three miles short of the border. He scratches his neck and stares at me. Finally he says, "Ok. Do you mean you just want me to take you to the border?"

"No," I say. "We want you to take us three miles from the border, let us out, and drive to the border to wait while we walk to the border. Then bring us back here to Van."

He shrugs and starts up the van. He stops three miles before the border and lets us off.

Gerdi gets off, too. She leaves her bike in the van. The driver will take it ahead to the border for her. Clouds cover the sun and a hard hail begins to fall on us. Ten minutes later, the hail stops, the clouds part, and the sun reappears.

With the border in sight, I stop for a bottle breaking ceremony. I write names of a few family and friends on each of the three bottles of sparkling apple juice I bought back in Van — Christian Stracke, Frank Kleist, Mom and Dad. I throw the bottles at the ground, but they just bounce back up and will not break. I throw them at the ground again, and again, and again, harder each time. They are apparently shatterproof. One of my friends brings me a large rock and suggests I try dropping it on the bottles. The bottles finally break, but then the road is full of broken glass, so Gerdi and I lean down and pick it out of the pavement. I don't want my celebration to cause someone else's flat tire.

The celebration finished, we walk the last half mile to the border, where Gerdi grabs her bike from the van, runs with it, swings her leg over the seat, and takes off into Iran.

I walk up to the fence marking the border. There are mountains on the other side, and they look just like the mountains on this side. I quickly swipe my little finger against the fence to make sure it's not electrified, and then I press all of my fingers through the chain link and wiggle them in Iranian airspace. I'm done.

79569207R00165

Made in the USA
Columbia, SC
03 November 2017